The Players of Religion

By

Nicholas Shaw

Shield  Crest

© Copyright 2009 Nicholas Shaw

All rights reserved

This book shall not, by way of trade or otherwise, be lent, re-sold, hired out, or otherwise circulated without the prior consent of the copyright holder or the publisher in any form of binding or cover other than that in which it is published and without a similar condition including this condition being imposed on the subsequent purchaser

ISBN: 978-0-9558557-8-8

MMIX

Published by
ShieldCrest,

UK: Aylesbury, Buckinghamshire, HP22 5RR
USA: Morrisville, NC 27560
www.shieldcrest.co.uk

ACKNOWLEDGEMENTS

I am indebted to the many authors and translators of the many books that have been needed in the writing of this book and I give all of them my highest regards and thank them deeply

I also wish to thank the many friends and my family for their support without which this book would not have been written.

Finally, I would also like to thank my agent for without them this book could not have been published.

AUTHOR'S COMMENT

From the origins to the creation of the Gods, the possibility that man creates the Gods becomes apparent and the consequences of the religions that are not willing to evolve become apparent in the later chapters.

The debates are far reaching, and the players bring new philosophical theories and possible consequences into many religions and their cultures theories and myths. Therefore, the theories on the Gods, chaos, ethics and particularly Mother Nature, and the consequences of defiling Mother Nature's creation through unsubstantiated beliefs are made evident throughout this work. This leads to the possible extinction of the human race and/or religions if some religions are not willing to resolve their theories and become less dogmatic and accept new scientific and philosophical understanding.

CONTENTS

Introduction 2-13

Chapter 1 15 - 31 - The Problems of Belief – the problems associated with the Divine

Chapter 2 32 - 42 - The Divine – the unlikely chance of a single Divine being creating all

Chapter 3 43 - 64 - The Creation – some of the differing theories associated with creation

Chapter 4 65 - 92 - The Coercion of Cult and Superstition – some of the means by which one religion corrupts another to convert their followers

Chapter 5 93 - 123 - The Natural Mind – the destruction of some beliefs through science and some of the consequences of not listening to science

Chapter 6 124 - 149 - Science and the Nature of Religion – shows the need for religion to evolve with science and not hinder the scientific process

Chapter 7 150 - 173 - The Realisation of Natural Ethics and Chaos – shows that the material pleasures brought upon by some religions ethics need to be revised

Chapter 8 174 - 208 - The Chaos of Truth – points to the chaos that is created by many religions theories in their efforts to create order

Chapter 9 209 - 230 - Predatory religions – makes evident that some religions predate and in predating can become the prey

Chapter 10 231 - 267 - True Understanding – points out how some religions use untruths within their scriptures and use these untruths to deny scientific evidence

Chapter 11 268 - 301 - The Final Death or Evolution (conclusion) – points to the probabilities of religious and human extinction if religions are not willing to evolve.

Bibliography 302

INTRODUCTION

The starting point of this book is The Problems of Belief, which begins to show the problems of the belief structure of religion. These belief structures have been shown to be unreliable in some of their scriptures, because many religions have been forced upon many populations by the victors of wars and another of the causes of this unreliability; is shown to be the problems of the definition of the soul or the self whilst it is held in bondage by the physical being, and controlled by the Divine, and the folk that are mythically associated with other worlds! After such association the players then assessed the possibility of the planets soul and the soul of the universe. Following on from this the players then discussed the problems that are associated with the definition of good and evil, and the improbability of a perfect and all knowing God. Hence the players followed on with the problems that are associated with the Lords of Karma and the Fates and Muses!

The next chapter on the Divine covers the probable origins of the One-God religions and it begins to show; how such religions God could be tyrannical and selfish through its heightened emotional state, and how through this heightened emotional state their emotions could be in control of the God rather than the other way round. Hence the emotional state and illusory world of maya enter the fields in which dependence and illusion begin to be discussed. Following that the idea that the self is the only unchangeable reality when it is realised by the individual and the theory that the Gods could realise their own reality, and therefore be changeless also emerges. Hence some of the verses in the Rig Veda were shown, because they pointed to the Gods not having complete knowledge of all, and to mankind [possibly] being able to go onto a higher plane of existence than the Gods. Once this was discussed the theory that the Gods were already complete in their evolution and unable to go any further came into being as well as the theory of the never ending circle of life death and rebirth.

The chapter on creation begins by discussing the scientific field of the big bang theory and the problems that are associated with some religions belief on the creation by a single deity. This idea of a single deity creating all becomes quickly realised as implausible and the problems of the realization of permanence and impermanence come into fruition; when the immortal soul or the self start to be discussed as a possible creator of the universe and the physical world. Hence the circle of life death and rebirth starts to be discussed along with the probability that if the self or the soul is immortal the chance that it has an outside agent for its creation becomes implausible. Such implausibility leads to the discussion of all creation coming out of the knowledge of past events, and how to have such a knowledge; would mean that if everything came out of the void; this knowledge would have been present in the void if any creation was to come into being. Hence the imperfections with the creation theories of some religions and the creation of time and the ideals that surround the Lords of Karma and fate began to be discussed, because the imperfections within the universe and nature come from the beginning, and in the beginning of most creations mistakes are made. The imperfections and self-creation of the self also entered this part of the discussion. This led the discussion onto the possibility that the self is self-creative, and that the deities are outside agents within the creative fields of the self. Following this it is shown that there are beliefs that have a Darwinian perspective within them, and the creation of water and animals come before the creation of mankind. Hence the discussion progressed onto the natural aspects of some of the deities, and the ways in which some animals and deities could be seen to be otherworldly figures. The connection between the fates, past events and the self follow on from this part of the discussion, because of the creative forces that would have to be present for such connections to be creative. Carrying on from this the areas of life, death destruction and creation are discussed, because all seem to need one another for them to be truly realised. Hence the self-creative aspects of the self and their connection with fate and historical thought processes emerge.

The Coercion of Cult and Superstition begins with the theory that all religions are self-created, and the realization that many religions have used nature; for the explanation and/or the show of power within their religious beliefs. Following this some of the consequences of ignoring superstition and the creation of scriptures written by the hand of mankind begin to emerge, and the reliance of the need of past events for these writings to emerge comes into being. Hence the writing of ethics through mythology and as a means of control through such mythology becomes evident. Following this it is shown that the bastardization of some beliefs can be used to further the cause of a belief that wishes to dominate [even if some of the bastardized beliefs are self contradictory]. Such bastardization is shown to be made through the demonizing of other religions God's, and other races to further the ideals of a dictatorial religion. After this the myth of Medusa is discussed and some philosophical possibilities for the creation of such a myth emerge. During this part of the discussion other myths of supernatural creatures emerge, and some of the so called ideologies that surround supernatural creatures and monsters are seen to have deeper and more philosophical meaning than they first appear to have. Hence the players discuss the monstrous aspects that are within the dreams and the creations of the human race, and also the probability that the human race is part monster. This leads on to how some of the religions use monsters demons and the devil to try to outlaw some scientific understanding, and control the masses through the fear of Divine retribution. Hence the realization; that it is probable; that the ideas of the minds; that create the demon or monster; are actually implanted with the idea by an outside agent emerges. This leads the players to discuss some of the means [such as hallucination through starvation] by which monsters and demons are created within religion and the coercion that is gained from such tactics. Following this; the realization that the word and emotion are the true creators of the superstitions within the human race becomes evident, as does the will to create such superstition.

The Natural Mind starts with the realization that the destructive aspects of some religions use natural forces for their selfish ideals, and in doing so; they try to hide the understanding of the scientific world. This leads to the use of demons and their God to create fear, and this also loses the realization of the true nature that they are part of. Hence the ideals of the religions that have a more natural belief emerges, as does the possibility that the religions that do not follow such beliefs and cause much natural destruction will be punished for their actions in the next life. Following this Mother Nature's creative abilities and existence are seen to be connected through evolutionary means. This leads onto the probability that the self cannot evolve without its natural experiences, because without realization that is made evident to it in the natural world it would not be able to realise anything at all and therefore it would not be able to exist. This leads to the possibility that once the self is enlightened the laws that surround its present physical bondage are dissolved and in being so enlightened the enlightenment does not stop the evolutionary process that the self is still part of. Following this possibility some of the misunderstandings and the consequences of misunderstanding nature within the scriptures of the One-God religion were discussed. Hence some of the possible reasons for such destructive desires are discussed, and one of the reasons for this was seen to be the undermining of more nature based religions. This was made evident by the way in which the One-God religions made some of the part animal deities and animal hides that were used in ritual appear to be unclean. Which followed on to the consequences of the deforestation through the greed and desires that have become prominent within the human race through dictatorial religions greed and selfishness. Hence the problems of the loss of awareness through the beliefs that caused such a problem come into the discussion, as do the problems that are caused by the loss of such awareness. This leads on to the discussion on the awareness of the evolutionary process of Mother Nature; more natural religions, and the surroundings of the individual. When this becomes discussed the consequences and the possible extinction of the human race start to become evident. Following this the misuse and outlawing of some of the scientific discoveries is discussed, as is the fact that some of the instruments of war could actually be helping Mother Nature keep the human races numbers down. This leads to the realization that many religions may be creating a demon of misunderstanding by misusing and outlawing some scientific discoveries. This leads to the realization that there would need to be some drastic changes within some religions if the natural world was to be truly explored and understood. Following this the need of food and water and things that are upon or part of the physical world that are needed for survival and true discovery are realised, as part of the spiritual journey, which also led to the realization that a healthy body is needed for a healthy mind, and that self starvation was not a means by which true enlightenment could be reached. This led to the realization that a world that was created by an imbalance–that appeared to be true–was paradoxical, because it was a truth that was created through a distortion and that distortion of the truth became the truth! Such a realization led to the realization; that some religions need to stop using only their prayers and ancient scriptures; to answer their questions about the natural happenings within the world.

Science and the Nature of Religion begin with the differentiation of invention and discovery, which leads on to Darwin and Galileo being discussed. This leads to the discussion making evident the contradictions between science and many religions. These contradictions are evidently uncomfortable for the religions that are contradicted by science. Following this some of the consequences of mistaken scriptures are discussed, and the unwillingness to change becomes evident in some religions dogmatic approach to new understanding. This leads to the discussion showing that the scientific theories of people like Darwin become uncomfortable for some religions, and in being uncomfortable for these religions, these religions still hold firm in their ancient scriptures, and try to bar the way to the progress that can be made through such discoveries. This leads to the discussion showing that such religions become unaware of the consequences of their actions on the natural world, which could lead to the planet becoming inhospitable for the human race. Hence it starts to become evident that some of the dogmatic religions are actually unethical.

This leads to the ethics that some religions use for their destructive actions to be shown for what they really are, and that is; a means of controlling the mind of the individual through the domination of their so called God; which misleads the individual into thinking that its race is the superior party upon the planet. The dangers of such a thought process are then discussed. Through such dangers it is made evident that the will of the Divine should not be a top priority in the ethics of the human race. Next it is made evident that the religions that do not accept the natural laws and only use science for its own selfish desires could be seen as suicidal. Some of the other nature based problems that are associated with the Godhead of such religions is then made evident. Following this it is made evident that the human race is in its infancy in evolutionary terms, and in its infancy the human race needs to be able to evolve its ethics without being hindered by some religions dogmatic practices. From this the morality and consequences of some actions are discussed and the planets natural values are seen to be above those of any political or religious agenda. This leads to the realization that over breeding will put a strain on the planetary resources, because the resources of this planet are finite. Therefore the need to allow ethics to evolve above religious ideals becomes evident. After this the survival needs and requirements of older times were discussed, because it was different tactics that were needed for survival in the natural world's different climates and conditions. This led on to the realization that many misunderstandings within the natural world are still being misunderstood through the dogmatic attitudes of some religions. This led to the relationship between Mother Nature, the Lords of Karma, and the Gods being discussed along with the needs of the planet in which we reside.

The Realization of Natural Ethics and Chaos begins by realizing that the concerns of the natural world need to be revised within religion, because most ancient religions deal mainly with the concerns of the human race and were not concerned with the future consequences of their actions within the natural world. This leads to the realization that the ethics of religion need to evolve along with scientific understanding and the evolutionary process of Mother Nature. Following this the debate continues with the ethics that surround the killing of another species and that of the survival of a human being. Hence the need to revise some ancient and outdated scriptures becomes apparent through the understanding that has evolved within the scientific world. The misunderstanding of the evolutionary process of Mother Nature is also made apparent in some religions scriptures, and such misunderstandings can be realised to be detrimental to the natural world in which they reside, and this is through the lack of respect of the natural world that is created when it is thought of as impermanent. Following this the realization that as we classify different species of a similar order [such as chimpanzees and Gorillas]; the human races culture and religions need to be classified in such a way for the understanding that is available or allowed to be available to them. This leads to the classification of religions in three orders, which are; hostile in natural understanding, natural moralists, and neutral with possible hostile tendencies. Following this the laws written within natural ethics are realised to be more important than those of some religions ethics, and therefore; they should come above any religions hostile ethical values. Hence the need for the freedom of speech and thought is analyzed, and it is decided that no belief should be outlawed but the actions of a belief that are detrimental to the natural world and the human race should be outlawed [which is necessary even though it does lose part of the free will]. Further on the unwillingness of some faiths to believe some of the scientific evidence that is put forward to them by some of their followers is evaluated. This leads to the discussion entering into a minor discussion on the chaos that is created by such actions. Following this the beauty of the chaotic universe and the implausibility of a perfect being are realised. After this realization the timelessness of evolution is also realised. Following this the destructive and chaotic actions within the universe are shown to be able to be used as an act of a Divine figure; that is displeased with the actions of mankind. Hence the problems of evolution within scriptures were discussed and realised to be a major problem for some of the scriptures for some religions.

The Chaos of Truth begins with the realization that whilst the universe is expanding to unknown limits and there are still unknown factors within the universe total prediction is not possible. Hence it is made evident that any religion that believes that their Divine has made total order within the universe is mistaken, because there are too many variables for this to happen. This leads to the realization that chaos and Mother Nature are closely linked, and that the religious ideals that surround the after death experience are just as chaotic, because the only certainty in death is the death of the physical being. Following this the chaotic nature of religion and the unexplored chaos within religions are realised. The lack of exploration and the disharmony that is created through such a lack are then made evident. Following this some of the means by which this disharmony is created through the individualistic and chaotic nature of the human being are realised. Then it was made evident that some of the Divine have chaos of their own making written within their own scriptures; even though they are considered to have made total order. This leads to the realization that some chaotic forces could be used to explain the wrath of the Divine instead of being truly realised for what they are, which then leads to the realization that there are some religions scriptures that show chaos; without truly understanding what they are making evident in these scriptures. Following this the realization that chaos can be present in some types of certainty emerges, which leads the players to make evident that what seems to be an ordered certainty can be chaotic, because much of the ordered certainty within religion is only of a metaphysical making. Hence the negligent ideals of the improvable [by the empirical means] aspects of most religions are shown as are some of the consequences of such ideals. Leading on from this the ideal of an all knowing being becomes illogical if immortality and infinity exist, because for both to exist it requires an end point for there to be complete knowledge of every thing that is and everything that is going to be. Following this it became evident that some events could be predicted and these predictions could be misused through the manipulation of the time frame in which they occurred. Such realization then leads to the realization; that with having so many different beliefs within the religions they are of a chaotic nature; which can become problematic when some religions remain dogmatic, and are not willing to fully evolve alongside scientific and philosophical understanding. What this leads to is the realization of the chaos of misunderstanding; through the incorrect assumptions of many religions dogmatic ideals that were created by their myths and/or legends.

The need for the people of religions that use misunderstanding to subjugate the people becomes evident, and the chaos that is caused by such a tactic is then realised. This leads to the realization that chaos must be as infinite as any Divine being if any kind of order is to come into being; which makes evident the improbability of there being only one divine being. This leads to the showing of events that are created through chaos, and the so called order within religions that can be the creator of chaos; which could be the first divine, and the probability that what it is would be what we call Mother Nature. Following on it is made evident that the creators of religions are not aware of the chaos that they are creating through what seems to be an ideologically assessed order; that is created by their Divine being. But this is shown to be problematic for many religions, because they are unaware of the chaos that is within their making. This leads to motion and the thought process being realised as connected and chaotic. Even if its creation through chaos is improvable it is likely that the thought process is created by chaotic means. Following this; the chaotic thought processes of the Divine, and the human race are made evident to be one and the same, and that the human race has lost this realization. Therefore religions are shown to hold back scientific and philosophical research to create the perfect order within their scriptures. This leads to the realization that it is possible that a Divine being could have a lesser conscience than the human being; although consciousness would remain the same because both are conscious beings. It is also made evident that there are different types of conscience that are created within religious beliefs. Following this it is realised that many religions are not able to alter their scriptures and in not being able to do so; the different types of conscience and the chaos that they are creating by their own dogmatism and mistakes would not be allowed to be admitted.

Predatory Religions begins with the realization that most religions are predatory and this predation is used for most religions appearance of superiority. Hence the warlike and dictatorial principles of such religions are made evident. This leads to the realization that such principles do not allow their beliefs to evolve alongside the war machine that they create. Following this the manipulative powers of some religions are shown to make the religions that are preyed upon become the predator, which is shown to create lies to hold on to ancient beliefs, and in creating such lies they are shown to actually go against some of their own beliefs. This leads to some of the coercive methods–again–being shown and realised. Of which the problems that are created by such a system also re-emerge. Hence the problems that are created by the predatory religions that are unable to realise that they are predatory also emerge. When that type of religion is at such a loss of realization, the unnatural actions of such religions become evident and such religions are then realised as being unnatural. This leads to the realization that such religions are like a plague and will inevitably wipe themselves out. But in being a plague they could renew themselves–and probably would–in a different form. Then it is made evident that such a plague will not evolve its beliefs and in not doing so it is not allowing free will, and in not allowing free will; it is shown to be controlling the mind and increasing its own population by manipulation. This leads to the realization that most religions are predatory through the nature of man. But some of these predatory religions are shown to create many problems when their beliefs lead them to stagnation. One of the major problems that this causes is the problem that arises when a religion splits and evolves into different predators. But this in itself is seen as problematic, because the new predators that evolve from such religions are still stagnated by their beliefs and the only way out of this is shown to be the evolution of the beliefs. This leads to the realization that when different predators emerge from the same religion and turn on one another [as they do]; they will probably make themselves extinct. This extinction would probably come about through the dissatisfaction of many of the predatory religions followers, of which; some would convert to other religions, which were not necessarily predatory. Hence the threat that non predatory religions pose to predatory religions is made evident.

True understanding begins with the realization that most religions are hindered by their ancient scriptures. This leads to the players making evident that partial understanding of science without the understanding of the consequences could be catastrophic. Following this the finite nature of our solar system and the universe is made evident, which leads to the limits of our understanding of the universe and other planes of existence being realised. Following this it becomes evident that a being that is immortal is not truly comprehendible by the human race in its present state. This leads to the realization that the chaotic nature of creation will remain within the human race, because anything that is not truly comprehendible will create chaos when it is investigated. Following this some of the reasons for the untruths within religion are shown to be unlike the mistakes of science, because science tries to discover the truth even if it shows some of its own mistakes. Such a search for truth was then realised to be uncomfortable for the many dogmatic religions hierarchy, and the rulers of the people that followed such religious practices. This leads to the realization that the scriptures that are proven incorrect by science could show that the God of such scriptures can make mistakes.

The use of things that are considered miraculous or acts of the Divine can usually be explained or put down to superstition. Superstition is then realised to be a powerful tool that is used by some religions to create many myths and legends; that are also used as fear tactics to control their followers. Hence the discussion enters the stage where it is realised that most religions are held in bondage by their none philosophical ways, and their explanation of what happens after the death of the physical form, which leads to an examination of the possible cause and effects of some near death experiences, which leads to the realization that the illusory world of maya could be inescapable after the present physical body is deceased. Due to this it is made evident that it is possible, that consciousness could move within a different time scale once the body has died. Hence the problems that surround the awareness of time, other dimensions, and other universes emerge. This leads to the realization that whilst the physical being is so constrained by its input capabilities it could have lost its knowledge of past universes. Hence the hiding of some truths is made evident when the manipulation of some religions is re-assessed. Following this it becomes evident that some religions are not interested in the truth that science delivers to them, because they are only interested in enslaving the population with their dictatorial beliefs. After this the issues that surround morality and metaphysics are seen to be problematic in their making, because of differing ideals. This leads to the use of the imagination to explain some scientific evidence as acts of a God. Following this it is realised that some of metaphysical theory only remains metaphysical whilst there is no empirical evidence for it. This leads to the problems that are associated with empirical and a priori reasoning being examined in a religious context. Hence it is made evident that many religions use a priori reasoning to explain the untruths within their scriptures. It is then made evident that truths can be lost and dissatisfaction can emerge when such reasoning is used. Following this it is realised that some truths can be misused and be unbeneficial to the human race [especially when scientific reasoning is ignored]. The use of a devil and demons are realised to be the main way in which religions can ignore what is proved to be unbeneficial to the human race within its scriptures, and to conspire against the truths that show some of the falsehoods within such scriptures. It is then made evident that some religions need to be caged and kept in check, because they could cause irreversible and unacceptable damage. Following this it is made evident that any true religion needs to be able to evolve and rectify its mistakes if it is to remain true. But following this it is also realised that the dogmatic religions are not liable to realise an important truth that goes against its scriptures until it is too late. Hence the reason for such actions become realised when it is made evident that in the short term it has benefited a religions hierarchy to dismiss evidence that has no short term benefit for them. It is then made evident that such a dismissal of evidence will only continue whilst the followers of such religions are held in bondage by the religions scriptures and/or hierarchy. Hence it is realised that the religions that enslave their followers in such ways are only creating disharmony, and are becoming unbeneficial to the human race and all other species.

The Final Death or Evolution gives a final conclusion on the events that have been theorized upon in some of these discussions. Therefore; the book needs to be read for this concluding chapter to be explained. In saying this, it should be realised that the end chapter is self explanatory through the title. Therefore and the reason that the book needs to be fully read before this last chapter can be fully understood this introduction skips the last chapter.

1

THE PROBLEMS OF BELIEF

After a deep draught of her tea Gaia says: "Merlin my friend, how do you theorise on religious texts that only have the Romans as authors. That is religions that are not of their own culture, but that are only noted by Roman authors?"

Merlin inhales long and deeply upon his pipe and replies: "my dear Gaia, I find it easiest to compare other ancient writings with those of the Roman authors, and then I try to find similarities within the separate texts. By this means of examination the validity of the Roman texts can be judged. I find this method essential, because the early roman authors tended to have rather contradictory views on the same subject."

Momentarily Gaia sits in deep thought, and suddenly she replies: "ah, but if you compare other religious writings with the Roman authors, the comparison can only be a comparison! Therefore, the comparison cannot be relied upon as a means to judge the other religions, because they are not of the culture that the Roman authors remark upon."

After stroking back, her long white hair, Pallas remarks: "if, you cannot use comparison to judge a culture that does not use the written word for its religious rites; then all you have is the written word of a victorious culture [like that of the Romans over the Celts], that use the word in its own religious and ethical teaching. Unfortunately that type of teaching has to be used and treated with some suspicion, because victorious races tend to think of the vanquished as inferior."

Merlin takes another long inhalation upon his pipe, clicks the fingers of his left hand and then he replies: "if contradiction and comparison are a part of the only sources of information that are available to us, we must surely start with the comparison, because if we compare we can use sources that are not necessarily of one cultural origin."

Gaia stirs a spoonful of honey into her tea and after taking a sip of her newly sweetened tea she says: "so, if we need to start with comparison we should compare the One-God religions with the many older Pagan religions pantheons of Divinities. I say much older, because the Pagan religions oldest written religion of Hindu predates that of the earliest written records of the One-Gods Hebrew scriptures."

Just before he comes into the debate, Michael pours seven glasses of mead, hands them around and then he says: "perhaps we should start this comparison with the Hindu, Greek and Roman authors!"

All nod in agreement.

As soon as Sankara has taken a sip of the mead he says: "perhaps we should start with the first part of dialogue 23 in the Uddhava Gita,[1] which is:

1 The Radiant One, Krishna, said, understanding essential oneness of Perusha (the transcendent self) and Prakriti (the origin of the universe) helps you to avoid making judgements about the nature and action of others.

2 To praise or criticize is simply to make a commitment to that which is unreal. This can only lead to a vision that is always limited to duality.

3 When an individual is dreaming of sleeping deeply he or she loses awareness of the external world. If you see only the world of multiplicities and do not extend your vision to the one, you will be like the dreamer or the sleeper and continue to enter the illusion of death.

4 In a duality that does not exist what is the real and what is the unreal? What is good and what is bad? Yet making such judgements and speaking about them gives them a reality in ones mind.

5 Reflections echoes and mirages-even though one knows they are unreal-will cause a reaction. Thus the body continues to inspire a fear of death as long as one identifies with it.

6 The supreme self alone is; it is the creator and the created; the protector and the protected; the destroyer and the destroyed.

7 Therefore nothing other than the self exists. That which appears to exist, that threefold category of the self of each being or object, the agency by which it exists and moves, and the thing itself-all exists within the self alone and only appear as separate on account of maya (the false knowledge or the illusion of that which is limited by measurement)."

---

[1] The Uddhava Gita Translated by Swami Ambikananda Sarawati Francis Lincoln Ltd 2000

Pallas takes another sip of her mead and replies: "this self seems to have similarities with the otherworldly ideals of the Celts and the Greeks. But in saying this it must be realised that these otherworldly ideals are very different, for instance; the shade of Achilles in Homers Odyssey is very different from the ideals of reincarnation in the Hindu and that of the Celtic ideals."

Gaia looks up and replies: "if the shades of the dead do not reincarnate, how did they come into being in the individual from wherever they came? That is if the shade or the soul is not able to reincarnate, then how did it come to be in the physical body?"

Pingala takes a long and deep draught of her mead and then she replies: "in being such a logical race the Greeks would not have considered the physical possibility of reincarnation, because they could have no empirical evidence of it, and this would be due to them not being able to realise the self through deep meditation."

After a long pause Gaia replies: "if deep meditation or a self induced trance is the only way to truly realise the object of the reincarnation of the self[2], why does the logical Greek mind miss this point?"

Pallas quickly answers: "that would be because the logical thinkers would have no realization beyond the empirical evidence of the physical world [that is evidence that is not open to the physical senses of touch, sight, smell, taste, and hearing]. In other words if it is not available to the five senses it does not exist within logical reasoning, because logic demands physical existence for the empirical proof that its reasoning demands. Therefore non-empirical theory is illogical and cannot be proven. So we must realise that the discussion can only continue in the realms of probability and metaphysics."

Merlin speedily replies: "Pallas my dear lady, what you are saying is correct, therefore we must lose the problem of the validity that surrounds the different authors of religious ideals and theorize upon the theories that they propose!

---

[2] The self is the soul in the Hindu scriptures, but this self has to be completely realised before the individual stops reincarnating and loses the illusion that is created by the physical world.

Although the last point on logic is correct the problem is more of how we use the senses for logical and metaphysical theorising, because the logical theories depend upon the physical world to reason, but this in itself is problematic, because the logical world still has the dream world of its members and this has the same problem as sight, which is: how does the grey mass that is our brain convert the greyness into colour? Like the colour dream our colour vision can only begin to be understood by metaphysical reasoning. Therefore empirical evidence must not be the only premise by which we judge our religious theories.

In having made the last point on reasoning I must now say that in every religion I have come across there are theories that seem to have no logical foundation. But in realizing this we must also realise that the theories that are proposed by all religions are logical in their eyes, for instance; the plague of locusts that were seen to be made by God in the bible; could now be explained by scientific means and accepted as a natural phenomenon by most people."

Pingala takes another sip of her mead and says: "the problem with Merlin's reasoning is that religious experiences can only be founded when that person has a passionate belief in their religion. Therefore we must realise that the belief in a happening—whether it is founded within science or not—can still be put down to an act of the Divine, because it could be said that the Divine used the scientific laws that created any natural event at any particular time. But this is problematic, because the belief that everything is a creation of the Divine is illogical, because logic is dependent on the five senses."

Sankara looks up from his glass, smiles and says: "do not our senses deceive us? And in deceiving us do not our senses need the instruments of science to make our understanding less corruptible? I would theorize so, but in theorizing that I would remind you that the human mind or the soul is the only means by which any theory can be perceived!"

Michael pulls his chair away from the fire and replies: "what you are saying is that all reasoning comes from the mind and in coming from the mind reasoning does not need to be influenced by external forces. Although we must realise that is not the means by which theories are generally formed, because most theories are formed by a logical and empirical process, but in saying this it must be realised that all and not just part of the theories are formed by the human will, that is the will of an individual that is forming a theory."

Gaia looks into Michael's eyes and then she says: "that seems to be Sankara's point but it must be realised that everything has to be influenced by something for it to be able to exist at this time or in the past. Although in realizing that we must also realise that the human mind or the soul is a very powerful creative force."

Pallas smiles at Gaia and then Pallas remarks: "of course there is another possibility and that is; that the human mind or the soul is not a creation of the Divine it is what it is, and in being what it is; it is as immortal as those that are considered Divine or timeless!"

Michael whistles softly and replies: "bloody hell Pallas; that is going very deeply into the Hindu philosophy of the self. In fact what you are implying is that the self is and always has been its own creator!"

Pallas looks round smiles and replies: "what I am implying is much deeper than that, in fact what I am implying is: the self is what it is and is the creator of its own destiny and reality; but in realizing this we must also realise that the self or the immortal soul must be Divine in itself for it to be immortal or timeless."

Merlin cuts seven slices of fruit cake that he has produced from his rucksack, passes them round and then he says: "does this not go deeply against the Christian, Judaic, and Islamic religions ideology of their One-God being the creator of all?"

Pingala takes a bite from her piece of cake, finishes it and replies: "are not these One-God faiths contradictory, because their bible does not believe that other animals have souls and in this book the blood is the soul and if the blood is the soul, then why do other animals that are not of the human race bleed if they have no soul?

Pallas finishes her piece of cake and replies: "my point is that in being Godlike the immortal soul has no dependency on the God of the Islamic, Judaic, or Christian religions or many of the divine entities of some other faiths. But in theorizing that we must also realise that the Divine have ways of controlling the soul that is dependent on its physical form. This means that whilst we are dependent on the physical form we are subject to the laws of Karma and are open to the effects of those that we consider Divine."

Gaia looks at Pallas, smiles and then Gaia replies: "so if the Divine are able to show and create a path for the physical being whilst the immortal soul is dependent on the physical beings existence for its awareness, the Divine must have some greater power than the immortal soul whilst it is imprisoned by its physical dependency."

Sankara smiles at Gaia and remarks: "perhaps the Divine do not predetermine the destiny of the immortal soul, perhaps they only act as a guide to our destiny. Therefore our destiny would be ordained by our own personal choices. This would mean that the immortal soul would lose the knowledge of its past incarnations if it did not reach a stage of enlightenment.

Pallas suddenly remarks: "what about the death of children and those that are never in a position to learn?"

Sankara smiles and replies: "perhaps those of us that are not fortunate enough to learn of the immortal soul in their present form: will be able to learn of this in their next physical form."

Pallas quickly replies: "does this mean that as we pass from body to body; we have no chance of this realization until we live in a situation that puts this knowledge within our grasp?"

Sankara puts another log on the fire and replies: "that is correct, but knowledge of the self or the immortal soul is not always grasped by those that have it within their reach. Therefore it is possible to have the knowledge of the ancients within our grasp and then be lost by our own stupidity or by the foolish actions of others."

Morrighan turns away from the stove, walks across the room, sits at the table and then she remarks: "of course Sankara is right, but there are those of other worlds and other realms that have not been acknowledged. Therefore I cannot hold everything you have said to be the complete truth, because once the other worlds are seen as they truly are; the realisation that these folk affect the path of our soul should come into existence!"

Michael finishes his piece of cake and replies: "what you are saying is that the path of the soul could be affected by the spirits of myth and legend or the phaery folk that are associated with this world."

After brushing her long dark hair away from her face, Morrighan looks at Michael and replies: "your thoughts of the other worlds and their connection to the soul seem to be almost correct, but you do not seem to have grasped the concept of the planet having its own soul–of which we are all connected to!"

When everyone has finished their cake, Merlin fills the bowl of his pipe with tobacco, lights it, inhales deeply, passes it to Morrighan and after starting the ritual he replies: "if the planet has a soul [of which I have no doubt it has] to which we are all connected, the ancient tribes, races, and species that are now extinct on the surface, must now, surely, live within the sole. Therefore the planet and all its beings can only go as far as physical destruction and not into total extinction if the soul is immortal."

After drawing deeply on the pipe Morrighan exhales and passes the pipe to Pingala and then Morrighan says: "perhaps we should go one step further and consider the universal soul rather than that of the individual being or planet!

After all that has been discussed so far the idea of the universal soul is the realization of the Atman[3] or the self and the universality of that theory. What I mean by this is that if the realization of the self is the one true reality, then all religions would become part of the self or the immortal soul if the immortal soul is the only true reality."

Pingala draws on the pipe, passes it to Pallas and then Pingala replies: "surely if the immortal soul encompasses all religions the immortal soul must have knowledge of all of them!"

Pallas inhales and passes the pipe to Sankara and then she says: "it is not necessary for the whole of religion to be encompassed by the individual parts of the universal soul, because each part only needs the truth that is applicable to it for them all to become universal knowledge, when they are

---

[3] Atman is the Buddhist version of the soul that is within the empirical being; in other words the Self of Hindu theology.

connected. In a sense this is similar to a single piece in a jigsaw puzzle–one piece on its own doesn't make the picture, but without it the picture can never be complete."

Sankara inhales, passes the pipe to Michael and then Michael inhales deeply upon the pipe and remarks: "if the immortal soul is a piece of the universal soul then why is there so much evil in the world? And why if it is universal is there no loss of knowledge if the evil piece of the jigsaw has a place within the universal soul?"

Michael passes the pipe to Gaia and Gaia inhales deeply and remarks: "my dear Michael if there was no evil then how do we define good–in fact how do we define good?"

Finally the pipe returns to Merlin and he empties it and puts it away.

Pallas suddenly remarks: "the act of evil appears to differ from faith to faith, but in general it appears to be whatever goes against the principles of the singular religion, for example: the ancient Greeks religion believed in human sacrifice as do the One-God religions, but in saying this the religions of the One-God are self contradictory, because they say that sacrifice to a God is evil and they have shed many lives in bloody combat and burnt witches at the stake in the name of their God and what is this if not human sacrifice! Hence it should become obvious that when they state that sacrificing a person to a God or Goddess is evil they contradict themselves when they state that their God is pure in its goodness!"

Merlin quickly replies: "this must surely mean that good and evil are part of every living soul and if this is the truth good and evil have no singular truthful definition, because it would be impossible to perceive one without the other and if one cannot perceive one without the other; then evil becomes a necessary form of judgement and once this moral code of good and evil is established it becomes the ethics on which the lives of a particular race or religion is run."

Pallas pauses for a moment and then she replies: "what you appear to be making evident; is that evil is as much a part of the soul as good is. With this being the reality the good and the evil that are within the soul are part of the divine and part of the universe and once this is realised, the truth of war, destruction and death; start to become apparent to those that wish to see the truth of their own being ."

Gaia swiftly replies: "blood and sand Pallas! What you are making evident is that immorality is as much a function of the soul or the Divine as morality is."

Pallas quickly replies: "morality is only defined by what is considered to be immoral; therefore the whole universe and the Divine consist of both other wise they would not exist at all!"

Merlin nods his head and replies: "so the immortal soul must be a divine reality if it has the understanding of good and evil, because in having this understanding the immortal soul must be divine for it to be immortal. But in realizing this it must also be realised that the soul being immortal or divine does not have to be of what people consider to be of a good nature for it to be divine, and this is probably where the confusing ideals of good and evil have their origin. I say confusing , because many different religions have many different ideals surrounding good and evil, and if we take this into consideration–along with the last remark of Pallas–it becomes quite clear that these definitions are not easy to define, because of the many different religions and practises, and in theorizing on these religions and practises it becomes clear that we cannot define good without evil, but good and evil can differ in different religions and therefore the relationship between good and evil should be linked to the universal soul for it to be able to be clearly defined at all."

Pallas smiles looks at Merlin and then she replies: "that is problematic, because when the differences on the religious theologies of evil are approached we will find that what is considered as evil is approached and defined in many different ways, for example; the One-God religions only accept the Gods and Goddesses of other religions as evil beings that are associated with their devil!

Therefore the concept of evil cannot be properly defined until we get to the root of the theologies that use evil as a means to make other religions seem Godless and in league with the devil!"

Michael suddenly remarks: "the major problem with the One-God religions is that; they have no theology that accepts that there is any truth or Divine beings outside that of their own theology. Therefore they consider any outside divine beings to be an incarnation of their devil or to be one of his cohorts, or to be part of the evil that is within their devils conspiracies."

Morrighan sighs, looks at Sankara, smiles at Michael and then she says: "what Michael has just said is a major problem for the One-God religions, because they believe their god is the creator of all and if he created all that is; this God must have evil within it as well as good for this evil to be able to exist at all."

Sankara smiles at Morrighan and replies: "of course there can be no other way for evil to arise; unless it is part of the creation of all and in realizing this we must also realise that there can be no such thing as perfection, when everyone's ideology of perfection differs. Therefore the theology that surrounds the perfection of the One-God is flawed; because they believe everything their One-God does is good—even in the action of killing thousands as in their biblical legend of Noah's ark!"

Michael looks at Sankara, smiles at Morrighan, brushes his blonde hair back from his eyes and then Michael says: "what you are implying goes against all the One-God's principles, because in their belief their God is perfect and does not make mistakes, because it is their belief that mistakes and evil come from the free will that he has given to all the human race."

Morrighan smiles and winks at Pingala, looks at Michael and then Morrighan says: "surely the perfect One-God that is the supposed creator of all cannot be perfect if his creations have imperfections within them. Therefore this theology cannot be factual, because humanity cannot agree on what their idea of perfection is; and if humanity cannot agree on their ideal perfection; is it not probable that the only perfection that is available to humanity or any intelligent being is their own singular idea of perfection? I theorise that the answer to this is yes, because there are so many splits in the different religious ethics that surround the One-God theologies; that the ideal of a singular creator of all becomes highly improbable, because if the One-God allowed so many different interpretations of his faith; it is showing its imperfection by not making its scriptures clear enough for its followers to understand. Therefore I suggest that with there being so many splits these splits imply that there is more than one creator."

Michael looks at Morrighan and then he replies: "it is possible that the One-God has many different aspects, like a cut diamond has many different facets!"

Pingala looks at Michael, smiles and replies: "if the One-God has many different aspects and all are one, then the evil that is within creation cannot exist unless evil is one of the aspects of the One-God, and if that is so; the One-God can never destroy the evil that is within the world without destroying itself. Therefore the major contradiction of the creation of the One-God's arch rival comes into being, because if the goodness of the One-God is true; then if it created all it created the devil and in creating the devil the One-God created the means by which evil is supposed to be created. Therefore he either made a mistake or part of his so-called perfection has evil within its being."

Michael puts his thumb to his mouth and is about to reply when Merlin suddenly remarks: "that will do you no good unless you have touched the salmon of wisdom!"[4]

Michael laughs, grins and says: "before Merlin was so bloody cheeky; I was about to say that the One-God theology does seem contradictory, unless the culture that received those scriptures was the only culture that those scriptures were written or intended for. Therefore the One-God theologies may not be applicable to other faiths and in not being applicable to other faiths it may not have evil within it, if the Divine of other faiths were where evil first appeared."

Pingala puts a kettle on the stove, whistles softly to herself and then she replies: "what you are implying suggests that the One-God faiths have no more power over the soul; than the individual has control over the soul after the death of the physical being and in implying this you are also implying that other Divine beings exist!"

Michael watches the steam rise from the kettle, smiles at Pingala and then he replies: "yes I am implying that there is more than One Divine being; in fact I believe that the God of

---

[4] The salmon of wisdom or knowledge appears in many pagan myths, but the one referred to here comes from the Celtic myth that surrounds the tree of wisdom.

the One-God faiths never actually denies this, because in Exodus 1-20 Moses begins by saying:

And God spake all these words, saying, I am the Lord God, which have brought thee out of the land of Egypt out of the house of bondage.
Thou shalt have no other Gods before me.'

Michael pauses for a moment and then he carries on: "what this scripture is saying is not a denial of other Divine beings or Gods: it is saying that his followers should worship no other Divine being except himself the One-God of their faith."

Pingala puts the pot of freshly boiled tea in front of Morrighan and then Pingala replies: "although the scriptures of the One-God religions do not deny the existence of other Divine beings; they still seem to think that their One-God will bring peace on earth. But this defies logic, because their scriptures show a god that is warlike on those that he considers to have defied him."

After letting the tea brew Morrighan pours seven cups and passes them around, and after taking a sip Michael replies: "do not Pagan divinities punish the living or the souls of the dead that offend them?"

Gaia stirs some honey into her tea, takes a sip, smiles at Michael and then she replies: "yes the Pagan divine do take revenge upon those that have defied them, but these Divine do not claim to be perfect or to be able to bring peace on earth, because what use would peace on earth be to a God or Goddess of war."

Pallas takes a sip of her cup of tea and says: "if some people would admit that their God is not perfect and able to bring about peace on earth, they would begin to accept that good and evil exists within all our souls, because with the realization that their God is not Perfect, they would begin to realise that one cannot exist without the other. So whether they admit it or not good and evil are as much a part of the Divine as they are a part of the human soul, because if good alone existed it would be impossible to acknowledge it without the knowledge and existence of what is evil. For example, how would we know thieving was wrong unless we knew it was bad to do such an act and in having such knowledge we must have it within ourselves to do so!"

Michael takes another sip of his tea and replies: "let us accept that good and evil are a necessary balance for either to exist. But in realizing this we must surely be able to realise what good and evil are."

Pingala looks across at Michael and replies: "this is problematic, because good and evil are not of the same theology in all religions. Although it must be realised that most religions have similar ethics on what they consider to be good and evil, but in realizing this we should also realise that some religions use their ideals to demonize others."

Sankara drinks the last of his tea and says: "good and evil can be theorized as part of the illusory world that humanity has created for itself. Therefore it should also be theorized that good and evil are not separate entities at all, because they are so needful of each other; they are at one with each other and neither can exist without the other, and therefore they are one within the soul and the degree of use of either entity is entirely dependent on the self."

Morrighan looks at Sankara nods her head and then she says: "in being responsible for our own actions we are still punishable for our wrongdoings by our own kind and our Divine entity or entities. But this is problematic, because there are differences in religious beliefs of what is or is not evil. Therefore the religions that do not acknowledge that evil is within the soul of all its followers and its own deity or deities is lost in a world of fantasy, because there is no way they can perceive one without the other. Therefore we must realise that good never totally vanquishes evil and evil never totally vanquishes good, because both are one and in being one they can never totally defeat the other that is part of that one, because to do so would mean that the self that it is within would have to defeat themselves!"

Michael looks at Morrighan and then he asks: "if the soul is good and the Divine are good and evil combined, is the soul as immortal as the ones that are divine? And if the soul is as immortal as the Divine, is the soul actually Divine?"

Morrighan feeds the raven that is perched next to her and then she replies: "the theories that some of us have suggested, do make the soul appear to be divine and this is very plausible, because in being immortal it would be as timeless as the Divine."

Merlin looks at Morrighan and then he says: "the soul could be a deity in training if the soul that is within the physical being has not realised its full potential, and therefore the soul that has done evil and has been cast back into a physical existence that is able to reason; is possibly a soul that is being punished for its previous life's reasoning or it could be a soul that has had an unfortunate past life that deserves another physical life to enable it to grow in spiritual awareness."

Sankara smiles at Merlin and then he replies: "that theory would make sense, but it does not reasonably assess the situation, because we cannot understand the reasoning that is available to a soul that has been condemned to be another member of the animal kingdom, for example; we could not understand the reasoning abilities of the soul that has been condemned to be a worm a thousand times for a thousand years."

Pallas turns towards Sankara and then she replies: "perhaps as the worm; the soul has the ability to reflect on its past mistakes and be able to rectify them when it reaches a form that can realise its potential as the Self."

Pingala picks up Pallas's flute, passes it to her and then Pingala says: "to be made to reincarnate as a worm suggests that there are forces; that have a way of directing the soul on its never ending journey and this journey is then–for a time–not in full control of the individual self.

Therefore it is possible that the evil that is committed by the individual is not solely of the individuals doing."

Michael suddenly asks: "if the individual soul or the self has a free will it would–surely–not be able to be controlled by any external forces?"

Pingala smiles and replies: "the self does have free will, but like the winds in the sails and the rudder that guides a sailing vessel upon the oceans there is no surety of time or direction if the wind dies and the rudder breaks, because like the sailing vessel there are external forces that are beyond the control and the power of the reasoning of the self. Therefore it would be possible for the self to be corrupted without its immediate knowledge, just as a sailing vessel can be sunk by the unseen part of an iceberg."

Michael smiles at Pingala and then he says: "are not the immortal souls all powerful and all knowing like the One-God faiths believe their master to be?"

Morrighan smiles at Pallas and then at Michael and then Morrighan replies: "any Divine or physical being that proposes to be all knowing is held in bondage by their own illusion of grandeur, because to be all knowing the being would possess knowledge of all future events and enable it to stop the persecution of its followers."

Michael puts some logs on the fire walks across the room, sits opposite Morrighan and then he says: "are not our paths in life predetermined by the Fates or Muses of some pagan religions and in realising this does it not imply that the Fates or Muses are all knowing?"

Merlin takes his harp out of the case, looks at Michael and then Merlin replies: "the Fates or the Muses weave many a path for a person, but the Fates or the Muses only know the outcome of a chosen path that a person is on, and with this in mind we must realise that the path that one takes is chosen by their own free will and not the will of the Fates or the Muses. Therefore the Fates or the Muses are not all knowing, they just know the consequences of the path that we choose."

Michael looks at Merlin and asks: "if the Fates or the Muses know the consequences of the paths that we take; then–surely– they are all knowing?"

Pallas looks across at Michael and then she answers: "the Fates or the Muses are believed to weave the paths of our physical lives; they are not seen to weave the paths of our souls or to have the knowledge of all creation."

Merlin gives a broad grin and replies: "perhaps the creation never existed at all, perhaps life and the universe is an entity that has no beginning and no end, perhaps it has always existed and it always will; and with this being eternal it is possible that in its infinity it can change an infinite number of times. Therefore the immortal soul–that is part of the universe–is capable of an infinite number of changes."

Pingala raises her eyebrows at Merlin and then she replies: "what you seem to be saying ties in with the theories that surround the Lords of Karma and the illusory world that is created by maya.[5] I theorize this because the illusion that is created by any kind of theology; that supports the theory that there is any kind of divine being, that holds all the knowledge of the future and the past; becomes illogical if the past and future are infinite, because anything that is infinite in existence requires infinite knowledge to understand all that is going to happen to it and all that has happened to it. This is problematic, because the infinite knowledge that is required of it can never be complete, because in being infinite it never comes to an end. Therefore the infinite knowledge can never be complete, because you cannot complete the end of something that never ends. Therefore the immortal soul of the individual cannot be predicted by any Divine being."

Morrighan nods her head, grins and replies: "the Lords of Karma and the illusory force of maya–from the Hindu and Buddhist religions–make the theologies that surround good and evil irrelevant, because the evil that we have done can be washed away when we realise that all we have done in the physical world that is considered to be good or evil; adds to the creation of our own illusion through our self interest."

Merlin starts to conclude the chapter by saying: "we have gone from realizing that the written word is not necessarily infallible, [because some religious theories are not written by the culture that the writing is about, but the culture that is victorious in a war with them] to the conflict of some of the different theologies that surround good and evil within the divine and the immortal soul.

From the evidence that has been attained within the discussion it seems highly plausible that good cannot exist without evil and vice-versa and the immortal soul and the divine beings–of which the immortal soul could be one–have good and evil locked together within themselves. But in theorizing that we

---

[5] Maya is what is considered to be the illusory world of experience in the Hindu religion.

must realise that the individual rarely realises the true balance, because they are wrapped up in their own religious beliefs—as are most of the deities in these religions."

Morrighan smiles and finishes the conclusion by stating: "from Merlin's statement and what we have discussed we should also realise that the Divine soul is not as powerful or knowing as those that are considered to be divinities. I theorize this because these Divinities are not open to the punishments [or do not appear to be] of the Lords of Karma. Fortunately this conclusion shows the need for us to examine the Lords of Karma and the Divine in more detail!

So as I and Pingala have passed the wine and the food the party should begin."

As Morrighan sings the flute of Pallas and the harp of Merlin begin to play for song and dance is now upon this day.

2

THE DIVINE

Amongst the dawn chorus the raven sings its song and Morrighan lets her voice flow.

A new day has dawned upon this winter morn.

The music of the harp the flute and the lute are upon this moot

The music declines and the debate begins....

Michael puts the bacon under the grill looks across at Merlin and says: "from what we have theorized, the One-God of the Middle Eastern cults is nothing more than a local deity, but in theorizing that it should be realised that through holy wars and terror tactics it has become a major figurehead. Therefore this One-God that controls the majority of powerful places in the Western world is actually becoming the One-God it wishes to be!"

Morrighan slices the onions, puts them in the frying pan, and says: "the whole idea of the One-God is problematic, because the One-God can only ever be the One-God of those souls his followers have deceived; by persuading those souls that it is the only true god in existence."

Pingala smiles at Morrighan and replies: "perhaps this One-God of the Middle East is the Egyptian Sun God–Aton–under different names. I theorise this could be so, because Aton, became a monotheistic God of the Egyptians when Akhenaton replaced the Amon cult–and the many deities associated with him–with this One-God ideal of the Sun God."

Pallas finishes buttering the bread, passes it to Michael and then she replies: "what appears to be emerging here is that the Sun God Aton liked the idea of being a god that shared his worship with no other Divine being. Therefore it is possible if not probable that this God uses many names for himself in the creation of the One-God cults of the Middle East."

Merlin helps to make the sandwiches passes them round and says: "what my dear Pallas seems to be suggesting is that the Divine beings are as open to jealousy and greed as are the souls of the physical beings."

Sankara eats a piece of his sandwich and then he says: "if the Divine being is open to emotional responses, then it is possible that the Divine beings are open to all the emotions that are within the immortal soul of the physical beings."

Gaia finishes her sandwich and says: "there is no reason that the Divine should not have all the emotions that are within the immortal soul of the physical being, and in realizing this we should also realise that the Divine beings emotional senses may be on a higher–or perhaps a lower–level than that of the immortal soul of the physical being.

It is also possible that a higher perception of the Divine beings could lose them control of their emotions, because in being heightened their emotions could be in control of them. If this is the case the Divine could be pure emotion and if this is what they are; then what they created is Divine, because it is and has part of the emotions that created it."

The meal is finished and Pallas replies: "if the Divine are pure emotion these emotions must be part of the building blocks of everything that appears in the universe, because nothing can be created without the will of the emotions."

Sankara walks over to the stove, puts the kettle on and says: "of course the Divine are pure emotion–of that there can be no doubt–because everything we experience as a physical being is dependent on our emotions, for example; the sensory action of taste can bring forward the emotions of pleasure and revulsion. Therefore these sensory feelings that are dependent on emotions for our existence are what the immortal soul is built of and deluded by."

Gaia looks at Sankara and then she says: "in being built of pure emotion the Divine are or can be as deluded as the immortal souls that are within the physical being. This is problematic because if the Divine and the immortal soul are deluded; what are they deluded by?"

Morrighan feeds the raven, smiles at Gaia and then she replies: "the ones that are deluded–and that includes the Divine; could be deluded by the illusion that is created by maya."

Michael looks at Morrighan and asks: "what exactly is maya?"[6]

Morrighan smiles at Michael and replies: "maya is the illusion of anything that seems real but is unreal due to it's impermanence in the universe. A simpler explanation of this would be that maya is the world of the physical reality that the physical being and some of the Divine are surrounded by."

Merlin grins at Morrighan and replies: "if some of the Gods and Goddesses are surrounded by this illusion of what is thought of as reality; then–surely–this idea of reality in the physical world is nothing more than a perception that is created by our emotions. Therefore the emotions of the Divine would be the creator of maya and the realisation of this could be the tranquillity that comes upon the self when this is realised."

Looking puzzled; Michael asks: "what is this tranquillity?"

Morrighan looks at him and replies: "this tranquillity is the realization that the only true reality is that of the self!"

Michael nods his head and asks: "when the self is realised and the impermanence of physical reality becomes obvious; does everything–including all the other Divine beings–disappears into oblivion?"

Pingala smiles and answers: "no, everything does not disappear into oblivion and the other Divine beings still exist, but what becomes apparent in realising the soul or the self is; the self or the soul realises that the only reality that is unchangeable is that of the self!"

Michael scratches his head and asks: "if a physical being has many lives, in many different circumstances and does many different things-why does the self not change?"

Pingala smiles and says: "because like the Gods and Goddesses the self or the soul has realised that the only true reality is that of the immortal self, because the self is the only thing that is always there, for example; the food that is on a plate that seems real enough until it is eaten or rotted away, and then it becomes nothing more than an illusion of past events."

---

[6] Although maya has been briefly explained it needs more than a few words in a footnote too show the complexity of this belief.

Merlin takes a jar of honey from the cupboard, places it on the table, and asks: "if the self is the only true reality; then how do we explain the realities of the Gods and Goddesses?"

Pallas looks at Merlin and replies: "perhaps a Goddess or God is what they are and need no explanation, because a Goddess or God would—probably—realise what they are, is what they are. Therefore they must have realised their self, because they would know that to be a Goddess or God of wisdom or war is to be just that."

Michael grins and asks: "Pallas my dear; is not Athena a Goddess of wisdom and a warrior Goddess in the ancient Greek religion?"

Pallas and Morrighan grin broadly at each other and then Pallas replies: "perhaps the wisest of all would need to fight most of all, because the greater the knowledge the greater the conflict!"

Gaia stirs the honey into the cup of tea that Sankara gave her and then she replies: "so, the Divine are complete in the knowledge of themselves and in this knowledge they are satisfied with what they are!"

Merlin takes a sip of his tea and replies: "if they are so content; why do they argue amongst themselves, for example; Loki is known to be at loggerheads with the other Viking Gods as Athena and Aphrodite are in the Trojan War?"

Morrighan and Pallas raise their eyebrows at each other and then Morrighan replies: "like Pallas has made evident; the wisest of all may need to fight the most of all, because the conflictions of separate theories and the passion that is involved in these theories will in some instances lead to conflict, and this would be due to the opposites and the diversifications that are needed to separate anything at all, for example; how could we realise tranquillity without knowing what we have been disturbed and/or disrupted by!

I would theorize that another reason that the Divine have such conflicts is because the Divine are as open to error as are the physical entities that are—at some stage— part of the self or the immortal soul."

Sankara looks deeply into the swirling liquid of his tea, looks out of the window and remarks: "the Rig Veda of Hindu scripture makes some interesting points and shows some uncertainties in the creation of the Gods and some of these are in the first few verses of the creation hymn, which are:

1 There was neither non existence or existence then: there was neither the realm of space nor the sky which is beyond. What stirred? Where? In whose protection? Was there water, bottomless deep?

2 There was neither death nor immortality then. There was no distinguishing sign of night nor of day. That one breathed, windless, by its own impulse. Other than that there was nothing beyond.

3 Darkness was hidden by darkness in the beginning; there was no distinguishing sign, all this was water. The life force that covered with emptiness, that once arose through the power of heat.

4 Desire came upon that one in the beginning; that was the first seed of the mind. Poets seeking in their hearts with wisdom found the existence in non existence.

5 There cord was extended across. Was there below? Was there above? There were seed-placers there were powers. There was impulse beneath; there was giving forth above."

6 Who really knows? Who will proclaim it? Whence was it produced? Whence is this creation? The Gods came afterwards, with the creation of the universe. Who then knows whence it has arisen!

7 Whence this creation has arisen—perhaps it formed itself or perhaps it did not—the one who looks down on it, in the highest heaven, only he knows.[7]

I must say that this seems to tie in with the point that the Gods and Goddesses are open to imperfection and strife, because there is uncertainty in the knowledge of their own creation. This uncertainty becomes even more evident in this next hymn's–The Unknown God, the Golden Embryo–verses 1&10:

1 In the beginning the Golden Embryo arose. Once he was born, he was the lord of creation. He held in place the earth and the sky. Who is the God whom we should worship with the oblation.

10 O Prajapati lord of progeny, no one but you embraces all these creatures. Grant us the desires for which we offer you oblations. Let us be lords of riches.[8]

---

[7] The Rig Veda p25-26 translated by Wendy Doniger O'Flaherty, Penguin books 1981

The two verses show that there is a gap in knowledge, because in the first verse it points to the creator being born and having arose, but it does not mention from whence the creator came and it took until verse 10 to actually name the creator that is worshipped and given oblations to.

After finding the creator to be worshipped, the next verses of the Hymn of Man could be theorised to show that Man has a higher potential than that of the creator, because it is said:

1 The man has a thousand heads, a thousand eyes, a thousand feet. He pervaded the earth on all sides and extended beyond as far as ten fingers.

2 It is the man who is all this, whatever has been and whatever is to be. He is the ruler of immortality, when he grows beyond everything through food.[9]

Having spoken those verses I must now ask; if the man grows beyond everything through food, does he outgrow the Divine? And if the man is the ruler of immortality, then–surely–the man must have been in existence before the Gods and Goddesses?"

Gaia sips her tea and says: "perhaps the wisdom that is available to the immortal self is not sufficient whilst it is encumbered by the physical being. I theorise this, because just like a bottle of water that overflows when it is overfilled, the physical body only has a limited amount of storage before it too overflows!"

Pingala sits next to Morrighan, lights some sweet smelling incense and says: "is it or is it not also possible that in being the ruler of immortality, mankind is being controlled by the power that is immortality and in being controlled by such a power, mankind can never realise this until it has destroyed the bondage of the physical being, by realizing the self, and in realizing this mankind would have reached such a high plane of reality that is true to the self and beyond the control of the Divine. In fact it is possible that the Divine are in the service of mankind."

Michael smiles and asks: "if the Divine are not in control of mankind, then why are the Divine able to kill the human being?"

---

[8] Ibid p27&28
[9] The Rig Veda translated by Wendy Doniger O Flaherty p30 Penguin books 1981

Morrighan quickly replies: "perhaps they cannot destroy the human being; perhaps they can only destroy the physical being or entity that incorporates the soul or the self. I theorise this, because one thing we seem to have forgot is the other worlds that–in many shamanic beliefs–the soul or the self travels to."

Michael prepares his watercolours, starts to paint and then he replies: "if the immortal soul or the self can transcend into different worlds, then–surely–the Gods and Goddesses must be able to do so, because their powers of reasoning and action must–surely–outweigh those of the immortal soul or the self, if they can destroy the physical being that holds the immortal soul or the self in bondage."

Morrighan smiles and says: "there is not much power needed in the act of destroying a physical being. So, if you do not need much power to destroy a physical being and the immortal soul or the self will transcend after its destruction; the hold of the Divine over it is broken when the self has become separated; from the prison of physical existence."

Sankara looks over at Michael's painting, smiles, gives a nod of approval and then he says: "this is problematic, because the self can only be free to journey when it becomes enlightened and freed from its physical bonds and from the Lords of Karma."

Michael asks: "does this theological journeying apply to the enlightened people of all religions?"

Merlin smiles and replies: "I would say not, because the One-God religions are limited by their ideologies on heaven and hell [although I must also say that this does not only apply to the One-God religions]."

Pallas looks out of the window, smiles, looks back and replies: "if the enlightened go beyond the realms of the Divine; by losing their need for the impermanence of the physical world, then they must–surely–become a Divine of the Divine, because if the Gods, Goddesses and the Lords of Karma no longer have control over them; then the self must be the most powerful of all the Divine and if this is so; then how did the lesser Gods and Goddesses persuade the self to enter the world of impermanence?"

Gaia walks over to the fire, puts another piece of wood on the fire and then she replies: "perhaps the Divine are the equals of the self and perhaps the self became part of the physical world of its own accord. I theorize that this is probably so, because if the self wished to gain complete enlightenment; then it would need experiences that are not a surety. Therefore it becomes simpler to understand that without the realisation of impermanence, the self cannot realise what is permanent."

Pingala watches the flames as they rise and then she says: "it must also be possible for the Gods and Goddesses to transcend to the higher plane if the self is able to do so. Therefore it is possible that the Gods and Goddesses are the self once it has become enlightened. Hence we must now realise that it is also possible that all the Gods and Goddesses have gone through the stages of physical impermanence to become enlightened, for example; if a Goddess or a God of war becomes that through enlightenment of the self, they would already know that there is no way of knowing what peace is without their wars [in other words how can one be seen to exit if there is nothing to exit]!"

Morrighan goes to the window to watch the oncoming storm and then she replies: "from what we have–so far–discussed; the Divine beings seem to be an image of the self that is in the physical being. But in theorizing this we must realise that the Divine beings that some physical beings give sacrifices, seem to be at one with what they are and in being at one with what they are, it is possible that even the dark ones have reached their own truth and enlightenment. Therefore it is also possible that they are no different from the enlightened self."

Pallas smiles at Morrighan and then Pallas replies: "perhaps, that is so, but that is problematic, because maya is the force that is behind the illusion of the impermanence that is within the physical worlds, and if the Divine are as affected by the power of maya as those within the physical worlds; then it is possible that the force of maya is a member of the Divine and not just a theological means of creating a force of illusion. I theorize this, because if the so-called reality of the permanence within the impermanence of the physical world is created by an outside agent; then the outside agent that is a creator of so many illusory forces must–surely–be Divine!"

Sankara smiles and replies: "that maybe so, but there are aspects of the Divine that cannot be explained by the idea of maya, for example; the Divine that realised their position and lose the illusory power of maya would-surely lose their position as well, because a God or Goddess of war can only be a Goddess or God of war in the physical world where wars occur!"

Merlin strokes his beard and then he replies: "if the Divine are enlightened enough to know what they are is what they are; then the Divine could have already lost maya, because they would be under no illusion of what their purpose is. Therefore the Divine could have an understanding that is beyond the reach of those that are influenced by the power of maya, because it is also possible that the illusion that is created by maya is not an illusion at all, because it is yet again possible that the Divine and the physical world are part of a never ending circle of life, death and rebirth."

Morrighan smiles and replies: "if the Divine are part of the never ending and never beginning circle of life; then it is possible that the Divine do not know how they came to be and if that is the truth; then how can we ever theorise the purpose of that which is unknown to itself? Perhaps we cannot, perhaps that is part of the power of maya!"

Michael smiles at Morrighan and then he replies: "this entire theory that surrounds maya is problematic, because most religions do not have any theories that surround the impermanence of the physical world. Therefore the Divine of these religions are not encumbered by the problems of the immortals enlightenment, and the realization of the self or the immortal soul that is being held in bondage by the physical being."

Pallas looks at Morrighan and Pingala and then Pallas replies: "perhaps the Divine that hold the physical being and the immortal soul in the bondage of their worship are fully aware of the concept of maya, but in being so aware these Divine entities have some kind of pleasure or need of the worship that the unenlightened self gives them while it is still held in bondage, for example; the shades of the dead that are held onto by the ancient Greek Gods appear as immortal shades of what they were as a physical being, and this could be seen as an unenlightened soul that is held in momentary stasis; by the Gods and Goddesses of this religion."[10]

Pingala looks and smiles at Pallas and then Pingala replies: "perhaps the reason that the Divine are so different in the diverse cultures that occupy the different regions upon this planet is, because the Divine are as different as the cultures that support them and if this is the reality of the mater; enlightenment may not have been reached by all of the Divine in all of the separate cultures."

Michael suddenly asks: "if all the divine were not enlightened; then what would the measure of enlightenment of the Divine be?"

Merlin smiles and replies: "perhaps the Divine are what they appear to be to the individual soul, and in being what they appear to be they are just that and nothing else!"

Sankara smiles and replies: "the individual soul can be wrong if it has not reached enlightenment. Therefore the realization that is needed to realise what the purpose of the Divine is cannot be fully understood until the soul has reached enlightenment. Hence we should begin to realise that each cultures Divine needs different stages or types of enlightenment for them to be fully understood. If this is the truth of the matter; this could be hugely problematic, because any writer of any religion would have to be enlightened in the ways of the Divine whose purpose they have discussed."

Gaia smiles and says: "it is possible that the Divine have always realised the impermanence of the physical world and are not concerned about a concept of non-reality; that is actually a reality within the Divine of the faiths that believe in the everlasting circle of birth, death and rebirth."

Morrighan smiles and replies: "the circle of life is only within the faiths that appear to be unconcerned with it and these faiths do not seem to have any reason to question what their Divine are, because there is no further explanation that is needed when the circle of life is accepted as the truth. Therefore these

---

[10] One of the finest examples of this ancient Greek belief is in book 11 of the Odyssey by Homer Translated by Robert Fagles Introduction and notes by Bernard Knox BCA 2003

types of faith would have no need to question what is when they already accept what is, is!"

After all these discussions it seems to be probable that there is no complete and singular version of religion that can define the Divine entities in all the religions. Therefore the idea of a singular Divine entity that created all seems highly unlikely, and as races and religions have victories over other races and religions; it also seems highly unlikely that any one Divine being or one pantheon of Divine beings will stay in power for evermore; and when we consider the wars, inventions, and the myths that are created by the unenlightened self; it is also possible that the self is as divine as the Divine, because of its creative abilities!

But in realizing that we must also ask; who or what is the real creator or who are the real creators of all that is?"

The discussion ends as the music begins and the voice of Morrighan and the Dance of Pingala set the scene.

3

THE CREATION

Their lunch is finished and they admire Michael's painting of the song and dance of Morrighan and Pingala.

Michael puts his paintbrush down, smiles at Pallas and then he asks: "if the immortal soul or the self is to become a divine being or is a divine being without the realization then what created the self? And did the self or the Gods and Goddesses that the physical beings give oblations to; create the physical universe and the self?"

Pallas smiles and replies: "there are many religious and scientific theories that surround creation, therefore I shall begin with the theory of creation that theorises; that it all started with a big bang and then the universe was started by countless tiny particles coming together, because for this to happen something must have created the bang and the particles, because nothing comes from nothing!"

Merlin, strokes his beard, looks at Pallas and replies: "so whatever created the particles created the impermanent universe, but it did not necessarily create the self, because the self would already be in existence [logic would demand so if we are theorising on immortality]. But in realising this it could make the self a creator of the universe."

Michael puts another canvas on the easel and then he asks: "why is it that most religions have their divine creating the universe?"

Morrighan puts the kettle on and then she says: perhaps it is because most religions have come into being; through the self having lost its connection with infinity and impermanence; and in doing so it has created the Divine out of those that have remained enlightened.

How could impermanence be realised without permanence? It could not!"

Pingala looks up from her writing and replies: "of course we would not be able to perceive what is and what is not without the opposites. But in realising this we must also realise that the permanence and impermanence can differ in different religions creation theories, for instance; the wheel of life that is an everlasting circle of birth, death and rebirth is completely different to the Divine retribution ideals of the One-God religions."

Pallas sits back in her chair, stretches and says: "I think that the real problem with creation theories; is that the creation ideologies of the One-God religions have stubbornly tried to refute and undermine the evidence of science and other faiths on this matter. Therefore we must approach all the creation theories that we propose and investigate with a hard line logical process."

Everyone nods in agreement.

Gaia looks at Merlin and then she says: "I think Pallas has a good point, because there are many creation theories. But the One-God religions have a problem with this, because they have a strict belief that their One-God is the soul creator of all that is; which of course seems to be madness to the more philosophical religions [like Hinduism and Buddhism], and in respect of other ideals we should realise that there are many other pagan faiths that have many creation theories. Therefore the idea that one divine being is responsible for all creation becomes implausible!"

Merlin strokes his beard and says: "this seems to make sense when the earlier comments on the self being the creator of the Divine [that is when the self has reached enlightenment and the full realization of what is has become one with the universe] is taken into consideration. Hence we could speculate that the deities of creation could be deities of the surrounding areas and cultures that are part of the unenlightened self that is wrapped up in its physical bondage."

Morrighan winks at Sankara and Sankara smiles, brings her a cup of tea and then Morrighan says: "that theory is problematic, because there are many theories that surround the wheel or the circle of life, and these theories show how incomprehensible creation can be, because in the theologies that surround the wheel of life; it is a continual existence of life death and rebirth-where there is no end and no beginning!"

Michael takes a sip of his tea and asks: "if creation has no beginning and no end; what created it in the beginning?"

Sankara smiles at Michael and then he replies: "that is what is incomprehensible about the wheel of life and the idea that it just exists, and the fact that we come to terms with the idea that it just exists [and that in the stage before enlightenment we do not have the capacity to understand the wheel of life] without a deity of creation or the action of an impermanent nature; means that we can never understand the circle of life."

Pallas smiles at Sankara and replies: "perhaps the circle of life is just what it is–nothing more, nothing less–and in being so the circle of life becomes quite comprehensible, because the circle of life only shows the never ending cycle of life, death and rebirth; that is the unchanging reality of the universe."

Sankara smiles at Pallas and says: "the problem with that theology; is that it does not explain how the cycle created itself!"

Gaia looks at Morrighan and asks: "was the cycle ever created at all? Or is the cycle just another Gap in the knowledge of the unenlightened self?"

Morrighan smiles and replies: "the circle or the cycle of life, death and rebirth is created by the enlightened self, because it can have no beginning and no end; because there can be no death without life and if life is the beginning which it has to be before death, it should be realised that life can be the only creator.

Surely there can be nothing that comes from nothing and without life there can be no concept of death; and without death there can be no concept of life; and if there is no death or life there is nothingness; and if there is nothingness these words could not be spoken or written!"

Merlin strokes his beard and replies: that would mean that the self is the creator of the circle of life, death and rebirth and the self is the creator of itself and all that is. But if this is the reality of the creation; then how can the self create itself if it did not exist before creation?"

Pingala looks up, smile's and says: "perhaps the self–like the Divine–had no creator, and if this is so; the reason that we would exist, would be; in being immortal the self would not be able to have not existed. Therefore the self is the creator of life, death, and rebirth, because that circle shows a never ending and never beginning cycle of life and death.

Even if we go to another place of existence; life, death and rebirth still carries on and the cycle does not end, just as it does not begin."

Michael scratches under his chin and asks: "surely; there must be an original creator?"

Pallas takes a sip of her tea and then replies: "there–surely–cannot be; a creator when the created has an eternal existence, because the circle of life death and rebirth must be as eternal as the creator for it too is able to exist throughout eternity. Therefore it would not be possible for a creator to create something that is as never ending and never beginning as itself, for example; how can a new born create something that is born at exactly the same time as itself? It cannot! Therefore the immortal soul or the self must be part of the force of creation, and in being so; the immortal soul or the self cannot have been created by an outside agent."

Sankara starts to prepare lunch and then he replies: "so the eternal circle of life, death, and rebirth has no creator, because it has to be the origin of everything, because to be eternal would mean that it could not have had a point of creation–in time–when it always has been and always will be."

Michael dips his brush and says: "in theorising thus we must–surely–acknowledge the theologies that propose everything came out of the void."

Sankara lights the oven and replies: "the void could also be considered as a lack of the knowledge of enlightenment, because it is a considered opinion that; if we presently realise that we know nothing at all; then we know everything there is to know, because there is no present, there is just past and future events and both are impermanent!"

Morrighan looks out of the window and replies: "that could be so, but if everything that is and was came out of the void through a lack of knowledge and non-existence; then it could not have existed in the beginning, because knowledge is dependent on past events for its existence. Therefore the void cannot be nothingness or a lack of knowledge, because any creation–whether it is a mirage or what is considered real in the physical world–cannot exist without the impermanence of past events, because every creation depends on the knowledge of past events!

Creation itself must then be dependent on past events and what is eternal.

How can history be destroyed? It cannot, because what has been has been and all records of a situation that has been can be destroyed, but this type of action does not destroy the happenings of past events.

With that in mind we must now consider that all knowledge that is lost into the void could culminate in a new creation or creations arising."

Michael tenderly strokes the canvas with his brush and then he says: "so, any creation could depend on lost knowledge coming out of the void. If this is the truth of the matter, this would lead us to the cycle of life, death and rebirth, because every new birth is a creation of parents and every parent was a new born of a parent and so life goes on!

Pallas smiles at Michael and then she says: "in that type of reasoning; the void can never really exist, because there cannot be emptiness when something is stored in it. Therefore the void can only be a void when it has lost the elements that get or are contained within it. Hence we can assume that the void only became a void after the creation. Therefore the circle of life, death and rebirth must have come before the void. Once this is realised it becomes clear that the void cannot have a permanent stage of emptiness if something came out of it. Therefore the void can only be the void when there is nothing within it that we can reach, and once this is realised the never ending circle of life, death and rebirth become the only possible explanation for creation."

Merlin smiles at Pallas and replies: "so, life is a creator of life and life has never been a void, because life has always been a reality, because–as we have previously remarked upon–nothing comes out of nothing.

Perhaps it is the understanding of time that is the major issue that surround the problems of creation!"

Pallas smiles and replies: "time is one of the area's of confusion that surround the issue of creation, because time cannot deliver a point in time when the immortal soul or the self was created, because time cannot be as immortal as the Divine or the self, because **time needed its concept to be created and without something to create its concept it could not exist!"**

Sankara grins and says: "this is the non-reality we should recognize and with this recognition of non-reality; we should realise that time was created by the self and in being created by the self it could not have been there before the self; after all time is nothing more than a measuring device!"

Pallas smiles at Morrighan, passes her some clay and then Pallas replies: "hence we can assume that the creation theories are just creation theories that are presupposed by the physical beings, and these theories are mainly; on the issues that surround life, death and the time constraints that surround our physical being."

Morrighan starts to caress the clay into the shape of a physical being and then she says: "we are—of course—assuming that the physical being does not understand that the life and death cycle is not contaminated by the idea of creation or the constraints of time, for example; the time that we live as a physical being will become a past tense and in becoming a past tense; the creation of that physical being will become an illusion to those that are in its future. But this illusion of past events brings old life to a future life, and so the cycle of life and death is renewed by past and future events. Therefore we should ask ourselves; is the circle of life, death so intricately entwined that the meaning of life is only present in those that have fully understood the concept of the relationship between life, death, creation, non-creation and future events."

Merlin opens his eyes—wide—and looks at Morrighan and then he says: "what you are implying is that the meaning of life is wrapped up and lost within the creativity of the theologies that encompass most religions. In fact what your theology suggests is that; to understand creation we must understand the meaning of life, and the only way to do that is to have completed the circle and have understood everything within that circle of life death and rebirth."

Morrighan smiles at Merlin and then she says: "yes that is exactly what I am implying!"

Pingala watches as Morrighan gently caresses a figure out of the clay and then Pingala says: "so, if the creation and the meaning of life are entwined; then it would be reasonable to summarize that the meaning of life and the creation are one and the same, because the meaning of life and the creation have always been a mystery to those who do not wish to comprehend them."

Michael smiles and says: "I think that you are implying that there are some religious orders; that are so wrapped up in their spiritual ideals; that they do not wish to acknowledge any theories or empirical evidence that goes against their teachings. This is problematic, because in this type of dogmatic belief these religions are able to hold back their followers from any other ideals that surround the Divine and creation, and in doing so; these religions are able to glorify their deities by making them figureheads that are capable of the most wondrous achievements. Therefore religions that hold on to a singular creation belief are able to use the wonders of the universe to enslave their followers."

Gaia smiles at Michael and then she replies: "hence we can theorise that the singular creation myths are nothing more than a means by which the human race can be enslaved by a single deity. But whilst they theorise that way and are held in bondage by their belief; there are those of us that realise; that the Lords of Karma could be–and probably are–in control when the physical being perishes and the immortal soul or the self that was within the physical being is not enlightened!"

Morrighan applies a little more water to the clay and replies: "what we appear to be theorising is that the creation never actually existed and that the theologies that surround the creation are only there as a means of control. But this is problematic, because creation has many forms and it may have been manipulated, and therefore it must be realised that creation also exists in the enlightenment, because the self has to create for it to be created.

If creativity is the means by which the self becomes enlightened; the self must be the creator of all it perceives. Therefore the self or the immortal soul can never have been dependent on any single deity for its creation. This is because in creating the images or the ideals that encapsulate the self; the self is the only entity that is capable of creating the circumstances that surround itself. But this does not mean that the self cannot be manipulated by outside agents, such as; disability, strict religious practises, being tied to a dictatorial regime, etc....."

Pallas smiles and says: "the Lords of Karma and/or those that weave the threads of fate must be outside agents that are involved in creation, because the Lords of Karma decide what we become; before we are enlightened and the Fates weave the paths that we follow before we become enlightened.

I must point out that the fates and the Lords of Karma are not necessarily responsible for the discomforts that are part of the lives of the individual selves, because they are just part of the imperfections of the creative self.

The Fates and the Lords of Karma never claim to be perfect. Therefore we should not believe that the creation of the universe and/or the physical beings should be seen to be perfect, because the whole of creativity is an experiment and when we experiment we make mistakes!"

Gaia gets the honey out of the cupboard and replies: "so, the Lords of Karma are entwined within the imperfections of the creation and creativity that is dependent on the individual self. Therefore the Lords of Karma and the Fates could be seen to be either the creation of the individual selves or a part of the self that is not truly recognized until enlightenment. If either of those is correct; the creativity of the self would be responsible for everything that is, because the self recognizes the impermanent world through the creation of its own senses. Therefore the creation of the universe is apparent through the recognition of the senses that are available to the physical being and in turn these senses only sense the creation, because the immortal soul or the self has allowed it to do so. Hence we should realise that the Lords of Karma and/or the Fates must be part of the same cycle of life, death and rebirth as the self that is entrapped within the physical being. Therefore the cycle of life, death, and rebirth must be the creator of all and this would have always been, because creation is dependent on creativity and there is no creation without creativity."

Morrighan starts to caress the features out of the clay figure and then she says: "So, creation and creativity could not be dependent on anything that is outside the circle of life, death and rebirth, because life, death and rebirth is created from the ashes of death and life is the creator of those ashes. Therefore the connection between life, death, and rebirth can only be creation, because the death of one living thing creates the food of life for another living thing."

Michael looks at Morrighan and asks: "what happens when all the stars burn out and the universe dies? Would there be nothing but a void?"

Pallas smiles and replies: "how can this void come to be when creativity still exists? I theorise it cannot, because creativity is part of the self and as long as the self exists the creativity that is within it can never die; because it is–and always has been–a part of the immortal soul or the self. Therefore the creative energy that is part or the self can never truly die, because if it could the creative forces that created the universe could not have existed if the idea of creation was not already there, for example; the first wheel would never have been invented without the first idea of it. Therefore creation depends on creation and the circle of life will carry on, because what has no beginning has no end; and perhaps that is the only logical answer to creation!"

Merlin grins at Pallas and then he replies: "your logic is fine and I must say that it does seem plausible; that if creativity has always been, there is no logical reason that it will ever cease to be, because it is feasible that; the creativity of the self will create another universe out of the death of the present one. But this does not mean that the next universe will be like this one"

Pingala looks at the ongoing creation of Morrighan and then Pingala remarks: "So, the whole universe is the creation of the self and the self is the creative force that is responsible for everything that is impermanent; and through this impermanence the self creates all that is permanent!"

Merlin looks at Pingala and says: "that maybe true, but the many ideals that surround creation, seem to have the physical being as being created along with the soul that is within it, but if the self is the true creative energy then it is also possible–if not probable—that the self created the physical being that it inhabits before enlightenment.

Although we have already made clear that the soul or the self could be the true creative energy that has always been; we have not considered the possibility that the deities are an outside agent of another world of creation."

Michael smiles at Merlin and replies: "the idea of other worlds that are beyond the present reach of physical reality; is present in many religions and this suggests that there is a possibility of more than one creator and more than one creation, for example; there is more than one theology on heaven and hell in the One-God religions."

Pallas looks at Michael and says: "the problem with the many religious beliefs of the other worlds is; there are many different versions of the religious beliefs of other worlds and this does seem to suggest that there is more than one creator, and if this is correct; the creator of each separate world could have a separate identity and these different identities show that there is a difference in their creative theories."

Pingala smiles at Pallas and asks: "could these different worlds and different ideals be part of the growth of the force of creation that has always been?"

Pallas smiles and replies: "perhaps that is possible, but we must also consider the possibility of there being more than one ideology of the self that is involved in creation. To enforce or dismiss this possibility I suggest that some of the European Pagan, and some of the Pagan religions of the indigenous people of America be compared!"

Merlin strokes his beard and replies: "one of the major differences is that the Native American people have a greater respect for the spirit of other living animals and in this respect their creation myths tend to involve animal spirits. Therefore their creativity seems to have a greater respect for the natural world, and with this respect of nature their deities tend to be of other animals rather than a human kind. Although in realizing that we must also realise that there are many European deities that are linked to animals, for example; Andraste—as a raven—is said to feed on the bodies of dead warriors and so the raven was seen as a powerful omen."

Sankara looks at Merlin and replies: "the native Americans use their animal spirits as their deities in their myths and legends. Therefore the deity does not become the animal, it is the animal! With this type of theology the animal spirits can be responsible for the creation of the human race [which in a way they are if Darwin's theory of evolution is correct]. But in theorising on that we should be aware of some of the many different theologies of the different tribes. Therefore I have selected a few of the creation myths. I shall begin with the Crow legend of Old Man Coyote makes the World and we shall follow that with Earth Making by the Cherokee; the legend of the Children of the Sun by the Osage and the legend of The Voice The Flood and The Turtle by the Caddo.[11]

Firstly I shall start by revealing an abridged version of the first legend that is mentioned above: Old Man Coyote is known as a trickster, but they believe that in the beginning there was nothing more than water and Coyote searched for other living things and found two ducks with red eyes. He then asked the ducks if there was anything below the water and the youngest duck dived for the longest and brought up a root. The younger duck dived again and brought up some soil and out of the soil and the root Coyote–of whom the ducks refer to as their brother–starts to make the world. After this the legend carries on to explain how Coyote created man and woman; and in the end it is fair to say that Coyote created new things out of elements that were already there."[12]

Michael smiles and says: "I must say that this legend does seem to incorporate the never ending cycle of life death and rebirth, because there is never any explanation of the water, the root, and the mud that Old Man Coyote used in his creation."

Sankara walks over to the stove and says: "like the Crow's legend the Cherokee's legend of Earth Making begins with the earth being covered in water and the animals are yet again responsible for land, but this time the animals are already overcrowded in a place above the rainbow and it is the water beetle that brings a dab of soft mud to the surface, but this time

---

[11] American Indian Myths and Legends Richard Erdoes & Alfonso Ortiz Pimlico 1997
[12] Ibid p88-93

it is an unknown magical power that spreads the mud and starts the creation of land.[13]

So the water is the starting point in both cases, but in the Cherokee legend the animals were formed before the land.

The legend also says that someone powerful formed man after they had formed the plants and animals."

Pallas watches Sankara pour the tea and then she remarks: "those two legends seem to have a Darwinian evolutionary undertone within their legend, because they both have the understanding that animals were on the planet before the human race evolved."

Michael smiles and says: "if the Cherokee refer to someone powerful they must be referring to a Divine being!"

Pallas grins at Michael and replies: "referring to a Divine being does not mean that the Divine being is human or alone!"

Michael nods his head and replies: "that is true, but the emergence of a power that is not connected to the physical world shows us that they are aware of; the realms beyond the physical senses. In fact this becomes more evident when at the end of the Cherokee legend they mention a need for a guide to the world that is below ours."

Morrighan smiles and says: "this appears to be very similar to the otherworld figures that are part of the early tribal religions of Europe [especially Northern Europe and the U.K.]. I say this, because these early religions had a shaman that had guides to such places and there are similarities in these beliefs, for example; these beliefs were connected by the idea that one of the entrances to the otherworld is through water. I theorize this, because some of the Northern European journeying is often achieved through a pool of water or a spring; whilst they are in deep meditation in a place of serenity."[14]

Michael smiles at Morrighan and then he says: "as we all know; water is the source of all life on the planet, therefore creation starts to appear with water and under the water is another world apart from the beings that depend on land. Hence

---

[13] Ibid p105-107

[14] The Lore of the Bard, Arthur Rowan p67-71 Llewellyn publications 2003 (Although they are not the same, there are many similarities between the practises of Bards, Druids and Shaman)

we should realise that the waters of life must appear–to many tribes–to be the creator of all known physical beings and to be an entrance or a gateway to other worlds. Therefore we must realise that water is not just another creative physical presence it is also a mysterious and magical element of many tribal religions."

Pallas smiles and says: "the myth of the Osage–The Children of the Sun–makes the spiritual being appear before the physical being and in this myth the water is already there and the animals are with them when the being arrives on earth.

The creation of the land is through the Elk, because when the Osage asked the Divine beings to help them they receive no answer and so they turned to the majestic Elk for help. So the Elk started the creation by dropping into the water; and they then go further to explain how the Elk is responsible for the mists of the land and everything that grows upon it.[15]

This whole idea of Gods and Goddesses not helping them does not mean that there are no such Divine beings, because the animal that helps the Osage has powers that could only be present in a Divine creature. Therefore it is possible that the Osage are suggesting that the Divine can come in animal form and this means that the other animals are not of lesser importance than the human being.

In Greek mythology the part goat and part human God Pan seems to show the power of the animals in the natural world; of which humanity is part. When we tie this with the natural spirit of the Elk of the Osage a realisation of the power of the animal world becomes evident on both sides of the Atlantic."

Merlin stirs his tea, takes a drink and replies: "there are also animal shape changers in the Northern European and Celtic deities; and there are many different religions that have animal headed deities; which does seem to suggest that animals are seen as a creative force that is equal or in some cases superior to their human counterparts."

Gaia sits back, stretches and says: "although the nature deities or spirits that have been mentioned–so far–have been seen as some kind of divine being; they are also seen as part of

---

[15] American Indian Myths and Legends, Richard Erdoes & Alfonso Ortiz p119 Pimlico 1997

or able to go to another world that is connected with our own. Therefore it should be realised that these other worlds that are above or below our own are always within the reach of the spiritual beings, because our soul or the self can be aware of these other worlds whilst it is in the physical being."

Sankara smiles at Gaia and then he replies: "the Caddo legend of The Voice The Flood and The Turtle shows the otherworldly aspects of the Turtle in this legend, because in this legend this Turtle or the Great Turtle as it is called; is sent by the Voice to kill the four monsters that were given birth to in the world before the flood; because these four monsters formed into one, grew roots, grew huge and started to kill. But The Voice sent The Flood and after The Flood; The Voice sent the Great Turtle to kill the monsters that had been weakened by the flood. This legend also has a great reed that the original couple [that gave birth to the monsters] led all the animals in two by two. Of course the Great Turtle does not need this, because it is part of the world of water and part of the world of land."[16]

Michael smiles and says: "this is all feasible in a spiritual sense, but those other worlds all seem to be part of a physical being of this world and in being so; the physical creatures of this world must have come at the same time as the other worlds, because each of them seem to depend on each other for its existence, for example; without enough heat water becomes ice and with too much heat water becomes steam and evaporates. Hence we can reasonably assume that everything depends on something else for its existence. Therefore creation depends on a creator and a creator depends on a creator for its creation."

Morrighan opens the window and breathes in the fresh, cold air and then she says: "this goes straight back to the never ending circle of life, because if a creator depends on a creator to exist; the creation can never have a beginning or an end, because nothing comes out of nothing. Therefore any theory that presumes that creation is due to any singular creator is illogical, because creation has to be part of a timeless cycle of creation and creative forces if it is to exist at all. This is, because forces are needed to create anything that exists and that must include a

---

[16] American Indian Myths & Legend, Richard Erdoes & Alfonso Ortiz p120-122 Pimlico 1997

creator, because a creator could not create without it coming into existence in the first place."

Michael looks at Morrighan and then he asks: "are you saying that a creative force is needed for a creative force to exist?"

Morrighan smiles and replies: "yes, because if we need a creative force to exist–and we do– this means that there is no logical method that can supply a method; in which a force can exist without something to start that force. Therefore the theology behind a single timeless creator appears to be illogical, but in realizing this it must be realised that even a circle starts somewhere before it is complete, and therefore all of creation could be part of a force that has always been.

One thing that we should start to realise is that the circle of life, death, and rebirth cannot start before the life; that is unless the circle is as timeless as its participants."

Pingala smiles at Morrighan and replies: "there is one thing that we have not yet considered and that is; are the spiritual worlds older than the physical world or are they just a creation of the self whilst it is in the physical world?"

Morrighan broadly grins and then she replies: "the self is the creator of all that is apparent to it, because the self is the only entity that can realise its own nature!"

Sankara looks at Morrighan and then he remarks: "if the individual self is the creator of all creation; then the individual self could [probably] be part of a bigger picture that is not whole without it. Therefore the other worlds that are part of the different individual selves; are–probably–all connected to the whole of creation, and therefore; they all exist in the creation of the individual selves that are responsible for their creation."

Merlin puts some tobacco in his pipe, lights it and then he says: "if that is the truth; the individual selves can be held responsible for all that is imperfect in creation, because if there is no individual power that is higher than the individual self; the individual selves would be responsible for all the imperfections!"

Gaia smiles, shakes her head and replies: "if the individual selves are responsible for all the imperfections in creation, they must also be responsible for perfection in creation, because it is not logical to recognize one without the other, for example; how can one recognize light without dark or heat without cold. Therefore the creations imperfections should be realised as unavoidable errors; that are part of the foundations of the creation of the universe; and without these building blocks of imperfection, perfections can never be achieved. Therefore imperfection becomes unavoidable."

Pallas looks into her empty cup of tea, smiles at Sankara and then she says: "the creation that is down to the individual self could also be shaped by those that weave the threads of fate; that is if the Muses or the Fates have any real control over our destiny!"

Sankara brings the pot of tea over to Pallas pours her some and then he says: "perhaps the Muses and the Fates; are the creators of all that appears in the physical world; and the self only became responsible for the creation of that world; when the self realised it was part of the never ending cycle of birth, death, and rebirth that the Fates and Muses are part of."

Michael looks at Sankara, smiles and then Michael says: "what that would mean is that the Fates the Muses and the self are part of each other, and if this is correct; the self is entirely responsible for the destiny it has created for itself."

Pingala whistles softly to herself and then she replies: "the self would not be entirely responsible for its own destiny if the Fates and the self were only connected to each other, because if the Fates or the Muses did not have a connection to the self and were a complete part of the self; the self would always know its future destinies, because a complete part of the whole would–surely–have a complete picture of that part of the whole. But if the self had no connection whatsoever to the Fates or Muses; the self would have no realization of the creation of its destiny; and if the self has no way of realizing its created destiny; then the self can realise nothing at all, because if it has no realization of what the Fates or the Muses have created for it; it can surely have no comprehension of anything at all. That would be, because the realization of any given fact or future probability depend on something that has already happened. Therefore the future that one creates for oneself is dependent on what has gone before, and a lot of those past events are out of the hands of the individual self. Hence we can surmise that the fate of the individual is dependent on past events; that at certain stages had nothing to do with the individual concerned, but these events can become connected through the fate of the individual, for example; a baby can have no control over the defects that it is born with if it is born with any kind of disability.

Michael gets a bag of nuts out of his pocket, offers Pingala some and then he replies: "so the Fates can be seen as the creators of past events; that can cause unfortunate future circumstances or happenings that create the physical beings destiny."

Morrighan looks at Michael and then she remarks; "If the Fates are solely responsible for the creation of the past events of the physical being; that would make the Fates the creator of the physical world and with the Fates being connected to the self–by their threads of destiny–the fates must also be part of the never ending circle of life, death and rebirth. Therefore the creation would become part of the never ending cycle of life death and rebirth and if this is correct it would mean that creation is as timeless as the Fates or the self."

It should also be realised that the creation is an ongoing event that can never cease, because there are creative forces in every thing that is born or destroyed."

Merlin strokes his beard, looks at Morrighan and asks: "what about the destructive effects of a nuclear explosion where everything is eliminated?"

Morrighan smiles and says: "a new space and radioactive fallout is created from such an explosion!"

Michael looks at Morrighan and asks: "if in destruction there is creation is creation destructive?"

Morrighan looks back and says: "creation is not always destructive. But; what we should also consider is that all physical bodies are born to die and all that is physical has a lifespan. Therefore we should realise that the creative cycle is as dependent on death as it is on life, because one cannot be truly realised without the other and that is because it would not be possible to understand physical life without physical death. Hence we should begin to understand that the creation of physical life is dependent on physical death, otherwise we would not be able to understand what physical life is. Therefore we must realise that if there is no physical death there is no understanding of physical life, because to know you are alive would mean that you would realise that your physical body is going to die!

Only when physical life has no more hold over its occupant; does the body reach its demise!"

Gaia opens her eyes–wide–looks at Morrighan in amazement and then Gaia says: "you make death sound beautiful!"

Morrighan gives Gaia a warm smile and then Morrighan says: "death can be beautiful or sorrowful and ugly, for example; in the Tibetan book of Living and Dying[17] a rainbow body is discussed and this body is only achieved after the death of the physical body of an advanced practitioner of Dzogchen[18], whereas the creation of war and illness cause many ugly deaths!"

Michael looks at Sankara and asks: "if creation and destruction are as entwined as good and evil; is it possible that one could exist without the other?"

Sankara smiles and says: "if something cannot be realised; it–surely–cannot exist. But in realizing this we must realise that creation and destruction cannot be considered as separate entities, because anything that is destroyed needs a creative action of destruction to destroy what is being destroyed, and therefore destruction is just another part of the creative force. But when this is realised we must also realise that the destructive force only has the instinct of the annihilation of an object; for a purpose that is only realised to itself at that time, otherwise pure instinctive annihilation would lead to nothingness and nothingness negates any idea of creation, because if nothingness comes into existence there would be nothing to realise it."

Pallas gives Sankara a broad grin and replies: "nothingness–surely–cannot exist if there is any consciousness in existence, because if something is conscious it would have a thought process that was created by it. Therefore the thought process must create a thought to even realise the existence of space.

---

[17] The Tibetan Book of Living and Dying, Sogyal Rinpoche p171-173 Rider 2002

[18] Dzogchen master; is one who has followed the path of enlightenment to become a Buddha. (ibid p154-156)

Hence we must begin to realise that nothingness cannot exist where there is any kind of thought, because once something is thought about; it is created by the thinker and where there is something–even if it is only a thought–there is something.

So where there is thought there is creation and where there is creation nothingness can never have existed, because where there is nothing there cannot be creation and where there cannot be creation, there can be no thought or any chance of thought, because if a thought process exists creation has to follow, because all thoughts are due to the creative energies of the thinker. Therefore it is not logical to assume that what is; was created from nothingness, because even if we are just the creation of a dream we are a creation and what created that dream; must–surely–have been created somewhere, by something, for it to be able to exist at all!"

Merlin waters the plants upon the window sill, looks at Pallas and then he says: "we must ask ourselves; if there was no destruction and creation reigned supreme; would creation exist at all? I theorise that it would not exist, because–as we have already begun to make evident–all of creation depends on the destruction of something else, for example; if we put something in an empty room it destroys the emptiness!"

Pingala passes Pallas's flute to her and then Pingala says: "that is if something is created, something must be destroyed for that creation to begin. This is logical, because even a thought destroys the emptiness–or the other thought that was in that part of the mind before it began–and therefore the thought is creative and destructive at the same time."

Morrighan gives Pingala a tender smile and replies: "it seems logical that all creation destroys something; but in its creative process, creation is intent on creating something out of its destructive process, whereas there are some destructive forces that are intent on total annihilation of the thing or things it wishes to destroy. But in realizing this we must also realise that when something is annihilated or made extinct a type of emptiness is created."

Merlin produces his harp and then he says: "it is becoming evident that creation is dependent on destruction for it to be able to move onward. But the forces that move creation throughout time and space are not yet fully explored or understood, because these forces that are connected to us are not yet fully accepted in the majority of the human race. Therefore we must try and answer this question; are we responsible for creation and if so why do we have so many creation ideals that surround the creation myths of all the religions?"

Sankara looks at Merlin and replies: "all the imperfections of physical life suggest a creation that is not fully understood, because the entity or entities that created it are not yet capable of understanding how they created or became part of the build up, of the creation of the physical world. In fact a figure that creates something new can never be sure of the outcome of a new creation, unless–of course–the whole of creation is a never ending circle of life, death, and rebirth. This is problematic, because if this is the truth of the matter, the whole of creation could be one huge and inescapable mistake. But in theorizing this we must realise; that the physical cycle can only entrap the self whilst the self is unrealised. Hence we should realise that; if the physical circle of life, death, and rebirth is inescapable, it can only become inescapable to what is considered a physical reality, because when the self is realised the self has escaped from this plane of existence!"

Pingala smiles at Sankara and replies: "if the physical world is escapable by the realization of the self of itself, then the self; must–surely–have a physicality about itself for it to exist at all, and I theorize this, because all types of energy have a presence that is realised by its action if it realises any type of existence at all. Therefore the self must be responsible for its own fate, when it realises that historical events lead to certain kinds of outcomes in the physical world will also lead to the outcome of their existence on this plane or any other plane of existence; of which the self is part of whilst it is restricted by the physical body that keeps it within this plane of existence."

Pallas smiles at Pingala, looks quizzically at Morrighan and then Pallas replies: "if we are theorizing that we are self creating, we must realise that to be so: we can never be in the grip of the Fates if we are self creating, because if we were completely self creating; we would have no need for history to give us any kind of guidance or would we?"

Morrighan grins at Pallas and remarks: if the Fates are not needed; would we have created them? I suggest we would not, because we would have no need of any kind of guidance if we were completely positive about our creations. Hence we must realise that if the Fates do exist; they are the controllers of our future and they do this by weaving the historical events into a known future that has already happened in history, for example; everything that is invented has its beginning as a thought, before it is put into action in the physical world. Therefore we should realise that all self creation begins with a thought and with this being the truth of any kind of reality we must ask ourselves: how that thought originates? The answer to this is that all thoughts rely on past events for their beginning and for them to come into fruition. Therefore self creation must rely on thought processes that are created by past events that were created by other thought processes; inevitably this leads us to a path that was created in the past and that is what the fates are weaving!"

Merlin looks at Morrighan and then he replies: "so creation is dependent on historical thought processes that are created by the Fates; which in turn must be part of us as are the Divine; otherwise we would not be able to recognize any of them at all!"

Pallas smiles at Morrighan, looks at Merlin and then Pallas remarks: "so the whole of creation is contained within the processes of the self, because; for the self to understand anything; it must have some kind of knowledge of that thing and the self must have confined that thing to its memory; of which that memory could not recall that thing from its past without it already being a historical thought.

Therefore if thought is creation and thought is dependent on history for its creation; then creation is forever trapped in the same cycle of birth death and rebirth. But in realizing this we must wonder; why many different religions have formed many different opinions on this matter and why these religions have formed hugely different theologies.

Michael smiles, passes some glasses and a bottle of wine around and then he concludes: "creation appears to be dependent on many selves and these selves seem to have been made dependent on other historical selves or Fates for their thought processes, but as we have already considered the consequences of other religions on this matter I think that this will need another discussion.

A soft singing comes from Morrighan and Gaia, and Michael and Sankara start the drumbeat as Pallas plays the flute and Merlin strokes his harp; the dance begins as Pingala starts to flow in a dance that begins the evening glow.

4

THE COERCION OF CULT AND SUPERSTITION

Morrighan opens the door and lets the cat out, deeply inhales the fresh, cold air and suggests a walk in the cool and refreshing midday snow. All agree and put on their coats and then they walk through the door. As the door closes the conversation starts to flow.

Gaia smiles and begins the conversation, by remarking: "how is it that the physical world appears the same to all religious cults, if this world is created by the self?"

Pallas smiles and then she stretches and inhales deeply, and then she replies: "whether we realise it or not; the selves are all connected whilst they are part of the physical world that they have created. Therefore their creation must be responsible for the creation of the cults and superstitions whilst they are part of the physical form. Hence we should begin to understand; that this physical form–that they are part of –is not only a creation that is made by their own physical senses it is also a creator of their own superstitious and religious beliefs."

Sankara looks at the snow upon the trees, smiles at Pallas and then he replies: "if the self is [truly] only dependent on itself; then there would be many more different worlds, cults and superstitions and they would not be able to intermingle, because if the self was completely self created it would surely have to be so complete that it would never be able to intermingle with anything that was outside its completeness!"

Pingala stretches out her arms and twirls as if to catch the falling snow in her open hands and then she replies: "perhaps the differences in religions and superstitions begin with the differences of the creation of nature, for example; some religions made a show of their power by showing no harm would come to them or their followers if a sacred tree or shrine of an opposing religion was destroyed by them."

Michael puts his hands in his pockets, smiles and says: "what you appear to be making evident is that creative energies– that make superstition evolve–are created by the knowledge of the individual religions, for example; there are many faiths that oppose the scientific theories that are made evident in the scientific search for the truth of a matter!"

Gaia points out a well coated red fox and then she says: "all living things are sacred, but the trees have been misunderstood because of their longevity, for example; there is a yew tree in the U.K. that is thought to be older than an ancient site in the U.K. called Stonehenge, therefore the trees that were known to have stood for many generations would have been seen to have been a symbol of long life and creation, because these trees will have seeded other trees in their long life. But this is problematic, because we must also realise that the ancient religions must have seen the death and destruction of some of these sacred objects."

Perhaps some of the ancient religions realise what a mess of its own food chain the human race would make when it lost the sacredness of all living things."

Merlin gets a large flask of coffee out of his rucksack, pours some and then he says: "hence it is becoming evident that superstition can have future implications if the natural signs are or are not acknowledged, because if the human race realised why trees were sacred in the beginning; some of them may have treated the woodlands and rainforests with greater respect [and the idiotic greed of some religions may not have been allowed to continue in the 19th 20th and early 21st centuries a.c.e.]."

Pallas smiles as she accepts the offer of coffee from Merlin and then she says: "some of the present day problems may be the consequences of ignoring some superstitions, but it does not explain how some of the more exotic myths and superstitions came into being, for example; the whole idea of Divine retribution is built upon the consequences of defying the ideals that are laid down by those that are considered Divine, but in theorizing this we should realise that the laws that are laid down by the Divine are written by the hand of mankind. Therefore the laws and ideals of the Divine are open to falsification and exaggeration!"

Morrighan looks at Pallas, smiles and replies: "I most certainly agree that anything that is written by he human hand is open to falsification and exaggeration, but all that is written by the human hand is in the mind of the writer of the words, and with this being the only way that text can be written; the idea must be born within the mind of the individual self, and with that being the only feasible way to create such myths and superstitions; these myths and superstitions must–surely–have a basis in history for them to be in the imagination of the self, because [as we have mentioned before] nothing can come out of nothing. Therefore the self cannot be the sole creator of the myths and superstitions it has written or been acquainted with. Hence we must realise that this whole concept must have originated; either before the individual self became aware of it or it was already implanted within the individual self and it was waiting for the right moment for it to come into fruition. The latter seems to be more likely, because, if the thought of the written word originated before the individual self became aware of it and it was not implanted; the thought would not have been able to be translated into a language that the individual self could understand, because understanding is based on historical evidence. Therefore the written word–and for that matter of fact, the spoken word–can only come into fruition through past events that have been implanted into us through the learning process. Hence it becomes obvious that superstition or myth is reliant on past events."

Pallas smiles, passes a cup of coffee to Morrighan and then Pallas replies: "what you are implying is that all myth and superstition is reliant on past events and that some of those superstitions of past events are born from natural truths, for example; many religions consider lakes and rivers as sacred places, and the pollution of rivers and lakes leads to the death of plants and animals, and in some cases part of the human race that is responsible for the pollution."

Pingala smiles as the coffee is passed to her and then Pingala replies: "the natural order of things is a fine reason to use the aspects of nature that are needed for the survival of life upon the planet for the myths and superstitions, but these are not the only myths and superstitions that have grown with humanity, and with this growth of superstition; the supernatural beings have emerged. This is problematic, because these supernatural beings or entities have emerged from somewhere– even if it is in the deepest part of the human mind–and some prime examples of this are the myths and legends that surround demons, vampires, and dragons."

Pallas smiles and says: "in legend and mythology demons are difficult to define, because demons are in many different forms in many different religions. Therefore it should be realised that; if we declare something as a demon we must find the form and meaning that is applicable to the entity. Hence we must begin to analyze and then realise that most of the forms of demons that are presented to us; are presented to us by the One-God propaganda machine that has misused Pagan gods, such as: Hearne, Pan and the Green Man for figureheads of evil demons and their devil. Therefore we must treat this subject with extreme caution, because most of the pictorial figureheads that the One-God religions use to show their devil or demons, have very little–if anything at all–to do with evil. Therefore we must look beyond the One-God religions for the origination of superstition-that is if the origination of superstition can be found!"

Gaia takes a jar of honey out of her pocket, stirs some into her coffee and then Gaia replies: "all religious thought is dependent on superstition for its survival, because the majority of ethics that are considered to be the way by which people should run their lives have consequences [if they are broken] in the afterlife or in the persons reincarnation. Therefore it is probable that myths and ethics were created side by side, because if we have something that is considered ethical it would be too easy to break if there were no dire consequences attached to it, for example; the One-God's devil and demons is a way in which their ethics have been forced upon the so-called civilized society!"

Michael smiles at Gaia and she passes him the honey and coffee and then he replies: "the problem with ethics and myths is that they reach throughout all religions and they do not always coincide. Therefore the different ideals that surround entities like Pan, Hearne, and Kali should be examined in the greatest detail, because [as we have already made evident] they have been seriously bastardized by the One-God faiths."

Merlin takes a sip of his coffee and says: "what we should also examine are some or the lesser known religious myths and superstitions when we analyze the ideologies that surround devils and demons. Therefore I suggest that we start with an Irish tribal myth; that is called; The Dawn.[19]

Similar to other religions and tribal myths [some of which have and will be mentioned]; The Dawn sees the Fomorians as demons or perhaps a prehistoric tribe with a demonic nature, for example; in this myth the invading Partholonians are said to have made this statement:

'The Fomor are not camped on the Plain of Ith.'
'How do you know?' Mercan asked.
'Aeolus informed me,' the prince said quietly. The demons are still surrounded by the mist....[20]

Hence we can see that certain invaders saw themselves as more civilized than the people of the territory they wish to take over. But it must also be realised that in these types of myths the demons are very rarely completely vanquished and in some cases—the Fomorians are a fine example of this—they can be linked with the ideals of another religion [such as the Christian in this case] and bastardised by them, because it is said that Parthenon who was the chief of the Partholonians was the good one of the descendents of the sons of Noah who came 300 years after the flood, and that the one who came first after the flood; was Noah's son Ham who was the founder of the Fomorians.[21] In fact this whole myth could be designed by the Christians; to show that there were no people alive after the flood of Noah. But this is a contradictory ideal, because in another myth it is said; that in the Northern Isles the Tuatha de Dannan learnt skills in magic and sorcery that surpassed the heathens of Ireland and the Tuatha de Dannan beat the Fomorians in the second battle of Moytura.[22] I suspect that this whole myth has the writings of Christianity indoctrinated into it, because who else

---

[19] Irish Folk and Faery Tales Omnibus Volume 2 Michael Scott p1-35 Warner Books 1993
[20] Ibid p29
[21] The Complete Dictionary of symbol general editor: Jack Tresidder p370 Duncan Baird Publishers 2004
[22] The Encyclopaedia of Celtic Myth and Legend, John and Caitlin Matthews p44-64 Rider 2002

apart form the Christians would call the original Irish Pagans heathens! Therefore we should ask ourselves why the Christians wrote of the old Gods if theirs was the only one and the supreme power."

Gaia takes a sip of her coffee and replies: "what that makes evident is that the victors over the Fomorians had stronger deities than they did, and therefore; were greater than them in warfare. Perhaps this shows why the Christians wrote up these myths and legends and that is, because if the Christians wish to be the only and the greatest religion within a kingdom they want to show that their God is the only surviving deity; even though in the Partholonians myth they all died of the plague after the Fomorians were beaten [this last part does seem contradictory, but that appears to be the way of many myths and legends and at the time of writing this could be seen as an uncertainty in their religious beliefs]."

Sankara looks at Gaia and replies: "magic is probably the root of all superstition and the demonizing of an older race that has been conquered; by a new race that thinks itself to be superior in the arts of war and magic seems to be nothing more than a misinterpreted spiritual creation. Therefore the question that we must answer is; what is a demon and are they any worse than the Gods or are they just another part of the Self that is necessary for the understanding of mankind?"

Morrighan looks at Pingala, smiles and then Morrighan replies: "one other question we must ask ourselves is; if there were not demons that are evil, what would the Gods have to fight against and how could we recognize what it is to be godlike or angelic; without there being demons with their demonic nature?"

Pallas smiles at Morrighan and then Pallas says:

"it is like all opposites; that is that one cannot be truly defined without the other. So, if we cannot define the angelic without the demonic counterpart we cannot logically have one without the other. Therefore the demons and the Gods must have grown out of the same creation for them to be able to be recognized, because if they were not created side by side; we would have no means by which we could truly recognize the angelic without having the demonic to compare them with."

Merlin looks at Pallas and then he says: "So, if we have a demonic person we would need an angelic one to measure it against if we are able to recognize it!"

Pallas smiles, and then she says: "There are very few things that can be truly recognized without their opposite, because theoretical or physical definitions depend upon comparisons and comparisons cannot exist without something to compare them against, for example; an apple and a pear look different and taste different and some people will like the taste of one more than another; or it is possible that some can be allergic to one without being allergic to the other and some people could enjoy the taste of both and be allergic to neither, etc.... Therefore I propose that what we consider demonic or angelic are down to the ideals of the different religions, for example; I am sure that when the witches were being burnt at the stake by the Christians the witches thought the Christians were being demonic; just as the Christians must have thought the Romans were being demonic, when the Romans fed the Christians to the lions."

Michael drinks the last of his coffee, collects some deadwood and then he says: "So, the idea of demons and gods are as necessary to one another as black is to white, but in this necessity the belief in individual religions corrupt the truth that lies behind these demons and they use them to gain the means for a victory. In realizing this we must also realise that a demon is as much a part of the self as is a god, because without each of them being a part of the self; the self would not be able to recognize either."

Gaia grins at Michael and then she says: "what is becoming apparent is that the self is as responsible for the creation of demons as it is for the creation of the Gods; that is if the self is responsible for the creation of Gods and demons. Therefore I theorize that it is unlikely that the self has both within it, because if the self is part of or connected to both, the self would be in a constant battle to keep both under control. Hence I suggest that the demons are not a different entity from the Gods they are just a God by a different name, for example; the Greek God of the underworld–Hades–would be seen as Satan or a demon by the Christians and most other One-God religions."

Morrighan smiles and says: "that is similar to the referral to Pan and Hearne that we made earlier; when the Christians idolized the Greek God–Pan–as their image of Satan. Therefore we must realise that Gods and Goddesses of other religions can be considered as demons by the religions that oppose them. If these Gods and Goddesses of opposing religions can be considered as demons; does this make them so? I suggest that it does in the religions that wish to make them so, but this does not make these Gods and Goddesses truly demonic, because–as we have already made evident–this demonizing of other religions is an easy way for a dictatorial religion to corrupt other religions!

So far that theory of demonic evil has evidently been a corruption of other races and religions beliefs. This corruption has been used to gain control, enslave and to wipe out opposing ideologies throughout history. Therefore the Demonizing of other races and/or religions [by religious and/or military means] is a means by which the enslaved parties can be controlled. I say enslaves, because the fear that is indoctrinated by demonizing an opposing religion is a means by which you can enslave the opponents mind and once an opponents mind is enslaved victory goes to the controller of the mind. Therefore we must realise that the demonizing of different races and/or religions is just a means of control that is used by dictatorial races and/or religions. But that does not mean that demons do not exist in a religious or spiritual context, because they most certainly do in the written or verbal lore of many religions, but there are also some religions that have no use for them [like the religion of the Sioux]. Although in saying this we must realise that the Sioux and other religions that have no use for devils and demons believe in monsters.

One of the finest examples of demons appearing to be of a different race comes from verses 10-12 in a hymn called The Birth of Agni, in the Rig Veda of the Hindu religion:

10 Let Agni's bellowings reach to heaven as piercing weapons to destroy the demons. His angry glare breaks forth in ecstacy of Soma.[23] *The obstacle of the Goddess cannot hold him back.*

---

[23] Soma is the ambrosial drink of the Gods

11 Inspired by poetry I have fashioned this hymn of praise for you whose very nature is power, as the skilled artist fashions a chariot. If you receive it with pleasure, Agni, let us win waters and sunlight with it.

12 'The bull with the powerful neck, increasing in size and strength, will drive together the possession of the enemy without opposition.' This is what the immortals said to Agni. Let him grant shelter to the man who spreads the sacred grass; let him grant shelter to the man who offers oblation.[24]

You must now realise that the One-God religions are not the only ones to use the demon concept; as a spiritual evilness and a way of demeaning their enemies and their enemies religious practices."

Pingala helps Michael collect the firewood, looks at Morrighan and then Pingala says: "so, we are in a state of realization that realises that demons and demonizing is used–through fear–as a means of control. But what we have not–so far–been able to certify is what a demon actually is and where if anywhere within the realms of the self and the physical being it could originate."

Sankara looks at Pingala and then he says: "the problem with the origination of demons is that the most ancient of the known written referrals is that of the Sanskrit writings of the Hindu religion, but this is not necessarily the origination, because some ancient verbal religions have monsters rather than demons. Therefore the concept of demons could be theorized as a linguistic creation; for the races that are considered to be below the races that are thought of as gifted by the gods; the people that are considered to be of a lesser or false religion; the people that do what is considered to be evil; the explanation for what is considered to be strange and unexplained events, such as earthquakes, volcanic eruptions [it should also be realised that these natural disasters could also be used for explaining the displeasure of the Gods or even the One-God] etc....Although in theorizing this these natural disasters can be explained by science."

Morrighan smiles, points to a log cabin and replies: "up to this point demons have appeared to be inadequates of a lower

---

[24] The Rig Veda translated and annotated by Wendy O'Flaherty p103 Penguin Classics 1981

race or a lesser religion; evil beings of destruction or Gods and Goddesses of another religion. Therefore the idea of demons and demonic beings has become the tools for the most dictatorial religions and/or races of the time.

What we must now realise is that the whole idea of demonic races and happening are rather successful propaganda tools that can be used to suit a party that is/or wants to be the dominant party of that era, for instance; what better way is there too subjugate a race than by demonizing its religion? My answer to this is that there is no better way, because–like we have already mentioned–to control the thoughts and the will of a race is to take over that race."

Michael smiles at Morrighan and then he says: "with demons having been shown to be a major element of control [through the fear of the unknown] within religion and race; is it possible that all superstition is linked in such a way?"

Merlin smiles, looks at the log cabin and replies: "unlike the demons; monsters and the Faery folk do not have to be what they are supposed to be, because monsters and Faery folk are defined in the myths that are associated with them. Therefore the myths and legends of these strange folk and creatures need to be examined as a feature of the religion that they are part of and not used as a propaganda tool to control the masses, for example: in ancient Greek myth; Medusa [who was one of the Gorgon sisters that were the daughters of the sea divinities Phorys and Ceto] was renowned for her beauty and beautiful hair. Unfortunately the Goddess Athena made Medusa's looks turn anyone to stone that looked directly upon her face and Athena also turned Medusa's hair into snakes, because Medusa had her virginity taken by Poseidon in a temple of the Goddess Athena and in doing so; Medusa was seen to have violated Athena's sacred place and punished. In the end of this myth Medusa is killed by the hero Perseus; who cuts off her head whilst looking at Medusa's reflection or by the guiding hand of the Goddess Athena. The hero Perseus kills Medusa, because his mother is held captive by the King Polydectes and this King gives Perseus the task of killing Medusa and bringing her head to him. But after Perseus uses the head to destroy his enemies he gives it to the Goddess Athena who wears it in her breastplate.[25]

It is said that a winged horse called Pegasus and a son called Chrysador came form Medusa's blood.

This myth could be seen as a warning that divine retribution would follow if any of the shrines or temples of the Divine are violated, because being a God or the daughter or lover of god does not stop the Goddess Athena seeking retribution.

It should also be realised that the Goddess Athena is known as a virgin Goddess and in realizing this the act of losing or having one's virginity taken in the temple of a virgin Goddess; could mean many things and give light to many different meanings, for example; it could mean that in the act of willingly losing her virginity or having her virginity taken by Poseidon–in the temple–Medusa took away the sanctuary of the place without the permission of Athena; and robbed the temple of its virginity and purity; or it could mean that Medusa was raped in the temple of Athena and Athena turned Medusa into a creature that Poseidon would not think of raping again. After Athena had done such an act and had Medusa killed the wearing of Medusa's head upon Athena's breastplate could be seen as a warning of what can happen to those who desecrate the Goddess Athena's sacred places."

Pallas grins at Merlin and then she says: "the myth that you refer to also shows that death brings life and that the wise can be as cruel and unforgiving as any tyrant."

Michael looks at Pallas and then he says: "the myth also suggests reincarnation, because if the blood is the soul and the winged horse and the son emerge from the blood it suggest that the soul can go onto a higher form or stay in the human form, but why Medusa's blood should give birth to two different forms needs further investigation!"

Pallas picks up some more firewood and then she says: "do not forget that Medusa was a daughter of Divine beings and in being so would be divine in her self. Therefore we must realise that when this body is lost and the blood or the soul is set free,

---

[25] The complete Dictionary of Symbols, In Myth, Art and Literature general editor Jack Tresidder p312-313 Duncan Baird Publishers Ltd 2004

what is within that soul is set free from the bondage of that body."

It is also possible that this myth is showing the power of the female deities, because in her death Medusa is able to create man and animals of the earth and sky [a horse is of the earth and a winged animal is of the sky]."

Gaia smiles at Pallas and replies: "hence it becomes apparent that the myth of a monster could be turned into or may even be a creation theory, because the creation of life is coming out of the blood of a woman. Therefore not all monsters can be considered bad, because if some good can come out of the bad it cannot be totally corrupt."

Merlin strokes his beard and replies: "it is true that all monsters cannot be seen as bad, because some myths show that some of them are used to explain natural phenomenon, that is if you truly think of mythical creatures as monsters, for example the Brule Sioux use the Four Old Thunderbirds as an explanation for weather systems[26] and there are many other legends and myths–such as that of Medusa–that appear to give meaning to our creation and to the understanding of the world that we live in."

Pingala nods and replies: "even with science the magic of this world is still apparent in its build up, because there are monsters within the planet and its natural systems, for example; a destructive hurricane or tornado could still be seen as a monstrous event. Therefore the idea that surrounds monsters does not mean that monsters are of a bestial kind.

What we should now realise is that anything that is considered monstrous or due to a monstrous event is open to the understanding of a personal and scientific nature. I theorize personal, because the understanding of one person or a group of people that are of different race and/or different religions are/or can be limited in their understanding by the hierarchy that they are associated with."

Michael looks at the building they are closing upon, smiles at Pingala and then he says: "so monsters and monstrous conditions can be seen as principles that are indoctrinated by

---

[26] American Indian Myths and Legends, Richard Erdoes & Alfonso Ortiz p218-222 Pimlico 1997

different races or religions to prove a point of view [be it good or bad]. But in realizing this we must also realise that we need to explore the monsters that are in the world that we live in."

Morrighan taps Pallas on the shoulder, points to the standing stones and then Morrighan says: "the monsters that are known in the physical world; are only thought of as monsters, because of a lack of understanding [one thing to remember is that monster can mean something, bad or just huge] of the animals or the weather conditions of the realm that that we live in.

The mythical monsters of religion seem to be of other worlds, but these monsters also seem to be based upon things that are known and misunderstood by the human beings physical and dream worlds, for example; the Centaur is a cross between a man and a horse and in the dream worlds the Centaur can seem as real as a man on a horse in the physical world. Therefore we must realise that in the exploration of these myths; the dream worlds—of which we are all part of—are as real to some as the physical world."

Pallas puts her arm around Morrighan, smiles at her and then Pallas replies: "there are some that think that monsters and dreams are nothing more than a figment of the imagination. But in their ideals they do not seem to realise that a figment of their imagination is a creation that is worthy of any Divine being, because the creation of the world must have had at least a figment of the imagination of a Divine being; before it became the reality of the physical being [that is if the world is created by a Divine being or beings]."

So the creation of the imagination can be as real as what we consider the physical world to be, because it has a creation and in that creation it has a reality and a purpose, for example; the Leviathan is of the Mesopotamian and Phoenician origin and is seen as a chaos God of the deep and in later Biblical [Job 41] works of the One-God culture it is seen as a terrible demonic monster that has scales, spits fire and cannot be killed by the likes of man.[27]"

---

[27] The Complete Dictionary of Symbols general editor: Jack Tresidder p287 Duncan Baird Publishers Ltd 2004

Sankara smiles at Pallas and then he says: "what seems to be emerging is that monsters are used as a mythical scare tactic and for an explanation of things that are considered evil–as we have previously mentioned. Therefore the adverse weather conditions and the natural phenomena of earthquakes and volcanic activity **can all be blamed upon the activities of the monsters.** Even the disappearance of people and the unexplained illnesses and deaths can be blamed upon monsters, for example; the creatures of the were [such as the wolf and the hare] in the Celtic myths and legends. Of course the wolf is a known and feared taker of animal life, but the strange thing about the superstitions that surround the hare; is that the hare is a vegetarian. But in saying this it must be realised that the tales that surround the werewolf can range from evil to loyally returning a favour that was done for it."[28]

Michael smiles, looks at Sankara and then he asks: "is it possible that these stories of supernatural creatures are based on a lack of natural understanding, for example some races and religions despise the wolf through their lack of understanding of the species whereas other races admire and respect the wolf, and with this conflict in understanding; is it possible that such creatures become misunderstood by the majority; if the majority is not willing to listen to the minority that understand the natural order?"

Pingala watches the snow fall upon her open hand and replies: "that is possible, but in being unwilling to listen it does not explain where the belief in shape shifting emerged from, and this also does not explain where the beliefs in the mythical creatures that affect the planets natural happenings emerge from."

Pallas looks at Pingala and then Pallas remarks: "beauty and brains my dear Pingala,"

Pingala sweetly smiles at Pallas and Pallas carries on: "this belief in shape shifting is common to many beliefs and many Divinities are thought to be capable of such actions, but for some reason the creatures of the were seem to bring fear into the superstitions of man, because of this and the previous reason

---

[28] Irish Folk and Faery Tales Omnibus Volume 2 Michael Scott p98-110 Warner Books 1993

of my own we should explore some of the myths that are associated with these creatures, because, although these creatures of the were [especially the wolf] are feared and seen as a great evil there is a particular Irish myth that shows compassion and loyalty within the werewolf."

Merlin looks at Pallas and then he says: "the family of werewolves in the myth; Creatures of the Were; The Wolves[29]; shows an animal that is capable of compassion, because this family give gifts and do not kill a frightened man that had [unknowingly] helped them in the past and for the favours he had given them [whilst they were in doglike or wolf form] he was given food drink and shelter and two cows were replaced that had previously been lost to the wolves.

The cows that were replaced were replaced with cows that had a massive milk yield and his farm was not troubled by foxes or hares; which were unlike his neighbours.

Every night the farmer left a little food out and it was always gone in the morning.

The farmer died two years later and the cows disappeared."

Gaia smiles at Merlin and then she says: "that myth shows a huge problem with the supernatural beings, because these beings that are of mythical character are open to many misinterpretations [as are most and probably all supernatural creatures]. Therefore we must realise that these misinterpretations are probably due to a lack of understanding and the need for the human race to think that it is the superior race in the world that we reside in our physical state. Hence it is evident that the human race wants to be and thinks that it is the superior race of the physical world."

Morrighan Grins and replies: "these [apparently] superior cults that are part of the human race–that are based on their religious beliefs–must be based upon myth for them to be superior, because they are dependent on creatures that they can overpower by their belief in their Divine. But in realizing this we must also realise that this is where differences occur, because these differences seem to depend on the races ability to accept the forces of the natural order rather than the power of their

---

[29] Ibid

Divinities. Therefore werewolves and other so-called monsters are used for the purpose of the show of power that is available to certain races through their Divinities.

So, if we realise that the Divine is not accepted [by some races and/or religions] as a force that is greater than nature, then we must investigate how these monsters that are greater than man came into existence; if the Divine is the greatest power and mankind is the divinities most intelligent and greatest creation or supporter."

Michael winks at Morrighan, looks and smiles at Gaia and then he says: "if the divine were so powerful and in control–then as Morrighan has pointed out–why are the creatures created if the Divine are truly in control?"

Gaia picks up some snow and watches it melt in her warm hand and then she replies: "why I think that nature and not any other divinity is the true controller of the planet is because the predator and prey aspects of the planet are needed to stop one species of the planet becoming too dominant. Therefore monsters are needed to keep other monsters under control."

Michael widely opens his eyes, looks at Gaia and asks: "am I right in assuming that mankind is one of the monsters that need to be kept in check?"

Gaia grins and says one word: "yes."

Merlin looks at Sankara and then Merlin says: "so the monsters that are created in the myths of mankind; could be seen as an extension of the will or the desire of mankind to control all their physical surroundings."

Sankara smiles at Merlin and replies: "perhaps the monster could be seen as such an extension, but the fact that they were created and the fact that in myth it takes a hero or a Divinity to destroy a monster; suggests that there is another controlling factor [such as Mother Nature]. Hence we must begin to realise that if we presume that Mother Nature is the controlling factor behind the myths and the creation of the monsters that are associated with the myths; we must assume that Mother Nature has an idea of the life expectancy of the monsters that have been created."

Gaia smiles and says: "perhaps Mother Nature had no concrete plan [to begin with] and perhaps there never will be any concrete plan, for example; the laser was intended to be a weapon of great destructive power, but this weapon has many medical uses and can even stop some people form going blind."

Merlin grins at Gaia and then Merlin says: "from what Gaia has said it becomes probable that Mother Nature is not in complete control over what she has created. If that is the reality of the creation it is also reasonable to assume that Mother Nature cannot control the physical existence of the beings that she has created, but in realizing this we should also realise that Mother Nature has the ability to destroy what she has created, because she holds the creative powers of the universe in her grasp!"

Morrighan laughs quietly to herself, smiles at Pallas and then Morrighan replies: "it is quite apparent that what we call Mother Nature or nature can be a monstrously destructive force.

Therefore we should begin to understand that; if the human being has come from a monster the human being must be part monster and in being part monster; the human race shows itself for what it is or what it can be when it creates monstrous acts. Therefore it is possible or probable that the creation of the myths of monsters; are just part of the whole–but unrecognized–creation of Mother Nature."

Pallas smiles and replies: "knowing that we come from a monster and we create monstrous acts seems to be part of the build up of the uncertainty that is within the physical being, but we must also realise that once this monster comes into fruition; it must also be part of the spiritual will for it to be able to act in the way it does. Therefore it is reasonable to assume that all monsters; are open to the free will of the human belief system and in being so exposed; these monsters come in many shapes and forms and are open to their own ideas being bastardized by a victor of another belief system."

As we have already mentioned; earlier Gods can become demons of other races and the demons can become monsters in their so-called acts of evil. Therefore we must ask ourselves; are the monsters and demons of this world; something that is actually within the entire human race or are they separate?"

Morrighan smiles as they close upon the log cabin and then she says: "of course we are all part demon part monster and part divine if the self is part of all that is!"

Pingala clasps her hands together, blows upon them, and replies: "therefore we should realise that the human race is–probably–as much demon and as much monster as the mythical beings it has created, because it is only the human race that gives these creatures or divinities their titles."

Morrighan grins and replies: "it is possible that some of the Divine create the problems that are associated with the definition of monsters and demons for their own purpose, for instance; the demonizing of Pan and Hearne [by the Christians] suited the idea of there being a singular God and in appearing to be so; this One-God and his followers seemed to be morally superior to those that this God and his followers wanted to overthrow and conquer. Therefore–as Pingala has already made evident–the Gods and Goddesses must be quite capable of persuading mankind to give monstrous titles to those that are in the way of their agenda.

The Christians the Jews and those of the Islamic faith are still at odds with each other and the rest of the worlds religions in their One-God ideologies and in being so; they could be showing what a monster or demon their One-God could be. Therefore the creation of monsters and demons could be; a creation of the linguistic abilities of the individual religions or their followers. I theorize that is so, because all individuals–be they religious or not–have their own very or slightly different ideas of what demonic or monstrous is!"

Pallas winks at Morrighan, smiles and replies: "the idea of monsters and demons appear to have been made apparent within the belief of the individual and in being so it is open to a serious amount of bastardization by the strongest ideals of the time. Therefore the religious ideals that surround demons and monsters can turn on some religions [as we have already made evident] and make demons and monsters out of their God or their Divine!"

Michael nods his head in agreement and says: "what this means is that any singular God or pantheon of Divine beings can be removed form their position; by the loss of belief in them; and this can happen at any time; especially if there is malicious linguistic misinterpretation."

Merlin lights his pipe and says: "such misinterpretation of language and pictures has been common practice for the One-God religions. This misuse is used for the dictatorial teachers of the One-God faiths; for their laws and their attempted control and abolishment of Pagan religions. But this is problematic, because such misuses and misinterpretations do not present themselves until the action is taken. Therefore this type of religion can become responsible for natural disasters and the monsters that they have created can rise up against them and destroy their own kind; and this destruction that is part of a natural happening; can be dismissed as an act of the devil or the monsters that are associated with him."

Pingala smiles and replies: "so, the action of scientific control can lose the ability to recognize the natural happenings within the universe; and create monsters and demons for the control of the main population. In this way of management the controllers are able to demonize any event that science could explain; by making the work of science illegal and appearing to be the work of a monster, demon or devil. When this type of control has been established the people of the faith of this type of scripture; become totally dependent on the scriptures and the priesthood or experts of these scriptures; for the answers to their problems. Therefore we must realise that these scriptures that are relied upon for the control of the main population; are controlled by the limitations that are placed upon them by their experts."

Morrighan raises her eyebrows and replies: "these scriptures that are used for demonizing and control are written by the hand of mankind and—as we have mentioned before—are open to criticism, because mankind is known for its falsehoods and exaggerations. Therefore we should eliminate such scriptures from our inquiry, because any written theory that tries to hold back its examination and uses sin to stop an investigation that is contrary to the beliefs that are within its pages; can be presumed to be hiding uncomfortable truths."

Michael smiles and remarks: "if scriptures and the modern word are not incorruptible; then all the theories on monsters have to be proved by scientific means, but this is problematic, because scientific theory is open to corruption and mistakes, because it relies upon the written word to contain its facts and figures."

Morrighan shakes her head, smiles and replies: "that maybe so, but true science does not try to stop people from examining it and trying to prove it wrong. Therefore we should realise that true science is the only non corrupt form, because it is open to examination and will freely admit to its mistakes."

Pallas smiles and says: "we have already discussed the probable reasons for the building of some myths and legends and with this in mind; we should have come to realise that these myths and legends are open to misinterpretation. Therefore we should also realise that some of the methods of building these myths and legends could be seen to be unreliable. This unreliability comes with the introduction of new religions and races that have different ideals from those of the original religions and races, for example; the earlier discussion on Pan and Hearne show how easy it is for a non scientific written theory to be used to coerce others..

But we must also realise that some of those myths and legends could have a deeper meaning than they appear to have; just like in our previous theory on the myth of Medusa."

Sankara looks at Pallas and then he says: "Medusa is a strange myth that hints at death rebirth and reincarnation. Hence we can assume that it is theoretically probable; that some of the myths and legends are based on the beliefs of a particular religion; rather than the written word of science. This is problematic, because beliefs are not dependent on anything but the word of man, which is; unknown in its origination!"

Gaia laughs quietly and then replies: "Could it be that some myths and legends were functional before the written word."

Michael gives a puzzled expression and asks: "how can something be proved if there is no written evidence?"

Morrighan smiles and replies: "if some legends and myths come before written evidence [as some have to in purely verbal religions] the evidence has to come about through purely verbal form, and when such a verbal myth or legend is carried on through many centuries–it is more than likely that it will get written somewhere.

Everything that is verbal or written has to start in the mind. Therefore the mind that has created the myth or legend of a monster or demon would have that image implanted upon it; before that image became a reality. This is problematic, because the mind that created that monster or demon; would have to have had that image implanted in it from somewhere outside that singular mind that created it."

Pallas smiles and replies: "what appears to be emerging is that the creations of the mind are based upon some kind of previous knowledge; that can only be made available to it by an outside agent that is not understood by the general population, for example; the legends of the giant squid that took ships are based upon actual creatures that were outside the human understanding of that time. Therefore it is possible that the creation of monsters and demons has a starting point for its knowledge, but this starting point of the knowledge is outside the full understanding of the time; and once this knowledge is filled by the factual world of science, the misunderstanding of a particular demon or monster is destroyed. But in realizing these it must also be realised that part of the myths do exist for the myths to start in the first instance. Which in itself is problematic, because there are still unexplained myths, for example; the myths that surround the Leviathan have seen this monster as a God of Chaos, a sea serpent, a whale etc...."

Merlin smiles and says: "what religion is being realised to be capable of is; the control of the imagination by the manipulation of the unexplained and then creating monsters and demons out of their manipulation of the unexplained. After this type of manipulation the individual mind is open to corruption and in being manipulated and corrupted in such a way; the individual mind is easier to control, because once the seeds of doubt are sown, the individual [generally] wants to lead some kind of satisfying life. But this is problematic, because the control that has been lost and regained through manipulation can only remain stable whilst the control is close to the individual."

Sankara grins at the person opening the door of the nearing log cabin and then he says: "the main manipulations that have been made evident are those theologies of the many One-God religions; that surround their evil being.

This evil being—be it demon or devil—has many forms and many allies that are easily portrayed as other religions deities. But in realizing this we must also realise that many of the one God religions do not seem to realise; that evil could be just as much a part of their God as evil is a part of man."

Gaia hugs Demeter, looks at Sankara and then Gaia replies: "perhaps it is possible that the manipulative ideals of the One-God religion; are driven by their need to abolish the pleasures that are associated with the flesh, because of the loss of religious thought that happens when the human kind are involved in such pleasures."

Demeter offers an open door to the travellers and then she replies: "the pleasures of sex and food; seem to be the main pleasures that are demonized and made monstrous by many of the One-God cults, but in realizing this we must also realise that many of the pagan religions use the abstinence of food to become closer to their spirituality. Therefore it is possible that this type of action could be seen as a sacred rite and in being realised as a sacred rite, the sacred rite becomes much easier to manipulate, because to break a sacred rite is considered sinful by most of the Pagan and the One-God religions."

Merlin looks at Demeter and replies: "what this is making evident is that if the Pagan Divine is associated with the pleasures of the flesh, they can be more easily demonized and made sinful; when over indulgence becomes a sin against God."

Michael shakes his head, smiles and says: "it is becoming clear that the physical pleasures of the human being; are being used as a tool against the enlightenment of the self or the soul; by some Pagan and many of the One-God religions."

Morrighan watches Michael put some logs on the fire and then she says: "the people of the religions that use demons and monsters as tools of their faiths enlightening power; only do so, because they have no alternatives. Hence we must realise that the demons and monsters that have been created out of other religions divine beings should be realised to be an act of psychological warfare. I theorize this, because in this way another religions Divine can be made to appear to be ugly and full of evil, and this would then make the original Divine unpopular and appear to be no good in the mind of the general population. Although in saying this I must also say that there are some pagan religions that have monsters that are of a beneficial purpose. But in realizing this we must also realise that the idea that surrounds the make up of monsters is of an individual belief and that belief depends on how the individual has been taught. Therefore we must realise; that the individual teachings of a persuasive religion–that are dependent on the attributes of others–are generally what convinces or corrupts the individual person's ideology, and this ideology includes monsters and demons."

Demeter puts her arm round Morrighan and then Demeter asks: "could the abstinence from food and procreation be responsible for the creation of some of the monsters and demons?"

Lug suddenly appears from the kitchen with a pot of tea and nine cups, pours the tea and then he says: "such activities as starving oneself and the denial of sexual activities can lead to hallucination and fantasy if the individual is not strong enough to control such urges. But in realizing this, a problem occurs, because a strong individual can be overthrown by a group of weaker individuals that would not be able to enslave the mind of the strong individual if they were alone, and once this will of the self is overthrown; it becomes easier to control through the effects of starvation."

Michael smiles at Lug and then Michael asks: "how can the will of the self be enslaved by physical starvation; when the will has allowed itself to be starved into hallucination and fantasy?"

Pallas grins and says: "the whole idea of hallucinatory monsters and the enslavement of the free will is problematic, because the free will can only reach such hallucinatory ideals by a misunderstanding of the natural world that is taught by a religion; that is not willing to progress, and realise that its original writings are not necessarily based on fact."

Pingala smiles and says: "all hallucination appears to be dependent on the will [mostly through starvation] misinterpreting natural happenings or entities. Therefore the hallucinations can be and in many instances are a creation of events, that are concocted into a vision by a chemical imbalance; that has occurred through a lack of nutrients and in this lack; this will has been easily corrupted–by others–for the acceptance of these hallucinations as visions; that have been presented to them by their new God that is the God of their new religion."

Gaia smiles and says: "hallucination may be responsible for some monsters and demons, but this is problematic, because hallucinatory thoughts cannot always be responsible for the monsters they appear to create. That is due to the fact; that what one mind sees as a demon or monster, another mind or self may actually see that monster or demon in its true capacity before any hallucination has been reached. Hence we should realise that any creation that has been made through hallucination is open to annihilation when a non believer has another explanation."

Morrighan smiles and says: "so far demons and monsters have been realised to be religious tools that have been used to demean other religions gods, and to explain natural disasters, and also to enslave the individual will. But in realizing this we must also realise that there are some exceptions–as we have already made evident–and these exceptions mainly exist within the natural world. Even Medusa is connected to the natural world, because Medusa becomes part snake and part woman and in transforming so; Medusa becomes a transformation that most of us would not want in the beginning, even though in her death her blood gives rise to a creation of beauty. This idea of beauty and the beast could explain one of the ideas behind creation, but I leave that for you to decide!

Those ideas of monsters and demons must be the beginning of superstition or perhaps the beginning of superstition is the unexplained natural world and the beginning of the universe?"

Lug smiles at Morrighan and then he says: "superstition must come before the conception of demons and monsters. That is if the human beings thought process is responsible for the language process that surrounds the ideas of monsters and demons, and if it is not the language of the self that is responsible for these demons and monsters; something else must have created them and that something else would have to rely on superstition to create such beings. Therefore the act of superstition must come before anything that is created by it."

Pallas stirs some honey into her cup of tea and then she remarks: "superstition may be dependent on language for its origins. But this is problematic, because the superstition that depends on language alone can have no physical form and [as we all know] there are many pictures and statues of physical creatures that exist within superstition. Therefore superstition cannot be dependent on language alone–for its creation–and if superstition is not dependent–solely–on language or words for its creation; then the only thing that we can assume is that superstition is another part of the self–just like good and evil."

Pingala winks and smiles at Pallas [Pallas passes her the honey] and then Pingala says: "in being a part of the self, superstition could still have an outside agent to the individual self, because superstition seems to be dependent on separate beings for its arrival. Therefore superstition does not need to be a part of the self until it has been realised by the self!

The self can only become superstitious if it incorporates the superstitions that have been made evident to it. But that is problematic, because the individual self can only realise that it is superstitious; when it becomes aware that these superstitions that it has been taught are based on conjecture."

Gaia smiles and says: "it is becoming evident that the whole of superstition is being planted by an outside agent and this outside agent; seems to be part of a force that is not truly recognized or acknowledged. Therefore it could be possible that the outside agent that creates superstition is part of the never ending cycle of life, death, and rebirth!"

Demeter stirs her tea and says: "perhaps superstition was not born. Perhaps superstition is a part of any language that language cannot do without, because once language has been created, things that are not able to be proven come into existence, for example; the creation of the universe and the creator or creators [if the universe was created by a creator or creators] of the universe are all ideas based upon conjecture!"

Morrighan smiles and says: "it is possible that superstition is created by the power that created the word and the word comes from superstition for its creation and can only be apparent in superstition; as two verses in the creation hymn of the Rig Veda show:

6 Who really knows? Who will here proclaim it? Whence was it produced? Whence is this creation? The Gods came afterwards, with the creation of the universe. Who then knows whence it has arisen?

7 Whence this creation has arisen—perhaps it formed itself or perhaps it did not—the one who looks down on it, in the highest heaven, only he knows—or perhaps he does not know.[30]

With this being made evident the idea of the Divine being responsible for the creation of superstition becomes implausible, because the Divine are part of superstition and in being part of superstition, it would be illogical for the Divine to allow the creation of a superstition that is against their will or purpose. Therefore the word that created a superstition—probably—has strength of will or power that is stronger than the will or power of the Divine, and this power of the word; has become more evident as we have seen how religions, have used the power of the word to cause fear of the unknown and to demonize and make Gods and Goddesses of other religions appear to be evil."

Pallas greases the cork of her flute and then she replies: "it is becoming evident that the word is responsible for all that is apparent to our understanding and in being so; the word itself—not the Divine—is responsible for all the creation myths and the science, because without the word there is no real understanding at all!"

Lug smiles and says: "it has become evident that the word is the beginning and the end of all myth and superstition, because without the word, there is no means of understanding the language of the universe and the language of the Divine. Therefore we must realise that the creation myths come from the word that has always existed, because even the first thought that was created after the creation of the universe was created by the word!"

Morrighan taps her foot to an imaginary tune, looks out of the window and then she remarks: "all written or verbal creation is dependent upon the word for its creation, but this does not explain how this process started before the word made these thought forms evident, for example; you do not need words to have the fear of death after falling from a substantial height,

---

[30] The Rig Veda translated and annotated by Wendy Doniger O'Flaherty p25-26 Penguin Books Ltd 1981.

because the fear is already there before the words are expressed. Therefore we should begin to realise that the emotions of love, anger, jealousy, hate, sadness and happiness must be in the individual before the word can become the creator of such emotions."

Merlin starts to uncover his harp as he replies: "so myth, legend and superstition are dependent on the emotions and the word for their creation!"

Morrighan smiles at Pingala and then Morrighan says: "without emotion the words of legend and myth become pointless, because emotion is the beginning of all creation; be it myth, legend, superstition or anything at all!

As we have made evident the emotional will of one religion can be the demise of another. But in realizing this we must also realise that the will of some deserted religions seems to live on, and re-emerge after many generations of desolation.

Pingala smiles at Morrighan, walks across the room to her and then Pingala says: "some of the races of Man have evidently created demons and monsters, out of the Gods and Goddesses of other races religions, and after doing so they use these new superstitions that they have created, to undermine these other races and/or religions."

Pallas takes her flute over to Pingala and Morrighan and then Pallas says: "with all the evidence of strife that has been caused by the creation of monsters and demons within superstition; the will to create these monsters and superstitions [in some cases out of other Gods and Goddesses] has become more potent when it is accepted by the majority."

Lug gets out his violin, smiles at Demeter and then he says: "it is becoming evident that the will of the race of mankind; is responsible for its own superstitions and it has been used to infiltrate other superstitions and religions, for the dictatorial ideals of one sect of mankind. These dictatorial ideals are shown by the non acceptance of other races and/or religions Gods and Goddesses."

Gaia moves over to Merlin and then she uncovers her harp and concludes by saying: "from all we have discussed; it seems fair to say that cult and superstition are entwined within the will of the human race and in being so entwined; the cults of one religion manage to manipulate other religions; by demonizing their old Gods. Therefore the cults of the One-God religions have become hugely successful, and this is because; if there is no other God but their own—which I think is a ludicrous idea, then these Gods of other religions can only be a manifestation of their devil. But this is contradictory, because the devil is a God of evil and still a God!"

The flute of Pallas begins to sing and the voices of Morrighan and Sankara stir the dance of Pingala and Demeter....

The discussion has ended and the party has begun.

5

THE NATURAL MIND

The feast is over and a new day of discourse begins.

Lug looks at Gaia and begins by saying: "so far we have discussed the theology and superstition that have led to the emergence of the One-God cults. But we have not closely examined the actions and the reasons that surround the theologies of Mother Nature; being the power by which every physical being depends upon for its survival!"

Morrighan looks out of the window and smiles as she sees the full moon shine upon this winters morn, and then she remarks; "the will of mankind has been used by some religions; to enslave the mind of others; for the purpose of being able to verify the destruction of natural entities for its own selfish uses!

The idea that the human being is in control of natural forces has already been seen to be false and has—in some past events—been seen to be the work of a demon or devil by some religious factions. Therefore the ideology that surrounds Mother Nature had to be controlled or demonized."

Pingala finishes her cup of tea, smiles and replies: "the demonizing of natural events can lose the people of that world their grip on natural reality, and once this grip is lost; they can then become complacent in their actions on the natural world, for example; if we pump enough of the poison of a bee into the human being it will die! Therefore it should be quite obvious that if we pump enough poison into the planet it will have the same effect. But this is problematic, because if Mother Nature has been demonized and all respect for her has been lost, and the needs of the planet—and its inhabitants—have become misunderstood then all could be lost!"

Pallas smiles at Merlin and then she says: "what is becoming evident is that the natural world and the life of the planet is becoming lost, and destroyed within the minds of some of the dictatorial religions. Therefore these religions should take more care in what they think they can achieve by their actions, but this does not appear to be in the mindset of a religion that believes its God will overrun all other religions and bring some kind of peace throughout the world."

Merlin takes a sip of his tea and replies: "we have already discussed how the devastation that is caused by natural events has been used to demonize other religions, but we have not discussed–in detail–how many religions have [in some cases] used natural happenings to explain the wrath of their Divine being or beings. The theory that I am proposing with this point is that if humanity uses such beings as the reason of the natural catastrophes; that are or can be humanities own doing; then the reason behind the catastrophes that can be caused by natural cycles, can be lost in myth and legend."

Pallas looks at Merlin and then she remarks: "most of the natural disasters that are blamed on a Gods revenge or a demons destructive will, have become tools of some religions destructive policies. Therefore the use of science to explain these beliefs is shunned by the majority of these dictatorial religions."

Lug looks at Pallas and then he says: "science and religion can contradict each other in many ways, but the natural world and the universe–probably–are always out of the realms of the complete understanding, because they are so vast!"

Morrighan smiles and says: "perhaps the understanding is not out of the reach of the human mind; perhaps the human race and the mainstream religions of the human race have made these issues too complex for their understanding.

We must also realise that the complexity of the world that is made by the humans is seen as nothing more than an illusion by some religions.

Nothing in nature lasts forever and all that is and has been will be lost from sight; is a theological idea, that is a part of some religions, for example; in The Tibetan Book of Living and Dying it is said that:

What is born will die,
What has been gathered will be dispersed,
What has been built will collapse,
And what has been brought high will be brought low.[31]

---

[31] The Tibetan Book of Living and Dying, Sogyal Rinpoche p26 Harper Collins Publishers Ltd USA 2002

Hence we can presume that nothing that is physical lasts forever, but in realizing this we should also realise that what we do in the natural world has consequences, because in the above mentioned book it is also said that:

He who binds himself to a joy,
Does the winged life destroy;
He who kisses the joy as it flies,
Lives in Eternity's sunrise.[32]

This little verse can bring many meanings forth and in theorizing that; I would personally think that it could show the journey of the soul whilst it is in the natural world, because it shows both aspects of the physical life that can be held in bondage by the things that we desire or it can show us that; we can let these desires fly by and become free, from the consequences of unsavoury actions in the natural world, because as the fourteenth Dalai Lama makes evident:

The natural world is our home, it is where we live. It is therefore in our interest to look after it. This is only common sense. The size of our population and the power of our science have become such that they have a direct effect on nature. To put it another way until now Mother Earth has been able to tolerate our sloppy habits. The stage has been reached in which she can no longer tolerate our sloppy habits.[33]

Therefore we must realise that if we defile the world that we live in we should be prepared to accept the consequences of our actions [in this life and the next], because if our greed is destroying parts of our physical world we are showing an imbalance within our personal ambitions, and our natural harmony."

Michael smiles and asks: "how can our selfishness in the natural world affect our entrance into the next world or worlds?"

Morrighan smiles and replies: "while mankind is being selfish it is not being aware of the bad karma it is giving out–particularly–in the Buddhist and Hindu faiths. Therefore the human or humans that do acts that are only beneficial to their

---

[32] Ibid p35: from 'Eternity' in Blake, complete writings, edited by Geoffrey Keynes p179 (Oxford and New York OUP 1972)
[33] Ancient Wisdom Modern Ethics for a New Millennium, Tenzin Gyatso the fourteenth Dalai Lama of Tibet (six times) p213 Little, Brown and Company 1999

ideals in the physical world; cannot reach enlightenment, because they cannot realise the truth of their actions, whilst they are held in bondage by their own physical desires."

Lug smiles and says: "there are many old faiths that believe in Mother Nature as a goddess in her own right, and some of these religions seem to be more aware of what is liable to happen if we defile her creations. But in realizing this we must also realise that a lot of the consequences of defiling Mother Nature are already evident (as has been referred to by the fourteenth Dalai Lama). In realizing this we should also realise that it is highly probable that the whole idea of Mother Nature has probably come into fruition, through the realization that woman is the one that gives life through birth. Therefore it is assumed that the planet that gives life to us is female."

Demeter smiles and says: "the whole planet is actually a living and breathing entity and once this is realised; the whole idea of Mother Nature as a spiritual and physically conscious being becomes more realistic, because when we infect her she tends to punish us, and when that is realised; we should also realise; that it is highly probable that Mother Nature is one or part of the Lords of Karma."

Merlin smiles and says: "it is probable that Mother Nature is the sole creator of all that is physical upon this planet, because as evolution has evolved our physical beings into what they are; we must realise that Mother Nature has allowed this to be so! But in becoming aware of this we should realise that Mother Nature allowed the dinosaurs to become extinct after millions of years; which paved the way for the human race to come into existence. **Therefore I suggest that; when she allowed the physical beings that incorporate the self to come into existence, and to realise what it is that Mother Nature gave our immortal selves as a gift; we should respect the gift for what it is.** Hence it should become apparent that; the natural beings that we inhabit before we are enlightened or go to another world are part of the building blocks of Mother Nature! Therefore whilst we are on this planet we should realise that Mother Nature is in control, and we have no right to try and manipulate and control Mother Nature!"

Gaia grins broadly and then she says: "what you are saying is problematic in many religions, because what is perishable can be seen as an illusion and in many people what is considered illusory is considered as unimportant. But if the circle of birth death and rebirth is truly realised; then nothing can be illusion, because what 'is' always will be even after its death, because you cannot lose what will always be reborn! When this is realised; we must also realise that what can be reborn; can be reborn on a different level of being. Therefore we must realise that; if we are reborn on a different level or as a different being; rebirth is never static and the physical entities that are perishable are perishable, and in being so they lead the immortal soul or the self into a new life, and a new being of existence. It must now become evident that all physical beings have the potential to evolve and in this evolution; the only thing that is lost is its previous existence. But what we should also realise is that in the cases of previous lives; what is lost has the potential to be found and remembered."

Merlin smiles and remarks: "hence we should realise that Mother Nature is the one that allows the evolution of the physical world and in this evolution; Mother Nature could be assumed to be the one that evolves the self or the immortal soul. Therefore it becomes just as important for the self to realise that it cannot evolve without Mother Nature [if its assumption is correct]; as it is for the self to realise that everything that is physical is perishable and in being so; some kind of physicality must have always existed, because nothing comes out of nothing!"

Michael smiles, gets a bag of nuts from his rucksack–offers them round–and then he says: "if physicality has always existed and Mother Nature is the creator of the natural world; then Mother Nature must have created the natural world out of parts that already existed in a different form, and that is problematic, because the parts that already existed must have come from somewhere!"

Pingala smiles and replies: "all parts that appear that are somewhere, must have come from somewhere, and Mother Nature herself must have come from somewhere. Therefore this arriving and creating must have come through different forms otherwise nothing new would be created, and if we carry on theorizing in such a way we will soon realise; that this type of theory has the possibility of carrying on throughout eternity; as it already seems to have done in reality!"

Pallas smiles and remarks: "this theory of nothing comes from nothing seems to go completely against many religious theologies, because–even some of the Buddhist philosophers that believe in nirvana come into question–when we theorize that nothingness can never have existed and never will; because if nothing comes out of nothing there would be no creation, because even an illusion has to come from somewhere and once something is created it exists. Even if what is created only lives in the dream worlds or fantasy it still exists!"

Sankara grins and replies: "nirvana is a philosophy that can also be assumed to show that nothing that is physical lasts forever, and that to be reborn on a higher plane of existence we should realise that our present physical existence came without our consent; and this could mean that we came from nothing, because before the sperm fertilised the egg that brought our physical life into existence–there was no present sentient being. Therefore we can evaluate that there was nothing before the conception as far as the awareness of the sentient being is concerned."

Lug smiles and replies: "that maybe so for the sentient being, but that sentient being was created out of something and without that something of the creation; the sentient being could not exist at all, because there would have been nothing to create it. Therefore creation must depend upon nature and the natural way of evolution for its existence, and this natural means of evolution; must be as immortal and timeless as Mother Nature."

Morrighan smiles and says: "the conception of the sentient being or beings must be as immortal as the immortal wheel of birth, death and rebirth suggests, because in the evolutionary process; the whole forward motion of the process has to evolved within itself, because if it did not; nothing could [ever] begin to evolve, for example; would the little mammals that evolved before the dinosaurs went extinct; have the slightest notion of what Mother Nature would allow them to evolve into? I really don't think they did!"

Demeter smiles and says: "that is problematic, because even the clouds that carry the rain come from water and how could that water originate that forms the clouds?"

Lug smiles and says: perhaps this is the entire problem of understanding the natural forces and Mother Nature, because when we try to realise and understand the creations of Mother Nature–we end up with more questions than answers! Therefore we tend to lose any conception of what is around us, and once we lose this; all we find is that we no longer possess any real perception of anything at all!"

Pallas opens a bottle of wine and then she says: "once we realise that all we perceived to be is lost, then we are truly lost within ourselves, because to conceive anything at all depends upon the elements that we provide for this conception; even if the conception of something we planned does not work as we wish–that is just another part of evolution."

Gaia smiles as Pallas starts to pour the wine and then Gaia says: if everything evolves; then the idea that surrounds an immortality remaining static is–obviously–incorrect! Therefore the idea of Nirvana is implausible, because we can never go back from where we came if we are constantly evolving, and therefore the other ideas that surround a continuous heavenly existence seem just as implausible; because the evolutionary process would mean that heaven would also evolve and where there is evolution there is change. Hence we should begin to realise; that during this evolution or change the Lords of Karma may be able to devolve our physical form [and put our realization back many more centuries than I wish to theorize upon], but this does not change the fact that evolution; will have evolved that original worm into the worm of today. Therefore we should realise that the evolutionary process does not go back to where it was and that the worm we could become today has evolved as the rest of the planet has evolved. Therefore we should realise that the worm we could become today would be far different from the worm we could become in a million years time."

Morrighan smiles as Pallas offers her some wine and after accepting the wine, Morrighan says: "it is becoming evident that the driving force of the universe is evolution and if all within nature evolves; the idea that the spirit is not able to evolve becomes illogical, because the spirit or the spirits that have passed through many lives will have evolved in their realization of past events! Therefore Mother Nature–as we have already made evident–could be the driving force behind any evolutionary process, because without any experience that comes through the physical being; the spirit cannot truly evolve, because without any experience that comes through the physical being, the spirit cannot truly evolve; because there can be no evolution, without there being physical experiences for them to evolve from."

Merlin smiles and asks: "why is it that the spirit cannot evolve without physical experiences?"

Michael grins and replies by saying: "what would the spirit or the self evolve from, if it never had a physical form?"

Gaia smiles and answers: "perhaps the spirit is nature and evolution combined and perhaps this combination is as immortal as the Divine. In fact; how could there be anything without the combination of nature and evolution? I suggest there could not, because from the moment we are born until the moment we have realization, we are evolving, and once we realise that the process of realization evolves with the experiences that evolve around it; we suddenly become aware of the fact that without physical existence nothing can evolve! Therefore we should begin to realise that; if the self had no means of evolution it could not realise itself and if the self cannot realise itself it cannot exist. Hence it becomes evident that the self could not exist without evolution and with this being the truth of the matter; evolution and the perishable physicality of nature's evolutionary process must be as immortal as each other!"

Pingala takes a sip of her wine and then she replies: "therefore we must begin to realise that the whole process of the immortal and natural evolution; is as dependent on the self for its creation; as the self is as dependent on the immortal natural evolution for its cognition. Hence we must begin to understand that if there is no natural evolution; the self has nothing to realise, and in having nothing to realise, the self would have no recognition of itself; and in not being able to recognize itself it would never have been able to exist. Just like nirvana could not exist if everything came from nothing and nothingness was the final destination, for example; nirvana can be seen as a state of enlightenment; when one has reached enlightenment and lost the accumulation of Karma and lost the bondage of the cycle of birth, death, and rebirth.[34] But this in itself is problematic, because if the enlightened lose this bondage; they must have been put into this cycle before they were enlightened and in being so they were bound by laws that were created for the purpose of enlightenment, but this is also problematic, because; why would we need to be enlightened if we are already immortal?"

Lug smiles and replies: "perhaps enlightenment is needed to gain true understanding of the natural world and also to realise; that the evolution that is granted to us in the natural world–by Mother Nature–is part of our spiritual evolution. When that is realised we should also begin to realise that evolution is a force that creates for ever. Hence we must realise that it is possible and highly probable that; once we are enlightened from the physical bondage that we are presently in; the evolution has not finished its process with the enlightened."

Morrighan takes another sip from her glass of wine and then she says: "one fine example of evolution; is the fact that the insects came before the bird and the bird hunts the insects and worms, but there are insects and worms that feed on the birds body, blood and the food it has inside it [just like the insects and worms that feed upon mankind].

Michael smiles and says: "what you are making evident is that everything in nature evolves. Therefore we must realise that in being a part of nature–the enlightenment that frees us from the bondage of physical life, death, and rebirth, does not necessarily free us from evolution, because enlightenment can be seen as another stage of the evolutionary process.

Sankara grins and replies: "perhaps evolution has a final stage and that is enlightenment, but I must say that this is unlikely, because evolution evolves all that is natural and in getting to enlightenment through the natural process; it is unlikely that the enlightened that has been dependent on

---

[34] The Complete Dictionary of symbols in Myth Art and Literature, general editor Jack Tresidder p342 Duncan Baird publishers Ltd 2004

evolution, will suddenly remain static when the rest of nature evolves."

Demeter smiles and says: "it is more than probable that the enlightened need time to evolve because the enlightened were and always will be part of the natural process, because in having gone through all their stages to reach enlightenment; they could not have reached it without realizing the physical world for what it is! Therefore we should realise that the natural world of Mother Nature is no illusion and those that see it as such are mistaken, because; nature exists and evolves and the only illusion that is needed is the illusion of permanence in the physical world, because everything evolves!"

Michael smiles and asks: "when the sun and this planet die do they devolve rather than evolving?"

Merlin smiles and says: "when something dies it becomes part of a new evolutionary process and that process is an ongoing something and therefore it is evolving!"

Pallas puts another log on the fire and then she says: "that maybe so, but Mother Nature is–constantly–evolving spiritually as well as in the physical world, because part of our enlightenment, could be to realise what a fragile balance there is upon the survival of species."

Lug smiles and remarks: "the spirit of nature–that is within us all–can be hidden away from us by our own negligence and by the religious beliefs of others; and when this happens the survival of other species can appear to be unimportant, even though the loss of species upsets the natural order and the balance of nature."

Michael grins and replies: "the hiding of the natural world becomes quite apparent in religious texts, such as one of the books in the Old Testament (Genesis 9, 1-3), where it is written:

And God blessed Noah and his sons, and said unto them; 'be fruitful and multiply, and replenish the earth. An the fear of a you and the dread of you shall be upon every beast of the earth and upon every fowl of the air, upon all that moveth upon the earth and upon all the fishes of the sea; into your hand they are delivered. Every moving thing that liveth shall be meat for you; even as the green herb have I given you all things.'

This piece of the Old Testament seems to forget that a hungry lion or a tiger shark would not fear killing a man for food; in fact some creatures would hunt man because he is an easy kill."

Gaia smiles sweetly and remarks: "these ideologies would come from a religion that has no real theories of the matters that concern the natural world and this is problematic, because the type's of theories that have, and are still having the wish to control the planets beliefs and natural functions; can destroy their own race by upsetting the natural balance; through their selfish and misinformed manner."

Merlin smiles and says: "it should also be realised that there are some animals that are considered unclean or abominations that are unfit for human consumption [such as camel or pig to name just two of such animals], and those that are considered unclean or abominations are not to be eaten, and this is shown in the book called Leviticus in the Old testament. Therefore I shall try and explain the verses on the unclean and those that are considered abominations and I will start with some of the verses on the unclean; which are in Leviticus 11, 4-6:

Nevertheless these shall ye not eat of them that chew the cud, or eat of them that divide the hoof: as the camel, because he cheweth the cud but divideth not the hoof; he is unclean unto you. And the coney, because he cheweth the cud and divideth not the hoof; he is unclean to you. And the hare, because he cheweth the cud and divideth not the hoof; he is unclean to you. And the swine, though he divideth the hoof and be clovenfooted, yet he cheweth not the cud; he is unclean to you.

Hence I must ask what is unclean about these animals, perhaps I can understand the pig, because the pig will eat dead things; including the human being, but in realizing this we must also realise that without some kind of scavenger to eat the dead flesh; it would just rot and go back to the ground and become food and fertilizer for many types of creature and plant life and therefore; it is always possible that some of the fruit, vegetables and other things that grow from the earth; have been nourished by the corpses of our dead. Therefore I suggest that the animals that are considered unclean have other reasons for their banishment from our table; of which I will discuss after I have shown some of the animals that are not to be eaten, because they are considered an abomination. Hence I will discuss the reasons behind this and the previously mentioned. So the scripts to be mentioned are Leviticus 10, 11-20 and they are written like this:

And all that have not fins and scales, in the seas and in rivers, of all that move in the waters and any living thing which is in the waters, they shall be an abomination unto you; they shall be even an abomination unto you, ye shall not eat of their flesh, but ye shall have their carcasses in abomination. Whatsoever has neither fins nor scales in the waters that shall be an abomination unto you.

And these are which ye shall have in abomination amongst the fowls; they shall not be eaten: they are an abomination, the eagle and the ossifrage, and the osprey and the vulture; and the kite after his kind; every raven after his kind, and the owl and the nighthawk and the cuckow, and the hawk after his kind and the little owl and the cormorant, and the great owl, and the swan, and the pelican, and the gier eagle, and the stork, the heron after his kind, and the lapwing, and the bat. All fowls that creep, going upon all fours, shall be an abomination unto you.

The whole idea of animals being considered as unclean is not a good thought, but to call some animals abominations as well, suggests that there are man made ideals in this script, because if the One-God of the One-God faiths is the perfect creator that he is meant to be; then this God would not have made an abomination or abominations.

Therefore I suggest that this One-God is not the creator of all that is and that Mother Nature–whose laws the One-God religions regularly break–is the true controller and the creator of the natural world."

Gaia smiles and says: "perhaps Mother Nature and the One-God religions God are at odds with each other, because the natural world in which the One-God believers live; can be as brutal to them as it is to the Pagans, because; when the planet decides to destroy areas it makes no distinction between race or religion."

Morrighan smiles and says: "the whole idea of animals being considered as abominations and unclean seems to be entirely man made, and was probably made of things that the writer of the scripts thought was vile."

Demeter smiles at Morrighan and then Demeter says: "the whole build up of the One-God cultures seem very unnatural, because these cultures do not seem to acknowledge the time and the beauty that Mother Nature gives to her creations, and therefore they have no respect for the planet and anything that is not human, because; they believe that they and their One-God is in control of all that is! Therefore we should realise that these religions that want domestication over all that is; lose the respect for the planet and in doing so; they are not the only one's to pay for the consequences of their actions, because in losing the natural thought process; they lose the reality of the fragility of the eco-system that we all live within."

Gaia smiles, sighs and replies: "the problem that is created when there is a religion that believes that there is one god; is that this type of religion cannot give respect for anything else that appears to be unholy, because in having such a singular attitude, it cannot live with the realization that there are other intelligent beings apart from them and their One-God.

Lug nods in agreement and then he says: "that is one of the reasons that some animals are considered abominations, and that is not the only one, because another reason is that some animals will partake in the eating of the human being and in some other cases; some animals are misunderstood and are used to symbolize the evil that is within this world. Hence it starts to become evident that the cults of the human race; that support the One-God religions need to feel that they can dominate the animals, and they do not like the idea that there are animals that can dominate them in life and death."

Pallas nods smiles and then she says: "most of the larger predatory species can kill and eat an adult human being that is in its prime. Therefore I suggest that in being at the top of their food chain, suggests that another animal can dominate the human being by being able to kill it or just by being above the human being in its own element, for example; a little owl cannot kill a human being, but it is essential for them to survive at the top of their food chain to keep a balance within the ecosystem that they are part of. Hence we must begin to realise that the religions that see such animals as an abomination are becoming egotistical, because they do not understand–and they do not try to understand–how anything apart from their One-God could have any kind of superiority over them."

Morrighan smiles and replies: "the One-God religions are so enclosed within their dictatorial policies; that they do not wish to acknowledge; that other animal forms could be just as important for their welfare; as water is for their lives, for example; without some species of bat there would be many more flying insects at night and in some places of the world, where many thousands of bats emerge from their resting places; there must be many millions of these insects that are eaten by the bats. Therefore we must realise; that if the bat is thought of as an abomination; it is an act of misunderstanding that could lead to all kinds of trouble, because when humanity thinks of something as an abomination; humanity tends to try and wipe it out, and if there are no bats in the areas where there were many thousands there would be plagues of insects [of course this does not apply to fruit bats or to vampire bats]."

Pallas smiles and remarks: "what is becoming more evident is that in abominating some animals the animals that are abominated are creatures that are misunderstood and inbeing misunderstood; they are abused by those that have no understanding of the natural world. This lack of knowledge happens through words that have been written in times long since past; and these words can blind many people from the evidence that is all around us. Therefore we should start to realise that these writings; that are made by the hand of humanity; could have been designed so that the human race could not become factually aware of the natural world. The reason for this could be that with understanding nature the human race could start undermining the Holy Scriptures and the words of these scriptures would then be questioned!"

Merlin lights his pipe and then he says: "the mind of the people that are dedicated to nature and the issues that surround Mother Nature, seem to hold all animals in respect and in doing so; they go against any teachings that are against the survival of many species. Therefore these types of people do not tend to be of a One-God kind cult, and in some cases they have been severely punished for this–and in some places this still happens."

Demeter smiles and then she says: "animal familiars are well known to the shaman and to the witch, and therefore it is highly probable that a lot–if not all–the creatures that are considered abominations or unclean; are known for their magical attributes that the shaman or witch gives them."

Michael smiles and replies: "what is becoming evident is that the One-God kind turned some of the animals that were considered sacred; into abominations and used this method to undermine the beliefs that supported and tried to understand the natural world."

Gaia looks at Michael, gives him a warm smile and then she replies: "the understanding of nature does not appear to be within the mindset of religions; that are convinced that their God will come to this world and put right all the wrongs of mankind, which is very problematic, because this selfish ideal can create a race of people without any respect for what this planet gives them."

Pallas smiles and then she says: "if there is no respect for Mother Nature within a race; the race that disrespects Mother Nature; needs to grow up and come away from their fantasies, and learn; that the planet that we live on is not a dump for their toxic ideals and waste matter!"

Morrighan Grins and replies: "it is becoming clear that the natural world that has been held with awe, respect and wonder; has become undermined by the beliefs that do not allow the worship and the respect of the other animals and living matter, for example; what reason could there be for calling a beautiful creature like a swan an abomination?

Lug smiles and answers: "the only reason to make a beautiful creature like the swan an abomination; would be, because in doing so it makes the creature appear to be below the beauty of the human race that this One-God has–supposedly–put in charge of all the animals. Therefore the beauty of the creature is denied by making it an abomination and in making it so; the One-God can also lose the magical qualities that are attributed to it."

Gaia smiles and says: "it is becoming clear that the idea of abomination is not only to stop man eating an animal it is also to stop the human race worshipping them [as we have previously mentioned] and holding them in a type of respect that holds them above the human race, for example; in one of the Greek myths, Zeus turns himself into a swan and ravishes Leda [who was the wife of a Spartan king]. Through this myth the swan was seen as a symbol of achieved passion and the decline or loss of love.[35] Hence it becomes evident that this bird can become a symbol of much passion and heartache and is abominated by religions that hold such natural passions as a sin if they are out of wedlock."

Morrighan smiles and says: "there are many other animals that are considered abominations and unclean in the Old Testament as well as the ones that are considered clean; which are all part of Mother Nature's creations and these creations have evolved through many thousands of centuries; as the human race has evolved. Therefore those that consider some animals as unclean and abominations should not be allowed to run the thoughts—of those that are not part of a sect that was in the minority and that is not willing to learn that their scriptures could be misleading and wrong!"

Gaia gives Morrighan a warm smile and then Gaia says: "the only reasoning I could think that would be behind such reasoning; is for the defilement of Mother Nature and once she has been so defiled and downgraded; she can soon appear to lose her appeal and magical ability [to the ones who used to worship her and hold her creatures in awe and respect]. But in saying this we must also realise that the human race—in general—is quite willing to accept a strong leader without asking questions that may offend them!"

Merlin takes a long drag of his pipe and then he says: "this disrespect of Mother Nature is possibly born from the Jews revulsion of the way they were treated by the Egyptians. Therefore many if not all the animals that are considered unclean or abominations; were probably worshipped by the Egyptians

---

[35] The Complete Dictionary of symbols in Myth Art and Literature general editor Jack Tresidder p284, 285 & p459 Duncan Baird Publishers, Ltd 2004

and some of these animals were part of the form of the Egyptians Gods and Goddesses."

Pallas smiles and then she says: "animism is part of many ancient religions, and if one race makes the Divine that are part human and part animal appear to be unclean or an abomination; that would be a good way to convince people that these Divine were demons and devils, rather than the Divine beings that they are. Therefore it is probable that these Divine beings and creatures; that are part animal and part human; have been deliberately targeted and made to seem evil by the defilement of the creatures that are part of them."

Michael smiles and replies: "this is not really surprising, because the Old Testament was written when the Egyptians were at the height of their power, and they had many part animal and part human Divine beings. Therefore it is not surprising that the God of the oppressed was seen to hold certain animals as unclean and as abominations in the Old Testament."

Lug grins and says: "that way of making certain animals appear unclean and abominations, would make many of the old Divine appear to be an evil being. Therefore the creation of demons and devils out of the old Divine of the Pagan faiths; would be that much easier if they were already seen as partly unclean or partly an abomination, because of the animal that was part of them."

Morrighan walks over to the stove, puts the kettle on and then she remarks: "the God Anubis is a jackal headed God of embalming in Egyptian mythology and this God that is part jackal would be seen as unclean by verses 27-28 of Leviticus which are:

And whatsoever goeth upon his paws, among all manner of beast that go upon all four, those are unclean unto you: whoso toucheth their carcass shall be unclean until the even. And he that beareth the carcass of them shall wash his clothes and be unclean until the even; they are unclean to you.

These two verses make evident that anything that has paws and goes on all fours is considered unclean as is the wearing of its carcass. "Hence we should realise that the shamanic and druidic practices that use the wearing of such carcasses would be considered unclean."

Pallas walks over to Morrighan and then Pallas says: "making the druids and the shaman appear unclean is beneficial to any religion; that is wishing to take over the mind of the people of other religions, because when someone is considered unclean or an abomination; people tend to make them an outcast and try to dispose of them by many different means. Therefore we must realise that the whole idea of this corruption of the natural world comes from the will or the greed of religions that want world domination. But this is problematic, because their greed is so great they also become blinded by their actions and in their blindness they become unwilling to realise that there are problems that are beyond the control of their God.

We should start to realise that the planet that we reside upon; should not become a playground for religious ideals because such ideals do and have had some disastrous consequences, for example; in some places around the world; they have massively deforested trees on hillsides; and had massive mudslides that have killed many people, and this has happened, because the trees roots held the soil together and with the greed that has become part of them through religious ideals, they lost the respect of nature and paid a huge price!"

Michael smiles and asks: "can we not blame this deforestation on the greed of the general build up of humanity, rather than saying this is through religious theologies?"

Sankara grins and replies: "not when a religion or some religions have led mankind to believe that Mankind and/or their God are in control of natural events!"

Pingala smiles at Morrighan and then Pingala says: "it seems to be becoming evident that the One-God religions are trying to take control away from Mother Nature and the self and in doing so; they are creating demonic cultures and races out of those that go against their beliefs, and therefore we must consider the whole of Mother Nature within science and religion.

In realizing that the planet that we reside in whilst we are in the physical state is not under our control or under the control of any single deity; we must realise that Mother Nature [although not in total control] will have the last word or action even though it may take many thousands of years, for example;

science now understands that the dinosaurs did not die out in one big hit, they had started to become eradicated–by evolution– many thousands of years before the big hit. In fact the dinosaurs didn't really die out; they just evolved into birds."

Morrighan smiles at Pingala and then Morrighan says: "Mother Nature appears in many forms and the term is sometimes only used to describe natural events and therefore; Mother Nature–in most cases–is not truly realised for what she is. But in realizing this we must also realise that as she destroyed the dinosaurs she has the power to destroy the human race. Therefore we must realise that if the human race carries on with the ideals of their superior God being able to put right all that they have done wrong; they will eventually become as extinct as the dinosaurs on this planet–in saying this it should be realised that this planet will eventually die anyway."

Gaia gets a pot of honey from the cupboard and then she says: "perhaps the nature of mankind has been lost through his beliefs, and as we have made evident; these beliefs can range from a single God that created all to the human beings immortal soul or the self being responsible for the creation. Although this may be partly correct; the self or the immortal soul appears to lose the realization of the natural world being partly created by it; when it is first born, and in the many possible reincarnations. Therefore it starts to become evident; that the self can become trapped within its present physical state, and when this happens; it loses the true awareness of the natural being. Hence we should start to realise that the loss of awareness; could become the beginning of a need to find a creative power that is beyond the understanding of mankind, and once this has happened; the creative power or powers can become so mighty in their appearance; that the self loses itself and in doing so all realization of any natural power is completely lost. Therefore we must understand that the self; that is entrapped by its belief in a God or Gods that are above Mother Nature; whilst they are on this planet; are probably mistaken in their conception of the natural world, because the natural world is or can be seen as where enlightenment begins. Therefore we must realise that if that is the truth of the matter [of which I believe it is] the loss of natural thinking is the enemy of the enlightenment of the self."

Pingala smiles at Morrighan, passes her a cup of tea and then Pingala says: "what you are implying is that some of the Gods could actually be an enemy of the self, because whilst the self or the immortal soul is trapped by its beliefs; these Gods or God become in control of the self and the thought process of the self. Therefore we must realise that enlightenment cannot be reached whilst the self is entrapped by a deity that holds back the truth of Mother Nature!"

Lug takes a sip of his tea and then he replies: "what we have made evident; is that most religions that are of the One-God kind are against the idea of Mother Nature, because that idea loses them control of what they consider to be their One-Gods creation; and in losing this control they would be admitting that there is more truth in nature, than what is written about it in there scriptures. And as Pingala has just made evident; this idea that surrounds Mother Nature could actually make the One-God and its followers an enemy of the self.

Do you recall the phrase 'you are your own worst enemy'! Perhaps when you go further with this phrase you will understand that when you get transfixed by a belief and do not accept any other evidence or proof; you are becoming a fool unto yourself, because you are losing that natural curiosity that would find enlightenment within nature."

Morrighan smiles and says: "perhaps it is time that we started to discuss some of the more natural religions rather than those that seek to gain something from its misunderstandings, because we have—so far—seen that few religions see Mother Nature for what she really is! Therefore I shall attempt to show that Mother Nature is a Goddess in more than a name, because if it was not for her spirit and creative energies the physical world would never exist!

What we must realise is that the term Mother Nature comes from many aspects of the natural world and this term is generally used; when an act of nature causes some kind of disaster that affects the human race. But in realizing this; what we also need to realise is that Mother Nature can also be used to explain some of the beautiful creation as well as the ugly ones that are within the natural world [it must also be realised that beauty and ugliness is down to an individual's perception]."

Pallas smiles and then she says: "it is quite obvious that Mother Nature creates the varied animals and life forms for reasons that are beyond the pleasing of human perception. Therefore we must look into the science of nature if we are to have any understanding of Mother Nature."

Michael smiles and asks: "if Darwin's theory of evolution is correct, was Mother Nature in full realization of how things would evolve and into what things would evolve?"

Pingala smiles and then she replies: "I would reckon than Mother Nature would be aware of what things would evolve into and when we realise that the complexity that surrounds Mother Nature is there for our understanding; we should also realise that evolution has an infinite number of possibilities and the human race is still evolving [in its physical form]. Although once this is realised it must also be realised that some religions would prefer it to remain static."

Merlin grins and remarks: "Perhaps the reason that a lot of religions disagree with Darwin is, because unlike Mother Nature; some religions are not willing to evolve!"

Demeter smiles and says: "There are many Gods and Goddesses from many religions that are creators of natural elements. Therefore Mother Nature can have many different faces and different names and therefore it is possible that she is the origin of the Gods and Goddesses."

Morrighan smiles and says: "The Gods and Goddesses–of many religions–are seen to have such elements as thunder and lightning within their grasp; in fact all natural happenings were [at one time] seen to be an act of the Divine. Therefore the idea of Mother Nature being the origin of such Divine beings; would not seem unlikely to the religions that give oblations to the Divine that are associated with natural events. Hence we should begin to realise that the Divine may be evolving as we are evolving; and if the Divine are as connected to us as we have made evident; then the divine must be evolving along with the rest of nature. But in realizing this we should also realise that evolution does not seem to have any way of knowing where this process will lead. Therefore, what we must now ask ourselves is; does Mother Nature have any knowledge of the results of the forthcoming events of any of her evolutionary processes? I suggest she does, but I also suggest; that she cannot be sure of the actions of her creations."

Pallas takes another sip of her tea and then she says: "the actions of the physical entities are more in the control of the Fates, the Lords of Karma and the Muses, because once the self is in the bondage of the physical body; it will only follow its own rules and the rules that seem appropriate to its physical being in its present state. Therefore the state of the physical being is dependent on its surroundings within the natural world and the political will of the area in which it is born. Unfortunately some of the politics of the human race go against the natural order of the world in which it lives, for example; the medical world wants the human race to live long comfortable lives [which sounds very nice], but the human race is overpopulating the planet and with overpopulation there will become a lack of resources. Therefore the human race should begin to realise that the planet only has so much of the resources that it needs to survive; and once this is realised they should accept that Mother Nature has limited resources; and if the human race exhausts them–it will become extinct through its own actions."

Pingala smiles and says: "What this could mean; is that with the combined energies of Mother Nature and the ideals that surround the Lords of Karma; if the human race creates its own extinction; those responsible would begin at the very beginning of a new time [but of a similar original creation] and be stuck in a loop of uncertainty within this new natural world."

Merlin smiles and then he says: "it is possible that most of the human race is already stuck in a loop of uncertainty; that has been created by the loss of the realization of the natural world and the natural order that is part of the creation of Mother Nature. Therefore we must realise that most of the human race is open to suggestions from religious ideologies; that promise what they cannot have whilst they are upon this world. Hence it is becoming evident that the human race has become reliant on non scientific theories, because the human race–in general–does not like anything that could prove that its ideals are flawed and in some cases totally wrong. Therefore we can assume; that it is probable that those of the human race that are responsible for the wars that surround their religions; are actually helping

Mother Nature by destroying themselves with scientifically designed products and/or methods, that can be uncomfortable for those that have used them, for example; the science that shows the evolution of the species, and the science that is used in arms manufacture may be totally different, but they are both sciences and there are those that would be uncomfortable in using either the weapon, and/or the theory of evolution, because both or just one of those can go against a persons beliefs and this can be problematic, because there are those that would quite comfortably use the weapon for their religious ideals, and some of these religions [that have used the weapon] ban the written word of Darwin. Therefore I suggest that it is probable that some religions; that would ban the use of any natural theory [such as that of Darwin] would try to demonize Mother Nature for their Divine; so that the priests and/or the hierarchy of dictatorial religions can appear to be in control".

Morrighan smiles and says: "it is saddening that the human race has got so wrapped up in its own selfish ideals that it has failed to recognize the warnings that Mother Nature gives to it, and this is due to the centuries old demonizing of the natural sciences. This has become problematic, because it has taken the human race much longer to realise the consequences of its actions and when it finally has it may be too late, because any natural being or entity can only take a certain amount of parasitism without having to do something about them or die. Therefore we must realise that it is quite possible that the understanding that has been held back by some religions will be a demon of their own making."

Gaia smiles and says: "what is becoming evident is; that the understanding of the forces of Mother Nature has made her into a—what would be seen as—demonic force. Hence we must start to understand that the religions that have changed her path; only have themselves to blame for the monster that has been created from their unwillingness to understand the natural world. But in realizing this we must also realise that most people are willing to be led like sheep; if they are comfortable with their present existence. Unfortunately the comfort that people are willing to accept as the norm can be and is provided by sources that are environmentally destructive to the individual; that is held by the comfort factor of its ideal and present situation. Therefore we must realise that the understanding process is held in stasis; by the world that is created; by the individuals that are comfortable with their beliefs; and are not willing to learn of other possibilities that are given to them, because they oppose their beliefs. This is problematic for the whole human race, because those that are willing to fight for their outdated beliefs—that arose in one particular area of the planet—are or could be slowing the development of evolution—in some concepts and speeding it up in others and in doing so they are upsetting the natural balance."

Michael grimaces and then he says: "This upsetting of the natural balance could lead to severe consequences for the entire planet—that is if it has not already done so! Therefore the loss of the understanding of Mother Nature; is of more consequence than the religions that are unwilling to accept her as a creator can ever understand, because those that are unwilling to learn cannot escape the bondage of the Lords of Karma!

Those that are unwilling to learn cannot escape the slavery that has been put upon them by their own beliefs, because when they blindly accept the dogma that is within their belief system; they lose any means by which they could accept any evidence; that is against the written word of their religion."

Sankara smiles and says: "one aspect that we have not discussed; is that Mother Nature could be the Lords of Karma or the Lords of Karma could be her creation, and if either is the truth of the matter; the misunderstandings of the past and present could hold most of humanity in eternal stasis, because the only way to gain enlightenment would be to realise the truth of nature! This is problematic, because it means that most of the human race needs to reassess its religions."

Morrighan grins and suggests: "if Mother Nature is part of or is the Lords of Karma; the true realization of nature would be the only means; by which the illusion that is created by maya could be lost. Therefore we should understand that the oblations that are given to some of the Divine would no longer make any sense; because the only way to reach enlightenment would be or is through the understanding of the world that is around us, and if we are tied to the dogma of some beliefs we can never be freed from them, because our search for true understanding would be limited by their rules!"

Pingala smiles and replies: "this whole concept of Mother Nature being the creator of all; seems to be a proposal that is becoming hard to argue against—without resorting to unproven dogmatic beliefs. Once this is realised we should also realise that some of the unproven dogmatic beliefs are very difficult to break; especially when these systems have been in place for many centuries and are still seen as evidence of a higher power—by those religions that are unwilling to investigate other possibilities!"

Gaia smiles and says: "this reasoning is problematic, because there are religions that are unwilling to accept strategies that are beyond their means of investigation—due to their laws. Therefore we must accept that the processes that define the laws that are part of the building blocks of religion would need to change quite drastically in some religions; if enlightenment is to be reached. Hence it becomes obvious that the elements of some religions would have to be questioned if their believers went through the process of experimentation; with their beliefs of the natural world. Therefore we should become aware of the consequences that surround the investigation of the natural world—and the understanding of the consequences will become evident when the understanding of the natural world becomes available through scientific and theoretical reasoning. If this is the truth of the matter [which in many situations it seems to be]; the understanding of Mother Nature is only open to those that are willing to evolve within their religion."

Merlin smiles and says: "it is possible that the process of evolution is about being willing to accept that we will evolve into something Mother Nature has already designed, and perhaps when we do evolve we will begin to understand the real creative forces of the universe!"

Morrighan smiles and says: "it is possible that we are beginning to become aware of the reasons of the ideas that surround enlightenment and these reasons are that; if the self wishes to evolve into its true spiritual form; it must understand that there would be nothing to become if Mother Nature had not evolved as we have done so. Therefore I suggest that the evolution process that we are part of does not stop with enlightenment—it is part of enlightenment!"

Michael smiles and asks: "if the process of evolution is the beginning of the realization of enlightenment; is there any escape from the natural world?"

Pallas smiles and says: "death is the only escape from the present physical state, but in realizing this we should realise that all states of existence must have a state of physicality for them to exist, because if they had no form at all the thought process would have no means of formation. Therefore I suggest that there must be some type of physicality even after the present physical state has gone; even if it is not recognizable in its present form, for example; would the caterpillar be able to realise its transformed form of a butterfly until it became that butterfly? I very much doubt it could, and therefore; it is quite probable that we cannot recognize our enlightened state until we have become enlightened!"

Pingala smiles and says: "what this could mean; is that enlightenment is an unknown entity of the physical world; that can only be reached by the acceptance of the natural world; as a living and continually evolving entity. If this is correct; the whole idea of the Divine; being in control of our destiny; would come into question, because evolution would be the true controller of our destiny and evolution is partly under the control of Mother Nature! Therefore we must realise that the whole of spirituality comes into question as well as the Divine powers, because the self or the reincarnation of the self; would become dependent upon its realization of the natural processes of evolution, and then it would realise that; all that is impermanent evolves!"

Lug grins and says: "evolution seems to be the power that is evident in all spirituality and natural happenings, because all are and must be linked, because if they were not, spirituality could not evolve and become enlightened; because where there is no evolution there is no fulfilment; because you cannot be fulfilled without being satisfied with your present existence!"

Michael smiles and says: "you can be satisfied and fulfilled in the physical world without being enlightened!"

Morrighan smiles and replies: "that is possible within a physical form that thinks it has no need for anything else; but we must ask ourselves if this is ever–truly–the case, because we all need food and water to survive whilst we are in the present physical form, and therefore; we always need something! Therefore we can never be truly fulfilled whilst we are in need! Hence we should also realise that whilst we try to attain enlightenment–the water and food that we need to sustain existence is supplied by Mother Nature. Therefore we must accept that the need of the food and water-that supplies the physical body of the self whilst it is trying to gain enlightenment; becomes one of the tools of enlightenment. Hence we should start to realise that enlightenment is totally dependent on nature and the natural laws that govern our survival; whilst we are in the natural or the physical form. Therefore we must understand that; if we wish any kind of spiritual enlightenment we must firstly understand the natural form that we are presently at the mercy of."

Sankara smiles and says: "just like the transformation of the caterpillar to the butterfly, the person cannot be transformed until it has been fed in the natural world. Therefore it does not matter what type of religious enlightenment a person seeks, because that person still needs feeding in the natural world! Hence it should become evident that the food that is supplied by Mother Nature is not only of concern to our physical welfare it is of great importance to the development of our spirituality, because if we do not have a well nourished body we do not have a well nourished mind."

Pallas smiles and says: "if that is fact, we must realise that the religions that support fasting are not supporting a well nourished body or a well nourished mind. Therefore it is reasonable to suppose that once the lack of food becomes a ritual; the body and the mind become open to ill health, and once this is realised–as the truth of the matter–the only true journeys that are outside the body would have to come through deep meditation!"

Gaia smiles, nods, and then she says: "fasting may be used in many religions for their journeys [outside the physical body] and for the realization of how thankful they are for the food that is provided at the end of their fast. But the problem with either; is that the journeys that one seeks through hunger are the journeys that lead them along the path of self delusion. I theorize that, because hunger can lead to the loss of our grip on the natural world [just as some drugs can]; through our organs and particularly our brain being starved of vital nutrients."

Morrighan smiles and says: "perhaps the hunger of long lost hunter gatherer tribes–that went through lean times–led to the beliefs of the delusions that some of them went through in these times; which also led to their belief that fasting would take people on incredible and otherworld journeys. Therefore it is possible that some of these beliefs have grown from times that food was in short supply [as it still is in many regions of this so-called civilized world]. Hence we should realise that the ideas of fasting can be seen to originate in less scientific and more difficult times, and once this idea had originated, it became a part of the beliefs and these beliefs stayed with them longer than the difficult years; because science did not manage to catch up with these beliefs for hundreds of years."

Sankara smiles and says: "although it is evident that starvation can cause hallucinations; these hallucinations still have to be created somewhere, and this somewhere has to be from within the knowledge of the self, otherwise it could not exist!"

Pingala smiles and says: "this is problematic, because the hallucinatory existence that is created– by the self–must have some origination, and that origination would have to be stored within the memory that was hidden to the self; until its present circumstances were put on hold by the lack of the nutrients that were needed to continue them. Therefore we must realise that the people that followed such beliefs and practise the fasts for their religious purposes; could appear to be closer to their Divine, because they were willing to undergo the practises that made them appear so spiritual or holy."

Demeter smiles and says: "it is also possible that the fasts that lead to other worlds and the feeling of closeness to the Divine; could also be part of a memory; that is confusing reality with the imaginative powers of the self, for example; a distorted mirror will create a distorted image. Once the realization of distortion is brought into the realms of hallucination, it becomes probable or possible that the hallucination is just a distortion of the mind; that is brought about through a chemical imbalance [through a lack of nutrients]."

Pallas smiles and replies: "that is possible, but it still does not explain how another world is created; unless it is a distorted creation of the world that we inhabit! Therefore this whole idea of distortion being the creator of another world becomes problematic, because if distortion is the creator of another world, distortion becomes a creative force and not just an image distortion of this world, because to create another world, the concept of that other world must have already been there before the distortion was reached through an imbalance within the human being, and if this is the reality of the matter; the distortion of the imbalance then becomes the truth, and the truth would only be gained through an imbalance within nature. Therefore it becomes paradoxical, because of the need to gain a realization of a balance through an imbalance."

Morrighan smiles and says: "an imbalance to maintain a balance that is already there is paradoxical, but we must realise that deep meditation that can achieve similar results; can be achieved without the need for any chemical imbalance. Therefore the imbalances that are used for spiritual awareness are not really necessary and in many cases these imbalances can have drastic results; that can lead to madness or physical death. Therefore we should realise that this imbalance of nutrients–that is apparently needed to maintain a balance–is not necessary and in not being necessary; the paradoxical ideal that surrounds this has no reason to exist; except for within the minds of the followers that have this type of belief."

Lug smiles and says: "what is becoming apparent, is that some religious followers can become confused when they create an imbalance within the physical being, this confusion can–probably–be used by the hierarchy of a religion; to mislead the followers of that religion, for example; when someone is hungry it would be easy to suggest a land of plenty that is reached through belief, and this belief would become open to the imagination; which could easily be misled [especially if it had an imbalance through the lack of nutrients] into believing this land exists after the death of the physical body!"

Merlin smiles and says: "in that situation; the suggestibility of the self–whilst it is within the natural being–is evidently due to the non realization of the natural aspects of its own existence. Therefore we must understand that the loss of the natural powers of deduction can be the creators of hallucination and the illusory ideals of dictatorial religions, for example; it is much easier to dictate to someone who is weakened by hunger, than it is to dictate to a well fed and well trained warrior of another religion. Therefore the hierarchy of a religion can use the lack of natural food as a tool of persuasion, and this tool can then be used for the servitude to a God or be seen as the revenge of a God when the crops fail. This whole approach of some religions becomes problematic, because it not only puts Mother Nature under the control of a particular God; it persuades some people into thinking that there is nothing they can do to stop this displeasure–except for giving oblations or praying for forgiveness instead of adopting a scientific approach."

Pingala grins and says: "science may be able to solve some of the problems that are created by untruthful beliefs, but science has created as many problems [if not more] as it has solved and a lot of these problems arise from when a problem is solved, because another problem can arise from the answer, for example; nuclear power can solve a lot of energy problems, but this creates the problem of how to dispose of a radioactive waste. Therefore we must realise that when science evolves the problems that arise from this evolution can rise at the same–and perhaps–a greater rate."

Gaia smiles and says: "that is true of some scientific discovery, but in the discovery of nature, the realization of natural evolution tends to bring more questions than problems. Of which these questions are to be answered by those that are willing to try to discover the truth when and if the question is answered. Hence we should start to realise that the questions that are to be answered within Mother Nature's world; are only answerable by those that are willing to go against some of the rules that were laid down in times of limited understanding. Due to that type of realization; some of the spiritual ethics of many religions can become their untruths; and in being lost these beliefs are no longer required by those who seek the truth."

Morrighan smiles, puts another pot of tea on the stove and then she says: "this loss of belief through scientific discovery can and does lead to many consequences within nature, because the natural understanding that causes such a loss has already been seen to be unwanted and classed as evil by some religions! But this theory can wait for the next chapter, because all that has been covered here leads to the need; for the science of nature to be seen as part of the realization of enlightenment—or perhaps it does not?"

The song and dance begins as the harp of Merlin and the flute of Pallas start to play

6

SCIENCE AND THE NATURE OF RELIGION

The dinner is served and the conversation begins....
Demeter finishes a piece of chicken and then she says: "if scientific reasoning and natural philosophy are the root of enlightenment; the whole of religions reasoning process must come into question, because most of the religions are not based on scientific foundations and as we have already made evident; some religions consider some animals as unclean and abominations. Therefore the scientific principle of research and empirical evidence gathering must be applied to religion in general."

Pallas takes a sip of her wine and then she says: "although empirical evidence is the only certain reality that we can attain whilst we are in the physical world, metaphysical theory has to be used in conjunction with this–when we are exploring religion."

Merlin finishes another mouthful of succulent pork and then he says: "science can be inventive and discoverable, for example; Darwin discovered the theory of evolution, he did not invent it, because it was already there and waiting to be discovered and Stevenson did not discover his train the Rocket, he invented it. Therefore there are–quite obviously–huge differences between discovery and invention, and in this context we must explore–some of the religious and scientific explanations–with the view that they can be either pure invention or a theoretical discovery that needs to be examined in the greatest possible detail!"

Lug pours himself another glass of wine and then he says: "Darwin's theory of evolution was seen as a heresy of the Bible and therefore it was against the beliefs of many of the One-God religions, but by the time he published this theory (1858 a.c.e.); the Christian faiths did not have the same power as they had when Galileo (1564-1642); started to open up the ideas that have led to today's understanding of the universe."

Morrighan takes the bottle of wine that Lug has passed her, pours some and then she says: "the One-God religions and science have been trying [and in some cases succeeding] to contradict each other throughout the Christian era [all the One-God religions dislike any science that goes against their scriptures, but the Christian era is when this disagreement has evolved alongside the evolution of science and technology]."

Gaia smiles as Morrighan passes her the bottle, pours some and then Gaia says: "the discovery of the laws of Mother Nature can only be realised when the sciences that aid such discoveries are given the right to do so, and are not hindered by religious ideologies. Therefore the natural sciences that try to determine the age of the planet; its place in the universe, and the evolution of species will be hindered, because ancient scripts that were not written with such an understanding can become as addictive as many drugs. This addiction is due to many of the people [within ancient religions] becoming uncomfortable with beliefs that are beyond and against their ancient scriptures. One example of that is in the Old Testament, where it says:

In the beginning God created the heaven and the earth. And the earth was without form, and void; and darkness was upon the face of the deep. And the spirit of God moved upon the face of the waters. And God said: Let there be light and there was light.[36]

These first few lines are contradicted by science, because science shows that the sun and light came before the planet Earth was formed. Therefore some of the very basics of today's astronomical knowledge–that tells us that the stars were formed before the earth–directly contradict the Old testament."

Michael takes a sip of wine, smiles and says: "this is not the only part of Genesis where the scientific and the religious theories conflict, because another part of Genesis [1, 14-16] is where God said:

Let there be lights in the firmament of the heaven to divide the day from night; and let them be for signs and for seasons, and for days and for years: and let them be lights in the firmament in the heaven to give light upon the earth. And God made two great lights; the greater light to rule the day and the lesser light to rule the night: he made the stars also.

---

[36] Genesis 1, 1-4

Here we are again—along the same path—suggesting that the earth was made before the stars; which is against the empirical evidence that has been discovered by astronomers, physicists, and mathematicians."

Pingala passes her glass to Morrighan and after a refill, Pingala takes a sip and then Pingala says: "the Old and the New Testament have many points that science and natural reasoning can dismiss as fantasy! Therefore the scriptural evidence of any religion that believes its scriptures or teachings are fact and without question will be mistaken, and should be easily—in some but not all cases—proven wrong, and dismissed so when they are proven to be so!

Pallas takes a sip of her wine and says: "this may be true for the dogmatic religions, but there are some religions that openly question their scriptures and their teachings—and when I say question I mean question! I do not mean ask questions on their scriptures and use these scriptures to prove themselves right—of which many religions do! Therefore I suggest that the Hindu and Buddhist ideals that surround their philosophies need to be brought into the equation, because whilst it seems to be mainly the dogmatic One-God religions that have a problem with scientific discoveries; there are certain places in the Buddhist and Hindu religions that can be brought into question."

Morrighan finishes her piece of beef and then she says: "all religions will have areas that they are dogmatic about. But in realizing this; the ethics of all religions would become the focal point of the discussion, therefore in this present analysis I suggest that the discoveries and the religious consequences that surround them should be the focal point."

Sankara finishes his last potato and then he says: "perhaps the focal point has already begun with the astronomical ideals of science and the Old Testament. Therefore I suggest that the science that surrounds the speed of light and the time and distances that are involved need to be determined; before we can truly realise how some religious texts are misinterpreted or are realised as just a creation of fantasy and/or myth."

Pallas finishes another piece of chicken and then she replies: "before the speed of light was measured; there was the uncomfortable science of people like Galileo that threatened the

Christian beliefs. But in realizing this we must begin to explore the consequences of such beliefs and we can only do so by theorizing on the scientific and religious texts; and comparing the science with the religious problems it has created."

Pingala finishes an apple and then she replies: "perhaps it would be more logical to start with Darwin's theory of evolution rather than the more ancient texts of people like Galileo, because evolution shows the possibility; of the human being evolving into something totally different to what it is today, and it also shows that the human being [in the physical sense] has evolved from other species! Therefore the creation of mankind from the earth does not actually come into question, but what does come into question is the method by which the species evolved from the earth, for example; in Genesis 2, 7 it is said:

And the Lord God formed man from the dust of the ground, and breathed into his nostrils the breath of life; and the man became a living soul.

Unfortunately that line goes against Darwin's theory of evolution, because the creation of man is before the creation of the animals that the physical human being is theorized to have evolved from."

Morrighan finishes another strawberry and then she replies: "Darwin's theory of evolution realises that the present physical form of the human being has been part of an evolutionary process that began many millions of years ago. Because of that theoretical reason; there are many places in many religions that contradict this theory. Therefore we must try to understand the reasoning that goes into the non scientific mind!"

Pallas sips her wine and says: "the mind can be controlled when it becomes comfortable with its surroundings and therefore; Darwin's theory will always be uncomfortable with those that wish to have a higher power in control of all that is around them, because any loss of control and any responsibility for your actions–that could become irreparable–would not be relevant; to those that believe a higher power will come and fix all that they have damaged!"

Pingala sips at her wine and replies: "the responsibility for our actions is part of many religious ethics, but the responsibility can be lost when our actions do not go against the ethics of a certain religion, for example; the cow is sacred in some religions and in others it is seen as nothing more than a food source! Therefore there is much confusion when the ethics of one religion clash with the ethics of science or another religion."

Lug sips at his wine and then he says: "ethics surround all religious ideals, but science does not follow the same ethical codes, because science is the route of all physical knowledge and therefore, the only responsibility of science should be that it should not–totally–wipe out anything that is around or part of what it is trying to discover.

Although the discovery of many things has cost many lives, the livelihood of the subjects of science should be its primary concern, but this is not always the way in which discoveries are made."

Demeter pours herself some more wine and then she says: "this whole region of ethics is becoming problematic, because what is seen as ethical by some is not necessarily seen as ethical by others [as we have already made evident]. Therefore any ethical debate should start with the basic arguments on what is considered ethical. Hence I suggest that we should start this part of the debate with the end point of Lug and that is on the concern of life and the destruction of life!"

Morrighan puts out the cheeses and the biscuits and then she says: "**the primary concern of any intelligent being should be for the welfare of the planet that is its host,** but when religious ethics come into being, their primary concern becomes the fulfilment of their deity's desire. Therefore we should realise that the desire that has supposedly come from a superior intellect becomes their primary concern, and their concern of natural needs is denied, and this means that the awareness of the consequences of their actions–in nature–also loses their primary concern. **This becomes problematic, because when the denial of the greater picture becomes lost–in what we can only perceive at any present stage–in time; the future becomes of no apparent consequence and therefore; the planet of its hosts can be thrown into chaos and this chaos has consequences far above what any dogmatic belief can comprehend!**"

Pallas smiles and takes a bite from her cheese and biscuit, finishes it and then she says: "the Gaia theory is relevant to this, because this theory of James E Lovelock says and makes evident that: *'the atmosphere is regulated by the biosphere and that all living things on Earth could be thought of as part of one being that could change its environment to suit its own needs. Gaia will ensure that conditions are right for its own survival even if that means conditions become unfit for the survival of the human race.*[37] Hence we should realise that if this theory is correct the planet will protect itself and the deity's of different religions will not be able to protect their followers if; they have been stupid enough to make the planet inhospitable for their life form."

Gaia butters another biscuit, grins and replies: "if this theory is correct [which I suspect it is] the controller of Earth is Mother Nature, and in this respect the ideologies and ethics that surround the human race; being in command of animals and having rights to abuse the land [in the ways it does] are unfounded, because Mother Nature is–probably–the primary controller of all development of life upon the planet, and if this is correct we must remember that Mother Nature's evolutionary practises replaced the dinosaurs. Therefore we must realise that any ethical ideology that makes the human race the controller of the planet is badly mistaken, for example; what idiots would constantly poison the air that they breathe and expect to survive? The present people that have been brought up for centuries with the belief that their God will come and fix all; is part of the answer to that question–I say only part, because there are non believers [some non believers do care about the planet and its future] and people that just do not care about future consequences."

Merlin finishes a slice of cake and then he says: "it is becoming evident that the whole theology; behind the idea of a Divine being or beings coming to fix all that we have done wrong; is unethical, because the ethics that surround such ideologies are created for a being that has no true responsibility for the mayhem that it causes–with the mass destruction of

---

[37] Encyclopaedia of Science p370 DK 2006

living matter—for the selfish and self satisfying desires it has been brought up with."

Demeter cuts herself a slice of cake and then she says: "selfish desire is a part of many religions, because this desire is the basis of control that is needed, for some religions to make themselves appear to be in control of all that is, and this control cannot be seen to be lost in nature, because if your deity has no control over the natural world, it would not be considered to be a force to be respected. Therefore we should begin to understand that the creation of all that is; is the way in which many religions use their deity or deities to appear to be in control of all that has happened and all that is liable to happen. This way of dictatorship has a possibility of becoming very disruptive [to the planet as a whole], because when the idea arises that there is a sole creator that is responsible for all and will fix all [for the likes of one species]; the loss of the Earth as a living being in its own right arises! Due to that idea, the welfare of the Earth can take secondary consideration to the needs of the dominant species on the planet [at this time the human race is the dominant species]. This is problematic, because once the respect of the planet takes a secondary place to the dominant species that is upon it; the planet has no choice in the matter of trying to rid itself of as many of the parasitic creatures as possible and if that means extinction of the species—that is what will happen."

Morrighan makes some cheese and biscuits and then she says: "that happens or starts to happen when ethics are not created in the boundaries of the natural world, and Mother Nature is ignored—by those that are blinded by their religions fanaticism! Hence we must realise that the ethics that are a part of any major religion need to be questioned and in mentioning these ethics we should try to realise that these ethics surround the survival of the natural world. For example, I would question the ethics that are part of the destruction of the balance of an ecosystem that a religion has destroyed in order to build temples or to destroy the shrines of another religion.

Michael smiles as he takes one of the cheese and biscuit snacks that Morrighan has offered him and then he says: "the problem with ethics is that; natural ethical behaviour does not seem to comply with the ethics of some religions, and these religions seem to hold the natural world in contempt; because they believe that their Divine have made this world for mankind to be the superior being. Therefore some of the religions of mankind do not realise that the consequences of their unethical actions on the planet are unethical, because they believe that their Divine will come and fix all that has been done wrong. This is problematic, because they consider their destructive actions as ethical; due to their deity giving them the Divine purpose of converting heathens and/or using destructive techniques for the good of mankind."

Pallas smiles and then she says: "the ethics of any religion become questionable when they try to go against scientific proposals and evidence; without any empirical evidence to justify their claims. Therefore the ethics of any religion that claims to be the one true religion is suspect, because they will mislead people into believing that; this religion is above the natural order and that the people of this religion are the only ones that can gain enlightenment. Hence it becomes evident that this type of ideological ethics can become dangerous, because once the ethics lose the investigative powers of science; the ethics are created from the wishes or the wants of certain cults within mankind!"

Morrighan passes some more of the snacks to Merlin and then she says: "the dangers that are apparent through such unsubstantiated evidence are of primary concern, because they lose mankind any responsibility; in the treatment of other faiths and others of their own species; as well as the most important responsibility of all, and that is; the care of the ecosystem that they are presently in [and this is because when they lose that care they could lose the planets compliance with their own species]."

Gaia smiles and replies: "the origination of the species is dependent on the planets compliance with them, and if one species is foolish enough to give the planet the means of its extinction through its own ethics and so called reasoning; that species is not as wise as it thinks, for example; if all giraffe were stupid enough to purposefully break all their own legs they would become extinct through natural predators. But they would not do so, because their natural survival instinct gives them no reason to do so. Therefore I suggest that the ethics of the human race should begin with the natural survival instinct. But that instinct seems to be eliminated by the need of the survival of certain religions, and the main science that becomes acceptable as the science that gives them an advantage in wars. This is problematic, because the existence of war is rarely concerned about the other species of life upon the planet; and this in itself is problematic, because in the misunderstanding of the ecosystem that the human race is part of, could contribute to its own destruction. Due to this problem, the ethics of the human race should concern itself with Mother Nature and the will of her evolutionary process, rather than trying to force a particular religion upon the whole human race, and therefore; the human race needs to respect the boundaries that Mother Nature has placed around them. Hence we should realise that these ethics should firstly be within the natural boundaries; secondly these ethics should concern themselves with morality and thirdly they should concern themselves with the will of the Divine. But in respecting the will of the Divine; the will of the natural world must come before the will of the Divine of any given religion, because if we are mistaken about the intent of the Divine, Mother Nature will not be compliant with our foolish misunderstanding of the natural process. Due to this Mother Nature could evolve, and as she evolves life will become at least uncomfortable and at the most impossible for the human race."

Merlin smiles and replies: "ethics is—as we are discovering—very controversial, because the ethics of a religion can lose natural responsibility, for example; some religions do not wish to believe in Mother Nature and her principles, and in not believing in her; all their ethics come from the belief in their God or Gods and its or their laws. That way of theorizing becomes problematic, because the laws and the ethics of such a religion; show that they are doing nothing wrong or unethical when they destroy large areas in the name of their God, because in such a religion they do nothing wrong as long as they carry on with the written traditions that they believe were written with the aid of their Divine! Once that type of theology is accepted; the problems of natural destruction and planetary changes become inevitable, because the ethics of the humans of this type of religion become over indulgent with their self importance and their wish to satisfy their desires and their Divine. This self importance creates the imbalance that becomes within the human race, and once this imbalance is created; the ecosystem that the human race is within becomes unbalanced and the natural order begins to change. That is again problematic, because once the natural balance is lost or altered; the creatures that are within the old ecosystem will have to change or they will become as extinct as the dodo!"

Sankara carries some plates over to the sink and then he says: "this change does not have to be physical it could be ethical [within the human race], but this is problematic, because the human race can be foolishly stubborn in its beliefs and its self interest; which can and does cause the continuation of the defilement of the planet and its ecosystems. Therefore these self interests need to be re-assessed and re-evaluated; but this cannot fully happen whilst the human race stays wrapped up in its dogmatic and unscientific beliefs, because many of these beliefs have ethics that are contrary to natural laws."

Michael puts the kettle on the stove and then he says: "it is becoming evident that natural ethics are the only ethics that religions need to agree upon for the balance of the natural world, but this is problematic when religions can [as we have already shown] misuse some of the planets living beings as a device to make other religions seem demonic or heathen."

Merlin smiles and says: "the ethics that are natural are problematic for religions, because the destruction of land and the extinction of any species [that appears to be in the path or slowing down the development and or the religious ideals of mankind] seem to be of little concern to some religions ethics! Therefore the ethics of some religions have grown within the concerns of humanity and without the concerns of the natural world within these ethics. This is problematic, because that type of ethics is still an ethical theory, but it has the ability to become very unethical; in any theory that is based upon logic and/or empirical evidence, because any theory that denies science within the publication of its theories; is potentially hiding from truths that are against their ancient laws! Therefore any ethical writings that deny any part or parts of the natural world and the sciences for their survival should be realised as the ethics of the unenlightened, and these unenlightened practitioners; should be realised for the distress and the disharmony that they have caused within the natural world."

Pallas smiles and replies: "the ethics of the natural world should be realised within all religions, but the religions of the One-God kind tend to be tyrannical and self righteous—without being aware of the planets needs. This type of religion can be and is very destructive to the natural world, because their selfish attitude leaves no room for the survival of other creatures that are not immediately beneficial to their well being. Therefore the ethics of that type of religion will appear to be unethical in the more natural religions, and this conflict of ethics; will not be resolved by those that do not want to accept the presence of other religions and their Divine beings! Hence a problem occurs, because when one religion believes its ethics are the only true ethics and are unable or unwilling to seek and understand the advice of other religions or scientifically based ethics—the whole structure of natural law can never be understood by such a religion, because natural law needs the sciences and religion; open for the discussion and the understanding of other religions means; and it also needs the evidence that is made available to them by these means."

Demeter takes a sip of her tea and then she says: "religious ethics that try to control the understanding of the natural world must be realised as unethical in the natural world, because this type of religion is controlling mankind with ethics that could destroy much of the life upon this planet, for example; there are many species that have become extinct through the acts of mankind. But this in itself can become problematic [and in many cases already has], because without the natural understanding that science has brought to the human race, it would make itself extinct at great cost to the rest of the planet [although in saying this we must realise that humanity has the type of science that could also wipe itself out, without a great loss to the rest of the planet]. Although this science teaches the cost of the destruction of species; this science also makes the destruction of lives and the annihilation of the human race much simpler, which is unfortunate for those that have a deep love and understanding of the planet, because the selfish and dogmatic religions can and do use the weapons that are created by science. But this—again—becomes problematic, because these religions that are unwilling to accept the natural scientific evidence; are willing to accept the weapons of destruction that are created by science. Therefore it should be realised that the religions that accept the weapons of destruction and annihilation without accepting the natural responsibility are in effect becoming suicidal, because no race or species will survive; if its only ethics are those that are presented to them with a lack of the knowledge that is of the natural laws!"

Morrighan finishes another snack and then she says: "natural ethics should be a part of all religions, but the understanding of the natural world that is evident within some religions; is usually due to very ancient writings; that were made without the script writers being aware of the natural laws and the age of the planet and its many varied inhabitants. This becomes problematic, because those that are unaware of the consequences of their actions can be dangerous to the survival of different species upon the planet, and the effects of the loss of a certain species upon the planet as a whole. Therefore we must realise; that the ethics that make the laws of some religions are severely mistaken, for example; in the Colossians of the New Testament 2, 8-9 it is written:

Beware that any man spoil you through philosophy and vain deceit, after the tradition of men, after the rudiments of the world and not after Christ. For in him dwelleth all the fullness of the godhead bodily. And ye are complete in him which is the head of all principality and power.

That is a problematic scripture, because it points to the sciences and the beginning of the world being deceptive, but in being deceptive to those that follow the search for truth beyond the Christ; the followers of the Christ lose control over those that become enlightened through the power of Mother Nature and/or the natural world and the sciences. Therefore we must realise that the power of the followers of the religion of the Christ and the One-God religions in general only hold control; over the people that do not hold the value of nature above the teaching of their godhead."

Lug smiles and replies: "the teachings that show any godhead above the creation of Mother Nature are suspect, because the God head itself; is created in the minds of the human being; by the force of the natural body that the mind of the human being is within, whilst it is being taught. Therefore the self that inhabits the human body needs to realise the natural world as an element; that the human race can alter through the misuse and the unethical actions; of those who believe that they have a path to a power that is greater than Mother Nature's creations, and greater than her evolutionary beings.

There are many within the One-God religions that have a deep respect for the natural world and the sciences, but most of these people are blinded by the ancient ethics of their holy scriptures. Therefore the natural ethics suffer–greatly–and the world is still abused; by those that think they know how to achieve their best performances without thinking of the consequences of their actions. Unfortunately these religions are not alone in being unaware of the consequences of their actions, for example; there are many Pagan religions that believe that it is good to have many children, but as the human race overpopulates the planet these ideals that surround the creation of large families are not being realised for the damage that they are causing.

Sankara smiles and says: "most people want their family bloodline to be successful, but as we have made evident; the ideals of the creation of large families can become problematic, because the need to keep large populations healthy costs the planet and its resources are not limitless. Therefore the religions that believe in large families need to rearrange their ethics and realise that; without the understanding of Mother Nature and her needs, the human race could become extinct through its own foolishness!"

Pingala smiles and says: "most religious ethics suffer from the neglect of natural ethics–within their principles–and this is because some of their scripts were written at a time when the human race was in its infancy [as it still is compared to the dinosaurs], and unfortunately within its infancy it has only become aware of the actions that are appropriate to its own well being. Therefore the actions that has and is having a wider effect upon the planet have only been realised when they directly affect the human race. Hence we must begin to realise that the religions that have grown up with humanity as its speaker; are open to the ethical dilemmas that are created when the human race misunderstands nature, because of its lack of scientific evidence and its willingness to wish for–and believe in–a creative force that will solve all the problems it has created for itself. This dogmatic way of coming to terms with the problems that the human race has created; is continually destructive, because they cause offence to others and are easily offended by the others beliefs. Unfortunately those that take offence and are offended create a vicious circle of misunderstanding; if none of the parties are willing to sit and discuss the problems of both sides!"

Gaia smiles and says: "it is unfortunate that some of the ethical religions still have some of their fanatical followers–of their old holy writings–as do some of the less ethical religions. This is one of the main problems of ethics within most religions, because the ethics must hold the responsibility of the survival of their beliefs above all others! This is problematic, because the followers of any religion that does not consider the well being of the planet their primary concern are unethical towards the natural world and this is due to the loss of the understanding; of the natural ideals that concern the survival of most species upon the planet, for example; if a top predator becomes too numerous it will start to die through the lack of food and the balance of nature will be restored. But the problem with this is that in the survival of the planet; the planet itself can–sometimes–eliminate the top predator and many of the species around it, and start again. Therefore the human race should realise that the planets ethics could need to eliminate their species from this planet at some stage (even planets die), which could mean that the road to enlightenment becomes longer, because those that are not enlightened will have to begin again with Mother Natures latest creation."

Michael nods and then he says: "the whole path of enlightenment is fraught with difficulties, because the human race has many difficulties in defining their ethics; this is due to the opposing religious factions, and the many opposing political factions ideals. Therefore the ethics that surround Mother

Nature should be of primary concern to all religions, because the natural world is the means of the human races survival. Hence all religions should realise that destruction and contamination of parts of the planet [on which they depend for their survival] is as important–if not more important–than their creation scriptures. This is problematic because; if some religions are unable to evolve within scientific discovery, they could make the planet uninhabitable for the human race! Therefore we must realise that the ethics that have evolved with the understanding of the human race are the human race's only true means of survival!"

Morrighan offers Michael some more snacks and then she says: "most religious ethics are not concerned with the natural world. Therefore those that will not be contaminated by religious ethics should write the ethics that surround nature! Hence we should start to realise that natural ethics should begin with the understanding of the natural world and not with ancient religious scriptures! Therefore the ethics that surround morality should be the first concern, because; the morals of a natural society will not always be similar to the morals that surround many religious ethics, because; the general ethics of a religion put the human beings survival before that of other living beings and natural habitats, for example; there are many religions and many people that would put the welfare of a single person above a small ecosystem or a herd of wild animals. This is problematic, because the survival of a single being could lose a complete ecosystem or a herd of animals, and upset the balance of nature in a way that is irreversible. Once this has happened and the process has become irreversible; the later consequences of this action could affect the whole human race. Therefore the action of saving that single human being has become immoral!"

Gaia smiles and says: "the natural morals would have to include the survival and the extinction of species. But the survival and the extinction of species should not affect the planet as a whole, because if any species becomes too dominant at the cost of others; it would become too confident and careless, and in this careless attitude it could hold its grip on the natural world and force its own extinction. In response to this extinction; Mother Nature's evolutionary process would– probably–replace such a creature with another and this would [as evolutionary evidence suggests] take many centuries! Therefore the human being [as we have said before] needs to re-evaluate some of its ethics, before it goes the same way as many of the creatures it has made extinct. Hence the human race should begin to realise that the issues that surround morality; should be made for total survival rather than the survival of one species, because as we have pointed out the loss of one species can lead to the loss of another and even the top predator becomes extinct when there is no prey. This fact appears to be difficult to understand for some religions, because they are so wrapped up in the ethics of their religion that the natural world seems to have no priority, because they believe that the morals of their religion are just and in being just; they are the only truth that has consequence. But this is problematic, because the justification and non evolutionary policies can be immoral and unethical; to those that have evolutionary policies and ethics that outdate the ethics of those who are not prepared to evolve with the rest of the planet."

Pallas passes Gaia a pot of tea and some honey and then Pallas says: "morality is dependent on the individual's beliefs, but true morality and the morality of natural consequences are not dependent on beliefs, for example; if someone removes trees from a hillside to build a temple or a shrine to their god and the hillside turns into a severe mudslide that kills one or many people; they would not consider their actions as immoral unless they knew that such an action would cause a mudslide. Therefore we must ask ourselves if the consequences of an unknown action that can create natural disasters; is it only the next consequence that is immoral or is the first consequence immoral also? I ask this, because the mass destruction of any living thing is known to have consequences and once these consequences are realised, the further mass destruction of any other living thing; should be realised as consequential in the natural world!"

Gaia takes a sip of her tea and then she says: "actions can only be immoral; if the consequences of the actions are known, and it is known that the consequences of such actions could be immoral, for example; if one village made a river dam that lost another village all its water; it would only be immoral if the village that made the dam knew of the existence of the other village that would suffer, and it would also be immoral; if they were irreversibly destroying an ecosystem that they were aware of. Therefore we must realise that the first actions cannot be considered immoral if they have unknown consequences. But in realizing this it does not mean that the consequences of the first action could not have been avoided; if they tried to seek the knowledge of the area that they intended to alter."

Merlin smiles and replies: "None of this alters the fact that there are always consequences to any kind of mass destruction or the major alteration of a planetary resource. Therefore the morals that surround planetary issues should [long ago] have been realised to be of the greatest importance, and be above political or religious ethics."

Gaia smiles and replies: "it is becoming obvious that the moral issues that affect the well being of our planet; must include all the species and the living matter upon the earth. Therefore the planet must come first, and the moral issues of man upon man must come second in any ethical thesis. But these morality issues that must take second place to the morals of the natural world, still become problems for humanity because the survival of their species would depend on some of these ethics. For example; if a persons survival depended on another animals death it would not be immoral for them to do so, but this becomes problematic when it becomes human upon human and one of them would need to eat the other to survive. This is problematic, because it is probable that the issues that surround survival through cannibalization can only be solved on a personal basis, because the ethics of one person can be the revulsion of another, and if cannibalization became the only way that the human race could survive; I am sure it would have no problem in resolving the issue and re-evaluating personal morals and ethical values! Hence we should realise that the morals and virtues of the human being should; firstly be to assure the survival of itself and the rest of the human race, and these morals and virtues should begin with the procreative values of the human race. Such values should begin with the understanding of over breeding within a given area, because if an area is overpopulated; the population needs to expand or succumb to the effects that mother nature will eventually place upon them, because as we have mentioned before—there is a **finite** capacity upon this planet!"

Lug smiles, nods his head and then he says: "what this is making evident is that the morals of humanity must have some kind of birth control; so that the planet can sustain its top predator (the human race is the planets top predator at this time). Therefore the ethics of birth and the human population need to be re-evaluated in some religions, because those religions that do not believe in birth control; must eventually realise that as the Earth evolves and the human race becomes more scientifically aware; the human race will eventually come to a place in time that is no longer sustainable. This is problematic, because the religions that do not believe in birth control are trying to look after the survival of their particular sect and in doing so they are trying to make the survival of the human race inevitable. But in being inevitable the survival of the human race needs population control whilst it is limited to one world, because if it has no control over its population; it will exhaust the resources of the planet and this could lead to its own extinction."

Gaia smiles and says: "the problem with the religious ethics that encompass birth control is that; when these ethics were written the people that wrote them were not as scientifically aware as the people of this era, and they did not realise; that through medical expertise the human race would expand so greatly. Therefore they did not realise that the expansion of the human race as it is today would become a problem for the planet. Hence it becomes evident that some of the ethics of some religions need to be rewritten, but this is not going to happen when some religions stick to their scriptures and in doing so condemn those who practise birth control! Although this type of condemnation seems unacceptable to those who realise the science and practise birth control when it becomes necessary; the majority of religions seem to be very slow to realise the consequences of some of their outdated and ancient practises. This dogmatic and unacceptable practise of condemning birth control will lead to wars, because when living space starts to become unavailable; different races—or even neighbours–become needful in the basics to sustain their lives. This need can become a warlike attitude where it is either killing or be killed and therefore, the ethics that condemn birth control can become unethical, because the actual ethics that were created to assure the continuation of life will be destroying life."

Morrighan smiles and replies: "the ethics of the ancient scriptures were not unethical in the time they were conceived, but as the human race evolves the religions and ethics should also evolve; but this evolution is not always accepted. This non acceptance does not mean that the ethics have not evolved, it means that those who have not accepted the evolution are becoming unethical and in many cases immoral. This is problematic, because once one part of the ethics is lost; the whole of the ethical ideals begin to crumble, because the whole of the reasoning that makes the ethics is unreliable when one part of it is wrong, for example; if throughout a lifetime a building has evolved and been maintained it stands a better chance of survival than one that is left alone, because Mother Nature's weather conditions erode or corrode most structures, and those that were built of wood or stone will be destroyed if they are not maintained. Therefore the human race should treat ethics like a building."

Pallas smiles and replies: "it is becoming evident that ethics need to be maintained, for them to be a comprehensive and realistic structure. Otherwise the only thing that will remain is their foundations and these foundations wll no longer have any viability, because the foundations of a structure cannot give the whole structure a long existence if it has been left to decay and the decay has been accepted as the truth of the structures integrity. Therefore without maintenance and the realization that the natural world evolves; the structure of words that have evolved along the natural path will become more than a historical foundation, and the structure of words that have not evolved will become static and in some cases worthless.

Gaia smiles and says: "the foundation of the words and theories that have evolved over many generations and within this evolutionary process will survive, but there are still those that are evident, that have not dramatically evolved and in some cases there are those that theoretically have not evolved at all. Those that have not–theoretically–evolved will be buried and the foundations could be dug up and survive for many centuries, but the foundations will be all that can remain, because the ethical truths are only available to those that are willing to evolve. Therefore we should realise that the foundations of an unscientific or scientific theory that is misled can become truthful; if it is willing to accept its mistake or mistakes and evolve within the scientific world. Hence we should begin to realise that science can help religion evolve and in this evolution–religion must be able to accept the ethical changes that science will give to them! Therefore the morality of religion depends upon its willingness to accept science and the natural world of scientific exploration, because the morality of people should respect the scientific theories that show the natural world that they live in; as a fragile and potentially hostile place, because if we treat these theories with disrespect; that disrespect [as we have mentioned many times before] could make human life uncomfortable or it could make human life become extinct."

Demeter starts to carve a piece of wood and then she says: "that disrespect could rise through religious ethics that believe themselves to be moral in their willingness to procreate and to fill the earth with mankind, but as we have already made evident this is an immoral ideal, because the world that the human race lives in has limited space. Therefore we must realise that without evolving; the ethics lose their worth, because they become immoral and unethical, due to the over indulgence of the race that they were designed to protect. Hence the human race should begin to realise that the ethical world that includes mass procreation will at some stage become immoral, because it will endanger he survival of humanity!"

Morrighan smiles and says: "the difference in the ethical structure of the natural world and that of religion; is that the survival of some religions seem to come before the survival of many parts of the natural world, and some of the ethics, of some religions; do not allow them to see what the consequences of their actions could be, because they have been blinded by the ancient beliefs and the scriptures that have tried to eradicate or limit the scientific exploration, and the theories that disagree with their beliefs and/or their scriptures."

Michael smiles and says: "if what is moral and is immoral is dependent on our survival techniques within the planet—why do some religions not mention these natural morals and why do they prefer to mention singular morals, such as; the moral issues of sex and murder?"

Sankara smiles and replies: "this would be, because the moral issues that surround personal conduct do not need a great deal of science for their truths to be found, for example; it would be considered immoral if someone murdered someone else so that they could gain some kind of profit for that persons death [be it monetary or otherwise]. But these issues that surround murder and sex are problematic, because different cultures and different religions have different morality issues, for example; there are some countries and some religions that do not consider the execution of a murderer as immoral and there are other countries and religions that consider execution as immoral, but murder would still be considered as immoral in the countries that did not believe in execution. Therefore morality and immorality can be different in different cultures and/or religions. Hence it starts to become evident that the personal ethics of a culture, and/or religion can differ and in both differences their personal morals are correct for each person!"

Morrighan smiles and says: "human moral issues will always cause conflicts, because the human mind is creative and within the creations of that mind; all the different religions that have appeared are different in their morals, because the morals of human beings tend to have originated through ancient actions. Therefore some morals could have been written to create a basis in which the people of a given area live within, but this is problematic, because different areas can require different morals for the survival of a race of people within a given area, for example; in the frozen arctic it was not unusual for a member of a tribe to offer his wife and bed to a friend, and this makes sense for the survival of a race in a hostile climate; where people and prey are scarce. But in the warmer and more dominated regions, polygamy can spread many diseases. Hence we must begin to understand that human morality can sometimes need to differ for a particular cultures survival."

Michael smiles and replies: "so morality within the human race cannot necessarily be the same in all cultures, because of their different survival needs, but in later ages the need that is no longer required can be seen as immoral by other religions and other cultures!"

Pallas smiles and replies: "although it could be seen as immoral the practise of polygamy; does not become so because of other people's beliefs!"

Gaia nods her head and says: "although the beliefs of other people are reasonable within their own culture and or religion; it does not give these other people the right to stamp out and in some cases outlaw the ethics of other nations and cultures. Therefore we should realise that the ancient culture that believes in polygamy should not necessarily be considered as immoral, because the ideals of such a culture could have grown through a physical need and in being so; these morals have become a part of their culture. Hence it is reasonable to assume that many cultural morals were not written or needed for all the cultures within the human race, but the morals that seem to be immoral by differing cultures; need to be examined for the truth of their circumstance, rather than through the ideals of another culture. Therefore we must realise that the only ethics that can truly recognize the need of all cultural ideals are not those of a religion that is outside the understanding of Mother Nature, because those that are unwilling to evolve and understand natural philosophy can never truly understand their own race. This unwillingness to understand natural philosophy becomes problematic, because in being unwilling they are losing the natural ethics and in losing such ethics they could heighten the chance or even cause; the extinction of their own sect within the human race; or **they could cause the extinction of the whole human race!**"

Demeter puts some logs on the fire and then she says: "the extinction process is usually due to Mother Nature, but humanity has the means by which it could make itself extinct and this could happen; through humanity being stupid enough to ignore the natural ethics and carry on poisoning, and by using its creative powers to make more powerful chemical, biological, nuclear and other types of highly destructive weaponry.

What the human race needs to realise; is that where as Mother Nature can recover and recreate; the human race is not in control of what form Mother Nature will give to her top being. Therefore whilst the self is trapped in the bondage of its physical being it should respect what is around it, because if we move on to her lives through the Lords of Karma; **it is highly probable that the creator of the natural world is one of them!**"

Michael smiles, looks at Demeter and then he says: "if Mother Nature is one of the Lords of Karma; would the immortal soul or the self be able to reach enlightenment, without realizing and living within the natural ethics?"

Merlin smiles and replies: "without realizing that all life is sacred, enlightenment cannot be truly realised, because without such a realization the natural ethics are liable to be broken, and in doing so; the human that breaks the natural ethics is not enlightened. Therefore the human would not become enlightened and be able to break the physical bondage that Mother Nature has placed upon them; until the human realises that the natural ethics of this bondage is inescapable, because [as Demeter made evident] Mother Nature is the major life force upon the planet, and humanity takes second place to her and her creative powers. Hence we should realise that the human race will never be able to be enlightened until the human race becomes aware of the consequences of its actions within the natural world."

Gaia smiles and replies: "the lack of awareness of consequences of the ethics within the natural world; does not mean that a person cannot be enlightened within its own religious ethics, but this is problematic, because if they go to the heaven of their Divine without natural enlightenment–the natural world would have no reason to exist! Therefore it is probable that the Lords of Karma are the controllers of all religions and there is no escape from them until the natural world is realised!"

Michael looks at Gaia in astonishment and then he asks: "if the Lords of Karma [of which Mother Nature could be one of them] are the controllers of the Gods, could the natural world be out of the creative aspects of the Gods?"

Sankara smiles and then he replies: "it is possible that the Lords of Karma are the controllers of the Gods, but in controlling the Gods it does not mean that the Gods and Goddesses are held back in their creative powers, because it still remains possible that the natural creations are of the making of Mother Nature's evolutionary process and this process of evolution is dependent on Mother Nature. Therefore Mother Nature is the controller of creation and in controlling creation; she would need to be in control of what being is inhabited by which self if the Lords of Karma were able to place a self into a physical being, because; if there were no controller of the physical beings, the Lords of Karma would have to put those in need of punishment upon the earth, without any realization of what being the self would inhabit. This would become problematic, because the human being is a physical form that is capable of wiping out much of the life upon this planet, and if this was done; there would be no where to put such an entity. Therefore there would be nowhere to put such an entity if there was not such a creative force as Mother Nature that could create new beings; for the physical bondage of the self or selves that are being punished; or the selves that have not realised or reached enlightenment."

Morrighan smiles and replies: "morality of the individual is usually realised by religious ethics, and the punishments that the Lords of Karma hand out to those that are in need of retribution; can only be realised by those that are in the present bondage of the physical being. This is problematic, because those people that are punished by the Lords of Karma may not be able to realise this whilst they are in the non human state. Therefore we should realise that if Mother Nature is one of the Lords of Karma, she would–probably–be the controller of the natural world and the jailer of the self that is unenlightened or being punished for past immoralities! Hence we should begin to understand that people that are being punished for their immoralities are not able to gain enlightenment; whilst they believe and will not alter the religious ethics that has lost them their understanding of the planets needs!"

Gaia smiles and starts to conclude: "what we appear to have made evident is that true morality is of a planetary and natural concern, because the end result of disrespecting the natural world could have consequences that the human race will not be able to recover from. Therefore we must realise that any ethics that see mankind as the only concern within the natural world are mistaken, because Mother Nature can survive and recreate. But if mankind is foolish enough to make his own environment and survival uncomfortable it would become the fault of mankind and his religious fanatics; if they drive themselves to extinction!"

Michael picks up a paintbrush and then he says: "what would these natural ethics include and would these natural ethics be much different from those of all religions?"

Pallas smiles and answers: "it should be immoral for hunting to be seen as a pleasure pursuit and for the human race to destroy areas for their unsustainable breeding and long term survival requirements within such areas. As well as this the greed of the human race should also be considered immoral when it affects the survival of other ecosystems! Therefore the ethics of religions that see other species and ecosystems as a piece of property [for the use of the human race and for the human race to be in control of its survival or extinction] should be seen as immoral, because this part of the human race is unaware of the consequences of its actions; through–in most cases–its willingness to hold back and ignore some of the uncomfortable scientific discoveries!"

Lug watches as Michael begins to paint and then Lug says: "natural ethics [as Pallas has begun to make evident] should not be held to account by religious ethics; that are not willing to accept the sciences that tell the human race that they are **not** the most important species upon the planet, because all life should be realised for the importance of its existence! Therefore the human race has no right to believe that it will survive upon this planet if it continually over exerts the planets resources."

Gaia smiles and says: "no planet lasts forever, and therefore the human race should look after what is impermanent whilst it resides upon it, because if the human race speeds up evolution through un-natural and immoral practices; the human race could become extinct before it has naturally evolved. Hence we must begin to understand that there is very little difference with the ideas that surround the care of the religious shrines and the temples to the Divine, and the care that should be taken in the looking after of the environment that Mother Nature has placed them within! Therefore, the morals that surround the survival of an ongoing breeding programme that will cause much extinction within a given environment and/or on a planetary scale, is immoral because such thoughtlessness can lead on and cause many disasters that could have been avoided. But this is problematic, because the survival of some religions depends upon the immoralities of their so called ethics, for example; some religions do not believe in contraception and such religions will over breed and strain the planetary resources without the thought of the future consequences within their own environment."

Morrighan passes Pallas her flute and then Morrighan remarks: "this whole debate has shown us that the ethics of religion have not caught up with the science of the natural world and such ethics that are not willing to evolve are capable of destroying many planetary resources. Therefore the need to re-evaluate the circumstances should be realised, and then people would not be tied to ancient and outdated scriptures that were written for the understanding of a being that was in its infancy!"

Pallas smiles and says: "perhaps it is time we re-evaluate the ethics that surround Mother Nature and in this re-evaluation we should consider the actual importance of the human race upon the planet."

The flute begins and the dance of life remains as the players feast on the art of peace.

7

THE REALISATION OF NATURAL ETHICS AND CHAOS

The feast begins and the players renew their time of debate; upon the fields of the natural world that is part of their concern....

Morrighan smiles and says: "the natural ethics of this world do not seem to be of many religions concerns and this is probably, because the natural world is not seen to be anything more than a gift to mankind [from the divine of their religion]. Therefore the ethics of nature were not realised for many centuries and this is problematic, because as science advances; most religions only accept the parts of science that were immediately relevant for their own benefit.

Gaia smiles as Sankara starts to bring in the food and then she says: **"Therefore our natural ethics that have not advanced alongside science should be revised right now!"**

Lug carves some pork and then he says: "what should be realised as unethical is the wanton destruction of life and ecosystems upon this planet. But in realizing this mankind would have to stop using the destructive forces of their science for personal gain, and the religions that are not concerned with their action upon the natural order should either be revised or abolished before Mother Nature takes her revenge.

I do not believe it is unethical for mankind to build its cities and try to improve its life upon this planet, but in his building of cities and his increased use of natural resources; his needs come into question, because in his need for greater energy use mankind is losing his ability to slow down and appreciate the beauty of the natural world."

Gaia takes a piece of chicken and then she says: "the religions of the world are mainly bound by the ethics that surround their own survival. This creates many problems for the natural world, because any survival ethics will not concern themselves with the survival of other species or religions that offend their laws and ideals. Therefore the ethics of the natural world need to be enforced and need to be outside and above the ideals of religions that are only concerned with their own survival and enforcement! Such religions should be forced to become aware of the consequences of their actions upon Mother Nature, because in having selfish ethical ideals; some religions could be altering the human race and speeding up the probable extinction of the human race. Therefore the ethics of the human race need to be within the awareness of Mother Nature, because Mother Nature can recover and restart the evolutionary process without the human race! Hence we should realise that natural ethics **do not** necessarily require the continued existence of the human race, but in realizing this we should also realise that the human race has the ability to outlive any species that have come before–if the human race evolves with Mother Nature!"

Merlin finishes a slice of beef and then he says: "nature should be the primary concern of any religion, and one of the moral issues that would surround such ethics would be the consequences of the death of a human to save other living creatures. Perhaps the place to start such an ethical debate; would be with the rights of a human to take another humans life when that human is trying to kill a species that is endangered."

Michael smiles at Pallas and then he says: "if that person's livelihood depended on the death of that animal that is going extinct; would it then be reasonable for it to kill one of that species, and in that respect, would it be reasonable for one human to kill that person that is protecting his or her livelihood?"

Pallas passes Michael a plate of lamb and then she says: "if the person is killing the animal to eat and there is no other means to survive; then natural ethics say that person like any other predatory animal has the right to survive! But if the person is killing an endangered species to make a profit out of its death, then the human that kills this type of human in the act of killing an endangered species has every right to do so!"

Demeter finishes a portion of chicken and then she says: "the act of one human killing another is seen as a sin in many religions [except in self defence]. But in this type of judgement; the action of killing to keep another species alive would not come into consideration in some religions, because all other species are considered inferior to that of the human race, for example; in Genesis 9, 1-2 it is said:

And God blessed Noah and his sons, and said unto them: Be fruitful, and multiply, and replenish the earth. And the fear of a you and the dread of a you shall be upon every beast of the earth, and upon every fowl of the air, upon all that moveth on the earth and upon all the fishes of the sea; into your hand they are delivered. Every living thing that liveth shall be meat for you; even as the green herb have I given you all things.

This is problematic, because this scripture is telling mankind that all beasts are afraid of him and that mankind should multiply, but I am very sure that the mosquito that passes the malaria through its need for blood [and the other creatures that make a meal of man] does not fear man, and another problem with this is that it does not theorize on the consequences of over breeding. For these reasons we should realise that these scriptures are not written by those that are concerned with the natural world, and this makes this type of scripture immoral, because if any human being does not try to understand the possible consequences of its actions; it is totally selfish and in being so selfish its actions will endanger many other lives!"

Morrighan finishes a piece of bread and then she says: "the lack of understanding of some religions, can make their scriptural ethics immoral, because if they are not willing to evolve with the rest of the planet; they are living in a past age that was not as reliant on the technology as those in the 21st century (a.c.e.). Therefore natural ethics should be aware of all the scientific findings and principles within the age of its writing."

Gaia passes Morrighan some beef and then Gaia says: "the law of survival should encompass all living beings, and this law should include the survival of those that need to kill in order to survive, but those who are to make a profit from the mass destruction of other beings should be made unlawful, because any type of mass destruction for a personal profit is unacceptable within the natural world. This unacceptability of the profit from mass destruction; would include the destruction of ecosystems for the benefit of one race [this would include all types of religion]."

Morrighan smiles after finishing a piece of beef and then she says: "therefore the destruction of a particular race of people would be acceptable if it was destroyed by Mother Nature, but; **if the destruction of a particular race of people is brought upon them by another race of people; this would be unacceptable, with the exception of; the destruction of a particularly destructive race!** Therefore the ethics that surround nature are not as complex as people would make them appear to be."

Merlin smiles as Morrighan passes him some of the beef and then he says: "the above ethics are clear and simple to understand, but this type of ethics becomes difficult to understand for those of the human race; that are convinced that their scriptures are correct and without question! Therefore these scriptures of ancient understanding can be unethical in this age. This is problematic, because in a rigid belief structure, their ethics can be detrimental to themselves and the rest of the human race, for example; in the Hindu Bhagavad-Gita (IX, 1-6) it is said that:

The Blessed Lord Said

1 But most secret and mysterious is the teaching I will now reveal,—[a teaching] based on Holy Writ consonant with experience:

To thee [will I proclaim it], for in thee is there no envy; and knowing it; thou shalt be freed from ill.

2 Science of kings, mystery of kings is this,—distilling the purest essence, to the understanding evident, with righteousness enhanced, how easy to carry out! [Yet] it abides forever.

3 Men who put no faith in this law of righteousness, fail to reach Me and must return to the road of recurring death.

4 By Me, Unmanifest in form, this whole universe was spun:

In Me subsist all beings, I do not subsist in them.

5 And [yet] subsistent beings do not subsist in me,—behold my sovereign power (yoga)!

My self sustains all beings, it does not subsist in them; it causes them to be.

6 As in [wide space] subsists the mighty wind, blowing [at will] ever and everywhere, so too do all contingent beings subsist in Me: so must thou understand.[38]

This part of the Bhagavad-Gita shows a God and creator of all, but this is as problematic as the One-God scriptures (although it has a different kind of problems), because these verses show that the recurring death or the never ending cycle of life and death is to be avoided by enlightenment, and if we avoid this cycle we can have no true respect for nature, which is part of the universe that this scripture claims that this God created. This is hugely problematic, because the Self can be the only true creator of the universe of its own surroundings, because the Self has the choice of its own actions within the natural world. This choice does not mean that the self is in full control of the universe it has created for itself, for example; if Mother Nature strikes someone with lightning they had no choice in the matter!"

Gaia smiles and says: "what this has made evident is that most religions–and perhaps all–can be unethical when it comes to nature, and this is because religions that believe in a creator of all things lose the natural balance, for example; in the Bhagavad-Gita it is said that *By Me, Unmanifest in form, this whole universe was spun: In Me subsist all beings, I do not subsist in them.*[39] This is problematic, because if something is Unmanifest and the universe is spun out of something that is Unmanifest; it cannot come into existence in illusion or anything else, and if people use this to believe that every thing is nothing more than an illusion, then those people will have no need to respect Mother Nature, because her and her creations do not truly exist! Therefore I consider this script as immoral, because in the impermanence of the natural world–evolution is Mother Nature's immortality!"

Morrighan smiles, finishes some rice and then she says: "this part of the script may be immoral, because of the loss of respect of Mother Nature, within the realms of this creator of all. But this loss of respect within the natural world; can also create a

---

[38] Hindu Scriptures, R. C. Zaehner p358-359 David Campbell Publishers Ltd 1992
[39] Ibid

loss of the road to enlightenment, because in an earlier part of the scripture it says:

Science of kings, mystery of kings is this,—distilling the purest essence, to the understanding evident, with righteousness enhanced, how easy to carry out! [Yet] it abides forever.

Men who put no faith in this law of righteousness, fail to reach Me and must return to the road of recurring death.[40]

Because of these verses we can see a need of scientific understanding for the natural world; if the followers of this religion wish to gain enlightenment, but this becomes problematic when [as Gaia has already pointed out] the following verse or verses show a God that creates all from nothing, and if nothing comes form nothing; why should we respect something that does not really exist? I suggest that we would not respect something that has no real existence, because there would be no reason to do so! Therefore the scriptures of any religion that deny the permanence of nature, become immoral and this is because, if you consider nature to be unreal, the evolution of the natural world would also be unreal, and we would then begin to lose the understanding of the permanence of evolution, and once that is lost; all kinds of natural immoralities appear, such as; the destruction of species would not be considered as immoral if everything was an illusion, because if in its illusion of permanence it became impermanent it would not matter, because once an illusion is gone it has no return, and therefore; the act of using illusion for the impermanence and the use of a God becomes immoral in the natural world, because the loss of the idea of life as a reality can lead to incompetence and mass destruction."

Michael smiles, finishes some fruit, and then he says: what is immoral about scriptures that say that there is One-God that is the creator of all, and why is the destruction of what is considered unreal immoral? And why does this come from incompetence of what is considered unreal?"

Morrighan smiles, finishes a piece of pork and then she says: "there is nothing immoral about the scriptures that relate to

---

[40] Ibid

there being One-God that is the creator of all! The immorality of these scriptures start through the loss of reasoning of the natural word, for example; if it is stated that: *As in [wide space] subsists the mighty wind, blowing [at will] ever and everywhere, so too do all contingent beings subsist in Me: so must thou understand.*[41] And in a later text in the same scripture it is stated that: *when men possessed of highest faith integrated and indifferent to the fruits [of what they do], do penance in threefold wise, men speak of penance in goodness way.*[42] These scriptures could both be pointing to the unimportance of what man does in the natural world. Therefore I suggest that any scripture or scriptures that lose mankind his responsibility for his actions within the natural world are immoral, because this gives mankind the freedom to upset the natural balance or order without the realization of the consequences of its actions."

Sankara smile and says: "**in natural ethics; anything that upsets the natural balance should be considered unethical and these ethics; will go against any ethics that are written for the sole purpose of the human race becoming enlightened, because natural ethics hold the survival of the majority of species at the cost of a singular species as moral. Therefore natural ethics would see the loss of a destructive species as a good result!**"

Gaia smiles and replies: "the extinction of any species can upset the balance of nature, but nature can and will recover. Therefore the survival of a singular species does not become a major issue for the natural ethics, but the survival of one species that is causing mass extinction should be against all ethical morals! Hence we should see some of the human race as a separate species, because the ethics of the followers of the natural ethics are so different from the ethics of those that are not enlightened within the desires of the natural world!"

Demeter smiles, finishes some of her meal and then she says: "perhaps Gaia is right and we need to reclassify the races and groups of people as separate species but of the same order,

---

[41] Hindu Scriptures, R. C. Zaehner p359 David Campbell publishers Ltd 1992
[42] Ibid p397

just as we would classify the Gorilla and the Chimpanzee as different species of the same order!"

Lug smiles, finishes a lamb chop and then he remarks: "this sounds like a reasonable idea, but the classification of different races and religions, is very problematic, because if we classify a race we must classify all the religions within that race as of that race, and there will be those within a particular classification that do not belong to the main religions within that order! Therefore we must realise that the races of man cannot be classified as belonging to any particular religion even if it was from that particular race that a majority religion developed, for example; there are people that convert from Hindu into Buddhism and other religions and vice versa. Therefore the development of a race needs a separate classification than that of its mainstream religion or religions!"

Merlin finishes some of his mushrooms and then he says: "when we start to classify separate races and religions and keep them within the same order as the human race; we need to give all races and religions the freedom to express their beliefs and their teaching in a non violent manner. This is problematic, because the majority of races and religions are run by hierarchies or followed by those that are held by their dogmatic belief."

Morrighan eats another piece of beef and then she says: "religions and races are generally only tolerant to the belief systems that they have been taught for centuries. Therefore the classification of religions and races would need to come through philosophers and theologians of all the mainstream religions, and this is problematic in itself, because many religions do not allow philosophy to undermine or interfere with scriptures that are of their ancient understanding!"

Pallas takes a sip from her cup of tea and then she says:

"That is why the classification must start with the ideals of the natural world!"

Pallas takes another sip of her tea and resumes: "therefore I shall start the first classification by stating that the races that are involved with the mainstream of the One-God religions; should be classified as hostile to the natural world, because these religions see their god as the creator of all and see mankind as being in charge of the rest of the planet; and as we all know mankind is definitely not in charge of the planets abilities. Therefore the religions that see themselves as above the understanding of natural ethics should be classified as **naturally hostile**. Secondly we should classify the religions and races that acknowledge philosophy and the understanding of the natural world as; **natural moralists**. These natural moralists would need to acknowledge the empirical evidence of the natural world, and in doing so, they would also need to be aware of the consequences of their actions and the probability of the human race–as we know it–becoming extinct through the evolutionary process! Thirdly we must classify the religions that use the ideas of illusion as the bondage of the physical being as **neutral and possibly bordering on hostile moralists**, because such beliefs do not corrupt in the greedy ideal of other religions, but in showing everything as illusion, the physical being of such a religion does not tend to have the concern for other living beings or species as those of the natural moralists,"

Michael smiles and says: "what you are making evident is that races and religions can be put into three separate categories, but this does not solve the problem of the true understanding of the natural ethics that we have been discussing!"

Sankara finishes his cup of tea and then he says: "the three categories would need many sub categories, and in the creation of these sub categories; the natural ethics of each religion would have to be the same, but this cannot happen whilst there are religions that believe their ancient scriptures are correct and unquestionable. Therefore the problems that surround natural ethics cannot be solved until all categories agree on the evolutionary process of Mother Nature."

Pingala finishes her meal and then she says: "evolution is very controversial within the different religious orders, and if the ethics of natural evolution contradict those of a religion, the religion that it contradicts could lose its free thought if other religions interfere. Therefore the ethics that surround natural evolution and natural thought–should be separated from religions ethics and any ethical process that denies the teaching of natural ethics."

Morrighan puts her arm around Pingala, smiles and then Morrighan replies: "what you are suggesting is that the natural ethics should be a law above any religious laws that contradict scientific findings without empirical evidence! Therefore the first law of any truly ethical society should be:

Natural ethics and discoveries must come before any religions ideals that could include the destruction of species for selfish and un-needed reasons!"

Pingala smiles at Morrighan and then Pingala replies: "the morals of any religion that considers itself above such a law should be seen as inconsequential, and ignored by those ethical cultures or religions; that administer the first law of natural ethics—as the most important law of the human race! Therefore the ethics of religion that appear unethical to the natural world; need to be either outlawed or ignored!

Pallas smiles and says: "true morality can only begin when selfish ideals are seen as a part of any culture or species that needs to be kept in check, for example; a pride of lions make a kill for their survival, just as a singular lion would do so. This is an act of self preservation and is a selfish act, because it depends on the death of another for its survival. Therefore we should now realise that there are necessary selfish acts!"

Merlin finishes his cup of coffee and then he says: "selfish acts should only become immoral when the selfish act is an act of greed; that is destructive to other environments, species and any of the human beings! Therefore the second law of morality should be:

Any act of selfishness can only be considered moral when it is being acted upon in the will to survive. But this can be considered immoral if the cost of the will to survive is greater than the benefit to the individual, or the race, or species, that wishes to survive!"

Gaia finishes her meal and replies: "all acts that are born through the will to survive are moral to the individual that is in a situation where it needs to act to survive, but [as Merlin has just reasoned upon]; this can become immoral when the survival of one individual or one idea costs the rest of the planet greatly. Therefore the ethics of a religion must not be taken as law without any empirical evidence. Hence we should realise that the third law of natural ethics should be:

Any religion or race that believes it is above natural reasoning without empirical evidence must be shown to be immoral, and must be realised to be a hostile party that threatens the natural balance!"

Michael smiles, finishes a piece of cake and then he asks: "if some religions are seen to be against the natural law: should there be any punishment and/or should they then be outlawed if they were not willing to change?"

Lug finishes his strawberries and cream and then he replies: "the problem with outlawing such religions; is that in outlawing something like a belief; you lose some of the ideals that surround the free will and the freedom of speech. Therefore we must be careful when we make laws that can affect other ideals and ideologies. **But in realizing that; we should also realise that scientific understanding and natural ethics need to be the main law givers, because most religious laws are based upon the needs of a religion to survive. Therefore we must realise the survival of a religion is not as important as the ethics of the natural world!"**

Morrighan smiles at Lug, finishes a piece of chocolate cake: "and then she says: "the natural ethics should be realised as the most important of all the ethical ideologies. This is, because the natural ethics should make evident—to those that are willing to understand—the consequences of the greed and the selfish desires; of some of the practises that are not willing to acknowledge scientific and empirical evidence! Therefore the law of the freedom of the will within the natural world should be:

No person, culture or religion, should be able to make laws that could affect the evolution of any of the species upon this planet, and throughout the universe!"

The above law and the other similar laws that we have mentioned should be of **primary concern** within the human race, but this type of ethical realization is not possible; whilst there are sections of the human race that are willing to defend their ancient scriptures; without trying to realise the consequences of their actions!"

Sankara smiles at Morrighan and then he says: "what Morrighan is making clear is that the races and religions that do not acknowledge scientific and empirical evidence; can and in some case are unbeneficial, and we must realise that; this type of belief can also hold back the evolutionary process. Therefore these religions and the type of people that follow them need to be realised for what they really are!"

Michael smiles and asks: "in realizing some religions as counteractive to the evolution of the human race; should such religions be able to exist within a naturally ethical world?"

Gaia puts her hand on Michaels shoulder, smiles and then she replies: "if the natural ethical people, allow the abolishment of a bad ethical religion; the ethics of free speech and the free will are questionable, because any ethics that allow the destruction of any thought process—be it good or bad—are destroying the free will that Mother Nature has given us. Therefore bad ethical teachings should not be destroyed, because in destroying bad ethical teachings they can re-emerge when the reasons for their destruction were lost. Hence we should realise that bad ideals need to be examined and re-examined for them to be realised for what they truly are."

Morrighan smiles and says: "what Gaia has made evident is that bad teachings need examination and re-examination, but the bad teachings must never be lost or be allowed to prevail!"

Pallas passes Morrighan a glass of wine and then Pallas says: "therefore the natural ethics should keep the unscientific religions in check.

But if the true reality of free will is to be established; the religions that are dogmatic and unscientific should be allowed to continue and not be abolished, because if people are allowed free will they have the right to believe what they wish. Although this is the only way of the human race being able to have any kind of free will; it can never be allowed to be totally free, because mankind is generally dictatorial and destructive."

Merlin smiles as Pallas passes him a glass of wine and then he says: "therefore the natural ethics must allow freedom of thought but not necessarily of action. This means that there must be this law within natural ethics:

The freedom of speech and thought should never be allowed to be made unlawful; but any of the actions that can arise from such a freedom should be made unlawful if they are against the first rule of natural ethics!"

Lug smiles, takes a sip of his wine and then he says: "freedom of speech and the free will can only remain free when the religions that do not allow such actions are abolished! Therefore there can never be true free will or freedom of speech, because if there was; there would be no need for ethics, because any kind of ethical values that create laws for the good of the human race depend upon some kind of denial of the free will, for example; the right to murder someone for selfish reasons is denied–and rightly so–and with this being denied it is a loss of part of free will! Therefore we must realise that all laws are made to deny someone the right to commit an action that is against the principle of another group of people or an individual."

Demeter smiles and says: "Hence we must realise that natural ethics must deny some people their freedom of speech and their free will, because without some kind of controlling factor; the more dictatorial religions would be able to take control–just like the warlike religion s throughout the ages."

Michael smiles and says: "therefore we must realise that the human race needs controls and cannot be allowed to have total control over its own actions at this stage in time, because the human race is very willing to follow its own desires, and it can be too easily led by an ideology that seems to suit its own desires. Being so easily led by a religion that suits its desires; can lead to many unethical practises and these practises can be made to be ethical within the religion that it was formed. Therefore religion and the human race need an ethical code that does not rely on religious practises and morals:

What it needs is an ethical code that relies on nature and the natural balance."

Morrighan takes another sip from her wine and then she says: "that is quite right, but this type of ethical creation and management would need a ruling class that do not consider themselves as superior to others of the human race! Therefore the ruling class that defines the laws would need to be changed on a regular basis, and such a ruling class would need to be able to stop any action that was against natural ethics. This is hugely problematic, because as we have learnt throughout history:

Power corrupts.

Therefore I suggest that the idea of a ruling class; that can be trusted is not a viable option within a world that is run by the ideals; that are created by religions; that wish to rule the world and ignore the science that can save many–including their own–species."

Gaia looks at Morrighan, smiles and replies: "this is a very disturbing and truthful reality that Morrighan has shown, because there is no way to stop the corruption that has dominated mankind for centuries; whilst there is any kind of free will. Therefore the domination of others by the corruption of religion and politics must be brought to justice by a force that is greater than either! But this is not possible whilst the human race thinks that it is the greatest race on the planet, and that each different race or religion has the only truthful God and reasoning within its scriptures."

Morrighan smiles, passes Gaia a bottle of wine and then Morrighan says: "everything that is created through the corruption of religions leads to chaos, because all religions can be corrupted to suit certain individual needs. This corruption can and in many cases has become problematic, because religions tend to born from the need of people to have a leader; that is all powerful and will help them win a war or win the domination of other races!"

Pingala sips at her wine and then she says: "religion has been seen to be dubious of anything that appears to make their scriptures incorrect and this is, because; if someone shows the imperfections within a religious figurehead's creations or truths, they undermine the ethics of that religion!"

Sankara smiles and says: "science can undermine many religions! Therefore the religions that are dubious of science must have something to hide, and if they have something to hide, they cannot be trusted, for example; religions tend to hide behind scriptures that cannot be proven and are scientifically improbable, like that of The Great Flood in the myth Noah's Ark (Genesis 7, 11-24):

In the six hundredth year of Noah's life, in the second month, the seventeenth day of the month, the same day were all the fountains of the great deep broken up, and the windows of the heavens were opened. And the rain was upon the earth forty days and forty nights. In the self same day entered Noah, and Shem, and Ham, and Japheth, the sons of Noah, and Noah's wife, and the three wives of his sons with them, into the ark; they and every beast after his kind, and all the cattle after their kind, and every creeping thing that creeps upon the earth after his kind, and every fowl after his kind, every bird of every sort and they went in unto Noah into the ark, two and two of all flesh, where in is the breath of life. And they that went in; went in male and female of all flesh, as God had commanded him: and the Lord shut him in. And the flood was forty days upon the earth; and the waters increased, and bear up the ark, and it was lift up above the earth. And the waters prevailed, and were increased greatly upon the earth; and the ark went upon the face of the waters. And the waters prevailed exceedingly upon the earth; and all the high hills; that were under the whole heaven, were covered. Fifteen cubits upward did the waters prevail; and the mountains were covered. And all flesh died that moveth upon the earth, both of fowl, and of cattle, and of beast, and of every creeping thing that creeps upon the earth, and every man: on whose nostrils with the breath of life, of all that was in the dry land, died. And every living substance was destroyed which was upon the face of the ground, both man, and cattle, and the creeping things, and the fowl of the heaven; and they were destroyed from the earth; and Noah only remained alive, and they were with him in the ark. And the waters prevailed upon the earth a hundred and fifty days.

From this there has become many scientific arguments in the religious fields, for example; how could a boat be built that could hold two of all the earths animals and how could they be fed and watered for one hundred and fifty days. This is only one of the scientific impossibilities that are thought to be true in this myth."

Gaia smiles and says: there are many myths like the one Sankara has mentioned; that are fanatically supported by the followers of their religions, and this is where many problems occur, because when some sections of the human race become unwilling to support such beliefs; the people that do not support can become outcasts and/or punished even if they support the faith that is punishing them, for example; Galileo who was a keen supporter of his faith was accused of heresy by the church of his people, and this is made evident in these three letters from Galileo:

The problem or the question of the centre of the universe, and whether the earth is situated there, is among the least worthy of consideration in the whole of astronomy. It has sufficed the greatest astronomers to assume that the terrestrial globe is of insensible size in comparison with the starry orb, and as to location it is either at the centre of the diurnal revolution of that orb or is removed there from by an insignificant distance. There is no reason to tire oneself out trying to prove that, nor that the fixed stars are situated in a space bounded by a spherical surface; it is enough that they are located at an immense distance from us. Likewise, to want to assign a centre to that space, of which the shape is neither known or can be known (or even whether it has a shape), is in my opinion a superfluous and an idle task. To believe that the earth can be located at a centre not known to exist in the universe is indeed a frustrating enterprise. (G W 411)[43]

2 The falsity of the Copernican system must not on any account be doubted, especially by us Catholics, who have the irrefragable authority of Holy Scripture interpreted by the greatest masters in theology, whose agreement renders us certain of the stability of the earth and of the mobility of the sun around it. The conjectures of Copernicus and his followers offered to the contrary are all removed by the most sound argument taken from the omnipotence of God. He being able to do in many, or rather in infinite ways, what to our view and observation seems to be done in one particular way, we must not pretend to hinder God's hand and stubbornly maintain that in which we may be mistaken.

And just as I deem the Copernican observations and conjectures inadequate, so I judge equally and more, fallacious and erroneous those of Ptolemy, Aristotle and their followers, when without going beyond the bounds of human reasoning, their inconclusiveness can very easily be discovered. (G W 417)[44]

3 I have said that I hope for no relief, and this is because I committed no crime. If I had erred, I might hope to obtain grace and pardon; for transgressions by subjects are the means by which the prince finds occasion for the exercise of mercy and indulgence. Hence when a man is wrongly

---

[43] Past Masters Galileo, Stillman Drake P89-90 Oxford University Press 1996

[44] Ibid p91

condemned to punishment, it becomes necessary for his judges to use greater severity in order to cover up their own misapplications of the law. This afflicts me less than people may think possible, for I have two reasons of perpetual comfort–first that in my writings there cannot be found perpetual shadow of irreverence toward the Holy Church; and second, the testimony of my own conscience, which only I and God in Heaven thoroughly know. And he knows that in this cause for which I suffer, though many might have spoken with more learning, none, not even the ancient Fathers, have spoken with more piety or greater zeal for the Church than I. (G W 436)[45]

These three letters show that Galileo was willing to question the ideologies of the scriptures and the theories that his faith had lived by for generations. But in doing so he had been punished by the hierarchy of his faith without losing the belief in his God. Therefore the people like Galileo that are willing to hold onto a belief in their God whilst they are disproving some of their faiths ideals tend to be made into outcasts and punished for their beliefs, because they are evolving or trying to evolve something; that the obstinate people of their faith; do not believe can be evolved."

Morrighan smiles and says: "although that type of obstinacy is obviously inappropriate for the evolution of the human race! That type of obstinacy is still used by many religions that still wish to gain the control of the world that we live in. In being so stubborn these religions are putting back the evolution of the human race, and they are becoming a danger to all the species upon the planet, because as technology increases the power of our destructive capability; the religions that are not willing to acknowledge evolution are willing to adopt the destructive technologies, for example; there are some Christian cults that see the destructive potential and do not believe in the ideals of war, but they still believe in mass population and/or they use many of the technologies that are environmentally destructive!"

Merlin passes a bottle of wine to Morrighan and then he says: "mankind's religions–in general–seem to have had a problem with evolution since the concept first appeared, just as they had a problem with the astronomy of people like Galileo. Therefore it is becoming evident that anything that seems to

---

[45] Ibid p92-93

contradict some ancient beliefs can be seen as heresy, and once they are seen as such; the people that have made these discoveries can be made outcasts and punished."

Michael smiles and says: we already know that Darwin was one of the people that made evident the evolution of species, but there have been many more scientists later than Darwin that live in fear of the Church or a particular religion because of their discoveries!"

Morrighan sips at her glass of wine and then she replies: "after Darwin; there would be many scientists that feared their religions reprisal; if they broke any of the laws or ideals that were laid down by their Divine being or beings, because anyone who has any kind of religious belief will fear any contradiction of that belief through their own discovery or discoveries.

Do not forget that there are still some religions and cults associated with them; that do not accept the theories; that surround natural evolution, and this is in the beginning of the 21st century!"

Michael smiles as Morrighan passes him a glass of wine and then he says: "from what you are making evident; it is doubtful that science and most religions will ever be able to negotiate in an uncompromising manner; whilst religion remains dogmatic in its beliefs!"

Demeter smiles, takes a sip from her glass of mead, and says: "that is also why the earlier proposals that surround natural ethics are unlikely to happen. Therefore the dogma that surrounds religions is still a major contributor to the warmongers and the selfish and self righteous people upon this planet. Hence we should realise that the dogma that is present in many of the early 21st century's societies; is still holding back the evolution of mankind!"

Pallas puts her arm around Morrighan, pours herself some wine and then Pallas says: "where religion and science mix, chaos seems to be the only outcome that is inevitable, because once they get attracted to each other, they start to repel each other when they reach a topic that conflicts. Therefore I suggest that the principles that surround the chaos theory needs to be brought into the field of discussion; when all that can come from two sides, that can be as opposed as good and evil appear in the same field of discussion.

The theory of chaos is [historically] the contrast between chaos, or the unformed, unordered, undifferentiated beginnings of things, and the cosmos which is seen as the ordered universe. This concept is implicit in early Greek Cosmogony. In modern scientific theories, chaotic systems are those in which an arbitrarily small difference in the initial conditions can produce arbitrarily large differences in later states. These chaotic systems can be deterministic, but are not predictable, because it does not matter how accurate a measurement may be, a variation smaller than any it can detect, could be responsible for a difference in the final outcome.[46]"

Morrighan smiles, takes another sip of her wine and then she says: "chaos would be a theory that many religions could not accept, because there are many religions that believe their God or their Divine are in control of all that is happening and has happened within the universe. Therefore we must realise that the theories; that surround chaos; are like a lot of scientific and philosophical theories—implausible to some religions!"

Michael smiles, pours himself some mead and then he says: "the religions that cannot recognize the chaotic actions within the universe are those that believe in a perfect God. Therefore we must realise; that those who are unwilling to accept the chaotic nature of creation cannot even begin to understand the evolutionary process, because if their God is perfect every thing it has created must be perfect in its perfectly ordered universe!

As we have already made evident perfection cannot exist without the realization and the creation of imperfection, therefore there is nothing that can be perfect, and there would be no being that could be perfect in the minds of all other beings, because there are imperfections in every being upon the planet."

Lug sips at his wine and then he says: "chaos is one of the beauties of the natural world, and this is because; if everything was in order; there would be nothing that could not be predicted, and there would be no discoveries left for man."

Pallas smiles, takes another sip of her wine and then she says: "there can be many things that are considered perfect

---

[46] Oxford Dictionary of Philosophy, Simon Blackburn, p61 Oxford University Press 1996

within the natural and the scientific world, but one persons perfection can be another persons imperfection, for example: the perfection of one religions God can be seen as an imperfection by another religion, and both religions could be seen as imperfect by scientific explorations and discoveries. Therefore I suggest that the complete perfection of any God or physical being; cannot be so whilst there is the chaotic principle of free will within the universe, because where there is free will; there is no true order within the beings of the universe!"

Pingala, smiles at Pallas and then Pingala says: "there is much predictability within a chaotic universe, but we must always remember; that within such a universe a miniscule and unexpected or immeasurable changes within the predictability; can completely alter what we thought we had predicted. Therefore we should realise that any religion that believes that there God or Gods are perfect cannot accept anything that is immeasurable, because if their god is so perfect he would not and could not have created an unpredictable and chaotic system within perfection, because if something is perfect all the circumstances of that perfection would have to be known for it to be perfect, and there is no known being that that has nothing about itself that cannot be chaotic!"

Sankara pours himself some wine and then he says: "if any being creates any type of chaos it cannot be perfect unless chaos is considered as the only true perfection within the universe!"

Pingala smiles as Pallas pours her some more wine and then Pingala says: "chaos is one of the true perfections, because chaos is perfect in its improbability, in other words; chaos is truly chaotic and has no need for imperfections within its chaotic creations, because once something has become or is un-chaotic it has ceased to be chaotic, and therefore chaos can never be imperfect, because when something becomes or is seen as un-chaotic it simply does not exist as chaotic!"

Merlin takes a sip of his mead and then he says: "it is highly probable that Pingala is correct, because chaos is one of the things that do not require any imperfection for it to exist, because chaos can be seen as perfect imperfection, and in this sense it can be considered completely paradoxical!"

Lug smiles and says: "that may be correct, but chaos is like all other truths and that is: they require their opposites for them to be recognized!"

Gaia takes another sip of her mead and then she says: "these chaos theories are entering into the realms of the existence of the universe, and the majority of science that dates the age of the universe is very problematic to some religions [particularly some of the cults within the Christian, Jewish and Islamic religions], because the universe and the stars are of such a great age; the approximation of this age can completely destroy some of the scriptural ideals; that have been thought of as being without doubt for many centuries. Therefore we must realise that the chaos theories that involve the creation of the universe; must have as great an age as the universe, and if the chaos principle is part of the creation; the chaos principle must also be part of the never ending cycle of life, death, and rebirth!"

Merlin takes out his pipe, fills it with tobacco, lights it and then he replies: "if this is correct; chaos would be as much a part of the universe as all the creations of Mother Nature, and if this is also true; Mother Nature would be the creator of the chaos that is needed for the realization of the order that is within the universe, because chaos and order are like any other realizations: they cannot be truly realised without each other!"

Pallas pours herself some more wine and then she says: "chaos seems to be a creative figure in many myths, but whether it is a deity or not in some of the myths is uncertain! Therefore the void that many deities seem to have appeared from can be seen as chaos by some religions, because in being uncertain of what chaos is; the idea of a void fulfils the need of something that cannot be or is difficult to be explained, and if there is no explanation it can also be theorized as chaotic, because if something is in order it is known of how that order came to be:

That is if there is any true order within the creation of the universe!

Perhaps the universe is a creation based on chance, and Mother Nature made her creation and just sat back and watched the results of her creation. But if this is true the never ending and never beginning circle of life comes into question, because if everything was based on the chance of that which comes from the original creation; the original creation of our universe must have been created out of something else for it to be able to exist in the first place. Therefore the chaos of the universe can become apparent, because if something is created out of, something else; there can be no beginning of its creation and no end to its evolution, because it cannot have never existed and it can never cease to exist!"

Morrighan takes a sip from her glass of wine and then she says: "chaos and order are principles that are within all religions, but there are some religions that seem to be more able to accept that there is chaos within the universe and that creation is not a complete realm without order. This is because, if anything is created there needs to be some kind of order for its creation; even if its creation begins through chaotic means, for example; a hurricane can create chaos throughout certain regions upon the earth, but a hurricane appears through a certain type of conditions and without any one of these conditions the hurricane would not exist, and therefore even the chaotic force of a hurricane needs a certain type of order for it to be formed!"

Gaia sips at her mead and then she replies: "as Morrighan has just pointed out; some chaotic conditions need a type of order for them to become chaotic:

Therefore the chaos that is within the universe is dependent on order for its chaotic conditions to occur—even accidents need an order of conditions for them to occur!

Once that has been realised, the religions that associate chaos with the aspects of everyday life can probably be accepted as the most natural religions on the planet, because if a religion believes that chaos arrives through order; the religion should come to realise that the vice-versa is also true.

Morrighan butters some bread and then she says: "science and religion have been seen to agree and to use each other for their own means only when it is necessary—or when they can gain some kind of powerful grip on their opposing factions. Therefore we should realise that the religions that need a perfect creator figure or figures; cannot have any type of chaos within their religion, because chaos comes through events that cannot be predicted in their original creation, for example; we cannot predict exactly when the next major strike of a meteor will hit the earth, until events lead to the oncoming happening come within range of our scientific means. Even though that meteor strike would cause major chaos: the religions that believe their Divine is or are all powerful and all knowing, would theorize that their Divine knew about this and sent the meteor to punish the human race for all its sins."

Gaia looks out of the window, smiles and says: "the sciences that realise that chaos is a part of all creation tend to be more philosophical than the religious ideals, because–as we have made evident–science is willing to theorise on future problems that cannot be precisely dated and are likely to be a consequence of the chaotic universe. Therefore true science is willing to explore realms that are outside the religious agenda of many religions, for example; in the Heifer of the Qur'An it is said:

28 How can you reject the faith in Allah? – seeing that ye were without life, and He gave you life; then will He cause you to die, and will again bring you to life; and again to him will ye return

29 It is he who hath created for you all things that are on earth, moreover His design comprehended the heaven, for He gave order and perfection to the seven firmaments and of all things He hath perfect knowledge.[47]

Hence we should realise that there are some religions–and this is not the only one–that cannot acknowledge the chaotic universe; whilst they believe in the perfection and the order that was created by their all knowing God, because if their God is all knowing and has created order and perfection there would be no possibility of chaos, because all would be created within the order of their God! Therefore the order that is created by an all knowing God; can only be created by one who controls all and one that cannot be seen as wrong by the scientific exploration!"

Michael looks out of the same window as Gaia, smiles and then he says: "that is one of the many reasons that the theory of evolution is so problematic for many of the One-God religions, for example; the science of evolution shows that a huge extinction was upon the planet at a very distant time, and with this being the truth the dinosaurs would be considered as a mistake, because they did not fulfil the expectations of the

---

[47] The Holy Qur'An Translated by Abdullah Yusuf Ali p6 Wordsworth Editions Limited 2000

religions that considered their God as perfect, because a God cannot be perfect if its religion denies the creation of something that could not survive upon the planet. This becomes even more strange when the Bible of the Christians and the Jews show some animals as an abomination and unclean–why create something you know to be an abomination or unclean!"

Lug opens the door, smiles and says: "there are many religions that believe in the perfection of their creator and cannot see the imperfections that are needed for any type of perfection to be realised. This is why many religions do not like the scientific evidence that contradicts the writings of their so-called perfect God."

Pingala walks towards the door, stops, smiles at Lug and then she says: "science has been and is seen to be the creator of natural ethics, because without the science that we have referred to, the natural ethics could not be truly realised. That is, because the natural ethics could not be truly created without the scientific and philosophical theories being able to contradict them, and in some cases demolish religious beliefs that are based solely on the material wishes and wants of mankind! Therefore we should now realise that such scientific theories as evolution, astronomy and chaos need to be part of the ethics that mankind lives by. The chaos theory is particularly relevant, because chaos is a theory that natural ethics need to realise that all is not necessarily well; when mankind creates something that is useful for its own purpose; without the realization that evolution is as dependent on chaos as it is on order!"

Morrighan smiles, picks up her rucksack and then she says: "therefore the ethics that we have made evident need to be realised as the truth of the world that we live in and these ethics should not be held to account by outdated religious beliefs, and the theories that are solely for the benefit of the material pleasures of the human race!

Perhaps we should now discuss the chaos theory in greater detail!"

The players gather their equipment and then they go out for a walk.

8

THE CHAOS OF TRUTH

The walk begins and Morrighan says: "the chaos theories are dependent on there being no complete perfection within the universe; that is, there is no dependence on everything that is available to our senses, but this does not mean that all is chaos and there is no order within the universe, because if there was no order nothing could remain stable, for example; if a beings genetic structure was continually altering within its body it would be continually forming into something else whilst it was alive! Therefore we should firstly examine the historical philosophies and theologies that surround the chaos theories!"

Sankara deeply inhales the crisp and clear spring air and then he says: "many theologies and philosophies begin [historically] with the universe being in chaos before the order of the universe was brought about by the will of their Divine being or beings. But this is problematic, because the universe is continually expanding and evolving, and there can be no total consistency while something is evolving or expanding to a limit or without any limitations!"

Gaia smiles and replies: "true order cannot be created within any unknown thing, because if something is unknown there are things within it that cannot be put into any kind of order, because if something has unknown things about it, its controlling factors cannot be correctly theorized upon.

Therefore we must realise that the order that appears within chaos can only appear when it is truly understood, for instance; the masses of individual people moving around in a city seem chaotic, but when we realise that each individual is going about their business in their own particular way; the chaos can then be understood and in some cases can be put into an ordered structure."

Merlin points to a peregrine falcon and then he says: "religion seems to think of chaos as the time before creation, but creation can only happen through chaos and order, because without a jumble of objects or things coming into some kind of order there could be nothing to realise the order. Therefore chaos must come first!"

Pingala smiles as she watches the peregrine and then she says: "chaos theory is a misunderstood part of many religions, because most religions see their divine creating order from the original chaos. But what most of these religions do not seem to realise is that chaos is a part of the world that is needed for it to exist, for instance; the weather patterns that establish themselves throughout the planet are still only predictable for a short term and even this short term predictability is not as precise–in some cases–as the human race would like it to be!"

Lug watches as the peregrine dives to take its prey and after its miss, he says: "order can be created from chaos, but total and complete order within the universe is not possible, because there are too many variables! Therefore any religion that believes their Divine have created a completely ordered universe that is in the control of their Divine are mistaken, because all creation depends upon a new order of things to come into existence from some kind of chaos, for example; a building or a wall that is made of ordered layers of stone; was at one time an unordered or chaotic order of stone."

Morrighan watches as the peregrine flies out of her sight and then she says: "even well built objects can become chaotic in their appearance, for instance; the mosses and lichens that grow upon some walls; were not intended inhabitants of these walls. Therefore we should realise that chaos can appear in many forms, and within this chaotic universe the order that is created is only temporary.

We should begin to realise that the chaos that is all around and within our own existence is the beginning of all creation, and creation does not arise from perfection; it arises from chaos!"

Gaia momentarily, watches the fish in the stream and then she replies: "everything that is created comes from some type of chaos, because whatever is created; is created from a mixture of some thing or some things! Therefore we should realise that there are many creations that are born from such a mixture of things, and this mixture is how religions are born from chaos!"

Michael watches the fish jump for the flies, turns, and smiles at Gaia and then he says: "if religions are born from chaos; chaos would be the creator of all that is and chaos would then be a Divine entity or entities, because chaos would be the beginning; before the Divine of religions!"

Gaia smiles and replies: "chaos is probably the Divine of all creation and Mother Nature and chaos could be one and the same, because if Mother Nature is the creator of all she must have put the order within the chaos for life to come into existence, and if she did so; she would need to be able to control the parts of chaos that would bring life into existence; and in being able to do so suggests that the chaos was of her making or within her being!"

Michael smiles and asks: "why does chaos need to be of her making or within her being for Mother Nature to be able to control it?"

Gaia smiles and answers: "because, if Mother Nature is the creator of all; her creations must have begun with chaotic form and if all form in the beginning was chaotic, Mother Nature must be chaotic if she is as immortal as chaos, and if she is as immortal then she could not have been created by chaos, because if both are immortal they would always have been!"

Morrighan watches the returning peregrine and says: "the problem with immortality and chaos is; chaos and immortality are both linguistic terms that are easily misunderstood, and in being easily misunderstood they are easily misrepresented. This becomes problematic, because our understanding is limited to what is mortal! Therefore anything that is considered immortal can have no true definition without the human race realizing the immortality of the soul or the self. But this is also problematic, because the only certainty within the death of the physical being is that it dies; which leads to the chaotic thoughts and theories that surround this process! Therefore I suggest that chaos and immortality are closely linked, because whilst there is no singular definition of the circumstances that encompass the self after the death of the physical body; chaos is the only element that can be considered a reality whilst our beliefs are in a chaotic form!"

Sankara smiles and says: "religion must then be responsible for much of the chaos that is within the present world, and when we consider that religion is formed after the construction of the physical being–which came from a type of order that was created from chaos–it is not illogical to reason that religion is as chaotic as the rest of the universe!"

Pingala sits on a fallen tree trunk, smiles and says: "whilst there is the chaotic evolutionary process within the universe, the chaotic creation of religions will always remain whilst there are sentient beings, because religions tend to be formed through the desires of sentient beings within a given area and a set of circumstances, and these circumstances and areas are constantly evolving."

Michael smiles and replies: "therefore all religions must be chaotic if they were developed from chaos, because total order would mean that everything was predictable!"

Pingala looks at the darkening skies and then she says: "although most religions will accept that order came from chaos, most religions do not wish to explore the possibilities that lie within chaos; any further than they have in their teachings, because chaos shows how unordered the world and the universe actually is, for example; the scientific knowledge that surround the universe is also constantly changing, because of the constant changes within the universe! Therefore we must realise that if the universe is constantly changing, there is no true order within the universe, because if something is constantly changing there is no end to its changes, and if there is no end to its changes; there can be no way of predicting the final outcome, because there is no finality in something that lasts forever!"

Merlin sits next to Pingala, smiles at her and then he says: "with there being no finality in the chaotic universe, this becomes problematic within many religions, because, many religions believe that their Divine brought order to the universe, and therefore; some religions try to belittle and even outlaw some philosophical and scientific theories. This becomes problematic, because whilst the sentient beings are being dictated to; they will be harbouring feelings of rebellion!

With the feelings of rebellion being harboured within the human being, the chaotic nature of such a being becomes obvious!"

Pallas sits cross legged in front of Pingala and then Pallas replies: "the chaos that is created by such beings is partly due to many of the human race being so willing to follow the practises of those that are taught to them! Therefore we should realise that the teachings within many fields become dogmatic, and unresearched until some of those beings become disillusioned with their teachings!"

Lug smiles and replies: "that disillusion will come from the nature of the human being, because in being created from chaos the human being will be indidividualistic, and in being individualistic there will always be some human beings that will disagree with some of their teachings! Therefore there will always be chaotic beings whilst there is a search for the knowledge that is unattainable through some religions, for example; in The Spider of the Qur'An (62) it is written that:

62 Allah enlarges the sustenance (which he gives) to whichever of His servants He pleases: and He (similarly) grants by (strict) measure (as he pleases): for Allah has full knowledge of all things.[48]

Which of course we know cannot be so if it is immortal, because it would mean that there is complete order within the world, and if there was complete order; there would be no use for science or other religions, because there would only be the one religion according to this assumption."

Morrighan sits next to Pallas and then Morrighan replies: "that begins to make evident one of the major problems with some religions, which is; the problem of being able to justify complete order when the chaotic nature of the beings within the universe make evident the complete opposite of any assumption of complete knowledge, because if there is complete knowledge there is complete order—and that is not so! Therefore I suggest that any religion that claims there is total knowledge within any of its beings; is either misinterpreting its own scripts or it is constructed around ancient beliefs that its followers are not willing to evolve from. But that—unwillingness to evolve—in itself is foolishness, because in being unwilling to evolve they are creating chaos within their own order, because dogmatic beliefs cause conflict and wars, because there will always be those who

---

[48] The Holy Qur'An p334 translated by Abdullah Yusuf Ali, Wordsworth Editions Limited 2000

are willing to evolve, and will not be willing to be held in check by ancient beliefs that have been outdated by scientific and philosophical understanding."

Pallas winks at Morrighan as she passes her the biscuits and then she replies: "the chaos that is created by such religions; is the chaos that comes from war and the misunderstanding of natural events. These wars and the misunderstandings of natural events are usually used as a payback to the human race, and this payback is meant to be created because of the displeasing actions of certain factions of the human race upon their [so-called] Divine."

Michael smiles at Pallas sits next to Morrighan and then he says: "the non realization of the chaos that is caused by war and natural events, can only occur within the religions that believe their Divine is all knowing, because such religions think that their all knowing deity or deities; is or are punishing the factions of the human race that do not agree with their ideals. Therefore such religions do not have the will to cause any kind of chaos that might affect their beliefs through scientific and philosophical research!"

Morrighan offers Michael the biscuits and then she says: "when the understanding of chaos is held in check; the only possible outcome can be unknown chaos and when chaos is unknown it can quite easily be made into events that are supposed to come from an outside agent. Therefore we should realise that the natural events and the wars that are supposedly created by a unsatisfied deity; are being used as a means of enslaving the mind and the bodies of races and religions that are not ready to succumb to beliefs that are not of their own making! This becomes problematic for many scientific and philosophical societies, because in not being willing to succumb to ancient beliefs; they become willing to fight for the survival of their ideals, and hence chaos begins–within the war that is created by the non believers of chaotic nature!"

Demeter sits next to Pingala and then Demeter says: "the non believers of the chaotic nature of the universe tend to contradict themselves, because order comes from chaos, and once order has been established there is still chaos that is present within the universe, for example; if the Divine create order from the chaos and then the Divine create a chaotic situation [chaos is still present] and this type of situation is made evident in the Bible [Genesis 1, 1-2]:

In the beginning God created the heaven and the earth. And the earth was without form, and void; and darkness was upon the face of the deep.
And later in Genesis [8, 18-24] it is said that:

And the flood was forty days upon the earth; and the waters increased, and bear up the ark, and it was lift up above the earth. And the waters prevailed and increased greatly upon the earth; and the ark went upon the face of the waters. And the waters prevailed exceedingly upon the earth; and all the high hills, that were under the whole heaven were covered. Fifteen cubits upward did the waters prevail; and the mountains were covered. And all the flesh that moved upon the earth, both of fowl, and of cattle, and of beast, and of every creeping thing that creeps upon the earth, and every man: all in whose nostrils was the breath of life, of all that was within the dry land, died. And every living substance was destroyed which was upon the face of the ground, both man, and cattle, and the creeping things, and the fowl of the heaven and they were destroyed from the earth: and Noah only remained alive, and they that went with him within the ark. And the waters prevailed upon the earth a hundred and fifty days.

Hence it becomes obvious that the one who created order also created chaos, because if any kind of true order was present there would have been no need for such a destructive force as the flood.

Pingala smiles and says: "any kind of flood that was seen to destroy the world of the people it was in would be seen to encompass the whole world, but geological evidence tells us otherwise, and we know that it would not have been possible for this to happen at that time. But in realizing this we must also realise that this evidence shows the chaotic world that weather and water can create!"

Merlin gets out a flask of coffee, offers it around and then he says: "water is one of the many chaotic things upon the planet and the use of water as a destructive force that is brought to bear upon mankind for its sins is a plausible way of explaining the unexplained. Therefore we should begin to realise; that anything that could be seen as part of the chaotic universe could also be used to explain the wrath of the Divine."

Morrighan smiles and replies: "any kind of unforeseen and natural event can be made to fit the wrath of the Divine if a particular religion wishes to use an act of chaos in such a way, but when they do use it in such a way they should–but are not willing to–understand that their Divine is chaotic if it creates chaos!"

Michael smiles and says: "any religion that believes it can cause perfect order through chaotic means is badly mistaken, because all that is within the evolutionary process comes from chaotic origins. Therefore we must realise that chaos is only chaos until it is put into some kind of order, which is problematic, because something that is created order can recreate chaos, for example; the will of each individual is its own will and is not confined to the will of other individuals; unless it wishes to be so or is forced to be so!"

Lug smiles and says: "the order that is supposedly within most religions can be the creator of much chaos, because if the individual has free will; this will create chaos when different ideals collide and in many circumstances war will ensue. Therefore the religions that come from the free will of the individuals are in effect–the creators of chaos through their ideals of order!"

Morrighan smiles and replies: "the ideals that create order are meant to be made by Divine that are actually chaotic in the construction of their own belief systems, for example; many religions cannot seem to realise that order can only come to be when chaos is put into order, and the previous example of Demeter; showed the chaos that was created within a supposed great flood that was created by their One-God."

Demeter winks at Morrighan and then she replies: "there are many other instances within religions that show the chaotic nature of many of their Divine beings; without realizing that they are showing the truly unordered form that is within the universe and its creations, for example; in the Rig Veda (X, In the beginning) it shows chaos, but does not show any realization of this chaos:

1Then neither being or not being was, not atmosphere, not firmament nor what is beyond.

What did it encompass? Where? In whose protection? What was water, the deep, unfathomable?

2 Neither death nor immortality was there then, No sign of night or day.

That One breathed, windless, by its own energy: Nought else existed then.

3 In the beginning was darkness swathed in darkness; all this was unmanifested water.

Whatever was that One, coming into being, Hidden by the void, was generated by the power of heat.

4 In the beginning this [One] evolved, became desire, first seed in mind.

Wise seers, searching within their hearts, found the bond of Being within Not-being.

5 Their cord was extended athwart: Was there a below? Was there an above?

Casters of seed there were, and powers; beneath was energy, above was impulse.

6 Who knows truly? Who can here declare it? Whence it was born, whence is this emanation.

By the emanation of the Gods only later [came to be].

Who then knows whence it has arisen?

7 Whence this emanation had arisen, whether [God] disposed it, or whether he did not,—only he who is its overseer in the highest heaven knows.

[He only knows], or perhaps he does not know![49]

This makes evident the non realization of chaotic realms, because it shows a creation that is not fully understood, and in not being fully understood certain types of realization are lost."

Sankara smiles at Demeter and then he says: "it is true that the realization of chaos is not made truly evident in these writings. But these writings do give a reference to a type of chaos, because it realises that there is an unknown and possibly an unknowable part of the creation of the knowledge of the universe. Therefore we can assume that chaos can derive from the unknown, and if chaos can derive from the unknown, chaos can then be realised. But this can be problematic in a religion that shows that the object of our life is to understand the Self

---

[49] Hindu scripture p13,14 R. C. Zaehner, David Campbell publishers Ltd 1992.

and become a part of their Divine, which is made evident in the Bhagavad-Gita (IV) where it is said:

6 Unborn am I, changeless is myself; of all contingent beings I am the Lord! Yet by my creative energy I consort with nature–which is mine–and come to be [in time].

7 For whenever the law of righteousness withers away, and lawlessness raises its head, then do I generate myself on earth.

8 For the protection of the good, for the destruction of evildoers, for the setting up of righteousness, I come into being, age after age.

9 Who knows my Godly birth or mode of operation?
Thus as they really are, he, his body left behind, is never born again:
He comes to Me.

10 Many are they who, passion, fear and anger spent, inhere in Me, making Me their sanctuary:
Made pure by wisdom and hard penances, they come [to share in] the manner of my being.

11 In whatsoever way [devoted] men approach Me, in that same way do I return their love.

Whatever their occupation and wherever they may be, men follow the path I trace.[50]

Because of this way of thought everything that appears chaotic in this script can be seen to go back to the order of the original being, but what is also being made evident is that there is more than one route to the original being and if there is more than one route, the chaotic nature of there being more than one route shows that chaos is within the original being!"

Morrighan smiles and says: it is quite easy to make evident the fact that any religion has chaos within its scriptures–whether it is intended or not–, because religions need a type of chaos for their explanation of wars and unexplained natural events that are within their scriptures, for example; a chaotic event, such as a flood; could be seen to be an act of their Divinities disapproval of the non conformist or chaotic attitudes of non believers and those who break the holy law!"

Merlin draws a bag of fruit from his rucksack takes an apple, passes it to Pingala and then he says: "the effects of chaos are within all religions and their scripts, but they are–mostly–not

---

[50] Hindu scriptures, R. C. Zaehner p335 David Campbell publishers Ltd 1992

realised as chaos. Therefore the chaotic acts of religions will remain until all religions agree upon one scripture, but that is not very likely, and even if it did happen they would all need to realise that the consequences of the chaotic universe; is that the universe is chaotic.

After taking and finishing a bite from an apple, Pingala says: "chaos will then become a major problem for most of religion, because most religions want to believe in the perfect order that their Divine can give them, and if there is no perfect order there is always uncertainty and chaos, but in saying this I must make evident that chaos and uncertainty are not always related, because we can be certain of something that is chaotic and this something does not have to relate to uncertainty, for example; if enough of the same type of triangles are made into a square or oblong the patterns would become chaotic in their appearance. Therefore we should begin to realise that there can become chaos within certainty and if there can become chaos within certainty, there are [probably] no realms that are not open to the chaos of the universe!"

Pallas smiles and catches the apple that Pingala has thrown toward her and then Pallas says: "chaos can appear to be present in many situations that come from what seems to be an ordered certainty. But the ordered certainty of religion is only metaphysically realistic and therefore, religion is open to all types of chaos that are present within its theories."

Morrighan finishes a piece of the pear that Merlin has given to her and then she says: "chaos and metaphysics are both theoretical terms that can come from non empirical evidence, but chaos can also become evident by empirical means, for example; a bird builds a nest and that nest appears chaotic in its construction, but the nest would not have been constructed; without the orderly actions in which the bird placed the materials."

Gaia takes another apple and then she says: "chaos is evident in many natural theories that are supported by empirical evidence, but religion has very little if no empirical evidence to support their beliefs. Therefore we must realise that the chaos within most religions is created by the natural world and by the wish–of some religions–to dominate the whole world, and therefore; some of the religions do not accept the chaotic natural world for what it really is, and in being so negligent they use the natural chaos to show the dissatisfaction of their Divine–on those that have offended it; or on those with a less powerful Divine being; or those that are considered to be in least favour of their Divine in a war."

Lug smiles and says: "there are many acts in many myths that can be put down to nature or the will of the Divine and if these acts are seen as both [which they are not], the will of the Divine would be seen to be chaotic and unpredictable and this type of theory would lead to the obvious imperfection of the Divine. Which becomes problematic, because there are some religions that believe their Divine is perfect [and as we have already shown this cannot be the case] in its entirety."

Michael smiles as Merlin passes him an orange and then Michael says: "chaos has many manifestations and because it has so many manifestations; anything that is considered chaotic cannot be considered perfect if it is not in total control of what it has–supposedly–created and therefore, the ideals that surround the perfection of a Divine being that is not totally in control are nonsensical, because imperfection is created by chaos [unless you consider chaos to be the only true perfection], because if everything has chaotic possibilities the only true perfection is the realization that everything comes from chaos, and in coming from chaos must be partly chaotic for any type of order to survive."

Morrighan finishes her pear and then she says: "chaos is very problematic for many religions, because it makes evident the unpredictability that is within the universe, and where there is unpredictability there is imperfection. Of course if there is imperfection there can be no perfect creator, because a perfect creator could only create perfection; unless the creator is part chaos in itself and if it realises it is part chaos; it would realise its own imperfection and have no reason to think of itself as perfect. Hence we must begin to realise that chaos cannot be verified by the religions that believe in the perfection of their Divine, because such religions believe the laws and ethics that their Divine has 'supposedly' given to them! With that type of reasoning the religions that believe in the perfection of their

Divine cannot allow chaos theory into their beliefs, because chaos theory shows the unpredictability within the universe, and if their Divine is perfect then it would know all that has happened and is going to happen; which means that chaos cannot and could not ever have existed. But this type of reasoning is problematic, because if infinity and immortality exist; there is no way that you can ever totally predict what is infinite, because to predict all that will happen in infinity would require an end point to infinity and without an end point there can be no total knowledge of something, and therefore; the total knowledge of infinity can never happen, because without an end there is no end to the future knowledge. Therefore infinity defeats the idea of a perfect knowledge within a [so-called] perfect being, and once the idea of a perfect knowledge are defeated; chaos reigns and chaos becomes the beginning, before order can be realised."

Sankara winks at Morrighan, smiles and then he says: "infinity and chaos [as Morrighan has made evident] must coexist, because all within infinity cannot be predicted if it has no end point and—as far as we know—time goes on whether there is anyone around to realise it or not."

Pallas gets some grapes from her rucksack, finishes some and passes them to Morrighan and then Pallas says; "trying to define infinity is problematic in itself, because if something is infinite it cannot have a beginning and if there is no beginning; how can it come into existence in the first place, and also if it has no idea of from where it came it must have a lack of that aspect of knowledge, and therefore; it cannot know everything; and if it cannot know everything; it has a certain aspect within itself that is unpredictable, imprecise, unperfected and chaotic!"

Merlin smiles as Morrighan passes on the grapes to him and then he says: "that would explain why the infinite ideals that surround the Divine are full of problems, but it does not explain how chaos came to be, and where the elements that created the chaotic universe came from—that is if there can ever be such a knowledge available to the Divine or the human race!"

Morrighan finishes her grapes and then she says: "perhaps there is never going to be any complete definition of infinity, because infinity is infinite and if something is

infinite it has infinite paths, and in having infinite paths, the knowledge of such paths can never be complete, because they are infinite! Therefore the only complete part of the knowledge of infinity is to realise that it is infinite, and in being infinite, we can never predict all its future events or circumstances, and therefore infinity is chaotic!"

Gaia finishes some of the grapes that Merlin had passed her and then she says: "this makes evident the realization that if the Divine are infinite in their lifespan; they are open to the chaos that is created by the imperfect knowledge of events that cannot be foreseen, because of the finite nature that knowledge requires for it to know all future events, because if all is known there must be an end point to all knowledge and if there is an end point to all knowledge [which includes the infinite numbers that are inevitable]; knowledge would be finite and infinity could not actually exist!"

Michael eats some of the grapes that Gaia has passed on to him and then he replies: "the chaotic nature of knowledge makes evident; that knowledge cannot be finite and if knowledge is not finite; it would also be chaotic in its origins and throughout all of its future discoveries, because order and precision can only be made when order and precision have gone past the original chaotic process, for example; the discovery of the means by which weather patterns are created upon the planet, brings part of the weather systems into an understanding; that was brought about through an orderly process, but when these weather systems originate is still down to speculation and remains chaotic in its predictability!"

Demeter eats one of the grapes that Michael has passed to her and then she says: "infinite knowledge cannot ever be available, because as we have made evident; predictability comes through knowledge that is finite, and therefore; if any being or thing knows all that is to know and all that there ever will be to know; this being or thing knows that the predictability that is gained by knowledge is finite and all will be predicted, and become predictable at some stage in time! But that is highly unlikely, because the knowledge that is gained by any being has its bounds, for example; the infinite largeness of numbers: 987,123,765,123,300,300,900,456,289,789,677,111,339,456,124,9

67,254,170,562,969,179,987,321,419,361…and forever this random sequence of numbers can go on as can many other sequences of numbers."

Lug smiles as Demeter passes him the grapes and then he says: "it is probable that the complete realization of infinity is beyond the grasp of anything, because—as we have already made evident—in being infinite, infinities end result is not predictable or realizable, because infinity can have no end, because it is endless and in being endless there will be endless chaotic creations that will appear to an endless being or thing."

Morrighan points to a hare and then she says: "therefore we must realise that the religion or religions that believe their Divine is all knowing must be mistaken if their Divine is immortal and timeless, because if it is timeless it cannot predict all that will happen in a time that is infinite!"

Michael smiles and asks: "is it possible that the endless Divine of some religions could be all knowing if they created all that is?"

Morrighan smiles and replies: "if the Divine created all that is out of chaos or out of pure energy; the Divine created something out of something within a span of time, and that span of time is always historical in its creations, because all creations come from something within a past event—even if the past event is only a thought it is still a past event! Therefore the prediction of future events becomes uncertain, because until the thought of a future event appears we cannot know of the future event, and once that thought has appeared that thought is historical and therefore, that thought of the future event becomes history. This historical thought becomes problematic, because the event it predicts has not yet happened and may not happen, and if it does not happen within a given time span; the time span can be extended until something similar happens; that a religion could use as evidence of its predictive powers.

Therefore the infinity of time can be used to suggest that something created all that is, because if we manipulate evidence to suit our means within time, all our predictions are likely to come true at some stage, for example; science tells us that the world will at some stage become uninhabitable, because of the processes that involve the sun, but this could also be seen as an act of the Divine in a far distant future, and those that are able to escape the planet–through science–would probably have religions within them that have adopted science to fulfil their prophecies."

Pingala smiles and replies: "the nature of religion is becoming–evidently–chaotic in its approach to science, because religion will pick up any scientific discovery that is applicable to its beliefs in its time, but most religions [especially those of the One-God kind] are just as willing to dismiss and try to outlaw scientific discoveries and theories that go against their beliefs. This attitude can become chaotic and problematic for religions, because when science is proved right and some of their scriptures are proved wrong, they need ways to get around these problems. And the only way to do this is to manipulate their scriptures in such a way that they are seen to be correct!"

Michael smiles and says: "this chaotic nature can only apply when people are bound by their religious beliefs, but there are so many religious beliefs, that the many religions have many scriptures and are in themselves chaotic, because when they believe their religions are undeniable, they lose the realization that there are so many differences within them; that they are more than likely to be wrong in some aspects of their beliefs, for example; the previously discussed aspects of infinity show the problems and the unrealistic ideals, that are associated with any kind of Divine that is supposed to know all there is to know!"

Pallas smiles and replies: "the issues that surround infinity and chaos have been made evident and in being made evident they have shown the all knowing aspects of any religions Divine; to be incorrect, because infinity has to be chaotic, because if there was any all knowing principle there must be total predictability and in being total predictability, there would have to be an end point to infinity, because you cannot truly know the outcome of all events until you know all there is to know, and if you know all there is to know there is an end point of knowledge. Therefore we must realise that there can be no infinity if there is an end point to future knowledge, because to have an end point means that there is an end, and where there is an end in something there can be no infinity!"

Morrighan smiles and replies: "therefore we should also realise that the manipulation that I previously suggested; is not true knowledge—it is just manipulated situations to suit a desired event or events within a religious context and therefore, these manipulations become chaotic, because events cannot be manipulated until they have happened in physical reality or a thought process, for example, science tells us that it takes millions of years for light to travel from far away stars, but there are some religions that consider these facts to be works of the devil!"

Lug smiles and says: "anything that is considered to be outside the beliefs of some religions can be manipulated in ways that demonize one or more of the Divine, but chaos itself cannot be applicable to a demon or devil if it is truly realised [which it never will be by some religion], because order must come from some kind of original chaos, because we cannot realise order without chaos, for example; the ordered structure of a building could not happen until the disordered materials and work force are put into order [architects for the design, organisers for the collection of the materials and the labour force and so on]."

Gaia gets up, stretches, smiles and then she says: "any work—just like Lug has made evident—needs organisation for there to be a non chaotic end result, and this makes evident; that to get any kind of work in progress chaos is present in the beginning. Therefore the structure of religions must have come from chaos, because order is not present until the chaos that surrounded that order has been put into some kind of order!"

Morrighan smiles and says: "the order that surrounds religions has originated with the original misunderstandings of the chaotic events that are present in a misunderstood world. Therefore the original misunderstandings that are explained in many scientific theories can become chaotic in themselves, because the theories that show religions to be [as we have already made evident] mistaken cause chaos within the religions that are not willing to let their original scriptures evolve!"

Pallas gets up, walks alongside Gaia and then Pallas says: "the structure of religion is like the structure of a city—it originates through the ordering of chaos within beliefs and needs, but this order becomes disorder when it grows beyond the original ideals.

Although the original ideals are still in place and there is order within the structure, the order becomes disorganized and chaotic in parts, because larger quantities of free willed beings need greater control, and just like an expanding city, the chaotic probabilities increase as it expands, for example; in a large city a catastrophe can occur that does not effect one part of the city, whilst the catastrophe would affect another part of the city."

Merlin stands up and walks over to Gaia and then he says: "it is becoming evident that religions are chaotic in their structures, because [just like the city] religions fulfilled the needs of people, before science could explain some of the events that they put down to the displeasure of their Divine [plagues of locusts, storms, earthquakes, etc...], and these beliefs or needs are hard to expel when the majority of people are brainwashed by ancient beliefs that have been created by the chaos of misunderstanding!"

Sankara walks over to Merlin and then Sankara says: "because there are so many religions and these different religions have been constructed, around the ancient needs of the people that require an explanation of unexplainable events; the religions are bound to become chaotic in their construction, because chaos forms in many different ways in many different places! Therefore we should realise that the chaos that is within religious structure; starts with a need for order, and when that order that is associated within their religious beliefs; is shown–by science– to be a part of a universal chaos; the religions try to dismiss the scientific evidence and the chaos of the misunderstanding is created!"

Michael walks next to Pingala and then he asks: "when the chaos of misunderstanding is constructed within religious texts and beliefs; **why do these religions that see some science as works of their devil; not realise that they could be wrong and in being wrong they are creating chaos within their religion?**"

Pingala restarts the walk, smiles at Michael and then she says: **"that type of realization can become impossible in religions that are structured, in a manner that believes its**

original writings are sacrosanct and that there can be no other truths apart from their scriptures!"

Morrighan walks alongside Pingala, smiles at her and then Morrighan says: "ancient scriptures become difficult to break, when these writings have been part of and constructed the political ideals, that are in the land of the people that are dominated by their order. Therefore the scriptures are used as a means for the hierarchy of a belief to remain in power, and for their belief to dominate the peoples thought process in their work and pleasure. But that type of reasoning will become problematic, because in creating an order that is without essential scientific understanding; it creates an order that will bring much grief upon itself and others; when it applies science without the true realization of the scientific consequences of its actions, for example; there is a cult called the end timers that believe that all out nuclear war is the only way to cleanse the planet in the way that their God has made evident in revelations, for they believe that only the righteous will survive.

Personally I think that type of ethics is a madness that is inherent within some religions!"

Pingala smiles and says: "there are many cults that are willing to create much chaos upon the planet without scientific reasoning, and therefore the religions that create chaos in such a manner are without true reasoning abilities, and as such; they become dependent on their scriptures for guidance. But this has become and will continue to be problematic, because in being reliant they also become totally dependent and brainwashed by their ancient ideals, and in being so; they lose the free will that gives people their true reasoning abilities!"

Pallas and Gaia catch up to Pingala and Morrighan and then Pallas says: "many religions need to keep the free will in submission, because the free will causes much chaos within religious order if it is not made to be submissive, and this is due to the free will being able to contradict, and show some of many religions scriptures to be things that are part of natural cycles, and not due to the whim of their Divine. Therefore some religions try to keep people submissive, because when people are allowed to have the freedom of exploration they can find truths that are not open to the closed mind, and in finding such truths;

some religions lose their credibility amongst their own people, and once this is lost, they have to resort to means that outlaw and cause bewilderment amongst their own people if they are to survive!"

Merlin looks at Pallas, smiles and then he says: "once religion has managed to create bewilderment amongst its own population it has inadvertently created chaos! Therefore the religions that try to gain control through bewilderment and brainwashing are creating the chaos [within their ordered structure] that they are trying to dismiss, because once bewilderment sets in: chaos reigns!"

Lug smiles and says: "as we have already made evident: chaos is present before any ordered structure appears and therefore, the religions that try to deny chaos within their structure are losing the reality of their own origin, and in losing this reality; they become less efficient in the understanding of the realities that science and philosophy show them, because in thinking that you are right on a matter that has had no true exploration could and does; lead to events that are not necessarily for the benefit of the human race!"

Pallas smiles and says: "most of religions unbeneficial actions are created when religions clash and the beliefs of the opposing religions do not coincide, and therefore; the chaos that is created by such events is not understood as chaos, because it is though of as a holy mission or war and this has the blessing of their Divine. But this becomes problematic, because in the loss of the true realization of the chaos they have created, they become more chaotic in their unscientific works, because if you cannot truly explore the world in which you live, you become negligent on some very important matters, and this negligence will lead to much disharmony in the world that they reside."

Michael smiles and asks: "are there any predictable outcomes of the loss of harmony within the world, and is chaos a part of that harmony?"

Morrighan smiles and replies: "as we have already mentioned chaos is needed for order to be created, but order and harmony are separate issues, because [unlike order] something can be chaotic and harmonious at the same time, for example; the weather patterns of the planet are chaotic in their predictability, but they are in harmony with the planets creative abilities!"

Pallas smiles and says: "Mother Nature is chaotic within her creations, but most religions wish for there to be an ordered structure that created the chaos that is present in the universe, and therefore; the nature of most religions is to make the chaos in the universe; present only with the compliance of their Divine. But this is problematic, because chaos is present before order [as we have already made evident], and therefore, the Divine of any religion must be partly chaotic, because in creating chaos it must have chaos within itself and therefore all of the Divine are partly chaotic, because to form chaos means that they must have chaotic principles, and in so being; they must be part chaos; which leads to the possibility of all the Divine beings originating from chaos if they are the originators of chaotic actions and harmony."

Pingala smiles and says: "chaos can be considered harmonious, because chaos has no limits of its chaotic abilities, and in being limitless it is in harmony within itself, because chaos is chaotic and needs no other explanation or thought process than that of a being of understanding, and that being of understanding will understand the harmony within chaos when it truly understands chaotic creation, because chaos does not pretend to be anything else!"

Lug smiles and says: "it is religion that pretends there is a controlling factor in the chaos that is within the universe!"

Michael smiles and replies: "although order can only come into being after some aspect of chaos has become order; it should now be realised that chaos must be as infinite as the Divine if the Divine made any kind of order!"

Morrighan smiles, winks at Michael and then she says: "perhaps chaos is the true Divine and in being the true infinite Divine there would be many of the Divine, because chaos is not created from a single form or entity, and therefore; the Divine must have come from many parts and in coming from many parts; it is doubtful that the Divine would have been created in a singular form, because chaotic creation tends to make many forms in its creations, for example; there are many different species of bird that have varying types of survival techniques, and therefore; I suggest that it is extremely unlikely that there would be just one Divine being–unless chaos is considered as the only true Divine being!"

Michael smiles and asks: "is it possible that there could be only one Divine being that was created by chaos?"

Merlin smiles and says: "it is possible that chaos could have created only one Divine being, but this would still mean that if chaos is the creator of the one Divine being; there would in effect still be two Divine powers, because if chaos is the creator and it still remains; chaos would have to be Divine to create the Divine and in doing so; chaos and the one Divine being makes two of the Divine, and therefore; there can be no single Divine whilst chaos is the creator of a Divine being, because one and one makes two!"

Demeter grins and says: "what you are making evident; is that chaos and order are defined by two separate entities, but chaos could derive from the being that creates chaos to create order and therefore, the order would come before the chaos, because if there was just a single power before creation, order would exist, because it is singular and in its singularity it would have order."

Gaia smiles and says: "not every singular form is necessarily ordered in its actions or its being, because a form or power can be chaotic without it needing anything else, for example; lightening from a thunderstorm flows through what attracts it, and it has no say of what the form its attractor will be, and it will also; not have any say in the consequences of its actions."

Michael smiles and says: "if a single entity or power can be chaotic; it must be possible for chaos to be a singular creator of all, and therefore; the singular creator could be seen as a single God!"

Sankara points to a butterfly, flapping in the breeze and then he says: "that would seem possible, but there are many separate circumstances that are needed for the creation of a chaotic event–such as a lightning strike. Therefore the chaotic creations should be realised as events that are created through more than one circumstance, and in being so; the realities of chaos would–probably–be the creation of a non singular event, and if this is so; it becomes highly unlikely that chaos arose through any singular action, and therefore it is just as unlikely that chaotic creation happened through any singular event and/or creation!"

Gaia watches as the butterfly lands and then she says: "just like this butterfly effect in the chaos theory, which is:

A butterfly lazily flaps its wings in Brazil and this causes a movement in the air flow that creates a slightly bigger air current to move, and this effect gets larger and larger as the air currents increase in size over a period of time and distance; until a major event like a tornado is moved to an area that it would not have been if the butterfly had not flapped its wings in that past event.[51] This makes evident; that the effect of a small singular action; can create unforeseen events if it creates other actions within other unforeseen events, and these actions multiply in their severity over a period of time and distance, or in some cases; just time."

Merlin smiles and says: "what that is also making evident is that through minor incidents; major things can happen, but this also makes evident that without the other minor things accumulating; the major event would not have happened or happened in the place that it happened. Therefore the events that religions cause can be seen as chaotic, because many minor incidents that are caused by religions can culminate into a huge event, for example; a religion can cause chaos through a war and this chaos is caused by their beliefs that in some cases are completely outdated. But this chaos that is created by these outdated beliefs is due to the chaotic nature of their so called Divine being, which in having come from chaos or having created chaos is chaotic in itself!"

Lug smiles and says: "what is becoming evident is that any creator is chaotic, because order only begins after chaos has been put into order, and therefore; any creators ideals must have originated within chaotic form, because order comes from chaos, and this original chaos must remain in some aspects for creation to continue and evolve, because [just like the butterfly effect] chaos can recreate itself from small and simple events that happen throughout long periods!"

---

[51] Coincidences, Chaos and All That Math Jazz p21-22 Edward B. Burger & Michael Starbird, Norton Paperback 2006

Michael smiles and asks: "when chaos can start from minute events; does this mean that original chaos could have created the Divine or the universe from many minute events or circumstances that were in the origins chaotic?"

Pallas smiles and replies: "many minute circumstances within chaos could cause the creation of a Divine being; when they come together and create order and/or the universe through a huge chaotic event, but in this creation the original chaos may be replaced with a new order and a new type of chaotic form! This new type of chaotic form would replace the old chaos, because before the origination of order there would have been no ordered form whatsoever."

Sankara smiles and says: "this makes evident the possibility of chaos being the true Divine and if this is the truth; it would probably mean that there would be many Divine that would be created from many circumstances!"

Gaia smiles and replies: "perhaps the Mother Nature that we refer to as the creator of all is the original chaos that has evolved by its own chaotic means—just like humanity and its religions! Although in theorizing that way we must realise that most of humanities original religions are not willing to evolve, because they see themselves as the true order upon the planet and in this way they become the order that creates chaos; without the understanding that is needed to realise this!"

Merlin smiles and says: "what you are implying is that Mother Nature is actually the original Divine and the original chaos!"

Gaia winks at Merlin and then she says: "yes that is what I was implying and from that we must realise that chaos/Mother Nature would be the creator of all the other Divine beings that we refer to!"

Morrighan smiles and says: "just like in the natural world, where large events tend to start with a multitude of small events happening over a period of time; the creation of the Divine and/or the universe would start with a multitude of small events; that evolved over a period of chaotic time, and in evolving they created certain types of order, and these types of order created new types of chaotic forms!"

Michael smiles and asks: "are you suggesting that the ones we know or assume to be the Divine and self creating are actually created by chaos, and in being so; if they are self creating and as immortal as we assume them to be; would they still actually be chaos?"

Morrighan smiles and says: "yes and they would still be at least partly chaotic, because they would have evolved from chaos and in being self creating and evolving from chaos they became the order within chaos. But in becoming the order within chaos; they also became a new type of chaotic order, because of their self absorbing beliefs and the beliefs that they indoctrinate into the true chaotic order–which we refer to as humanity!"

Pallas smiles and says: "what is being made evident is that in creating order from chaos–chaos is being recreated within the order that has been created within it, and therefore the creator that arose from chaos actually creates chaos within the order it has created. This ordered creation of chaos is not realised as chaos by those that are trying to create order by the destruction of other orders, because all such orders realise; is the ideals that surround their actions and they think that they have no need for any realization that contradicts the ideals that are written within their scriptures. Therefore they have no conception of the chaos that they are creating and the chaos that is inherent in their beliefs and their ethical structures."

Pingala smiles and says: "if there are people that do not have the realization of the chaos that they create through their religions; it is probable that there are some of the Divine that were created by chaos; are unaware of their chaotic nature! This unawareness within some of the Divine shows the imperfection within the structure of the Divine, and this imperfection within the structure make chaos even more evident. Due to that reason we should begin to realise that chaos is hidden by some religions, because chaotic forms will always have originated with chaos and the only perfection that is available to them originates with chaos!"

Michael smiles and asks: am I right in supposing that this makes evident; that all Divine create chaos in trying to create order and there are some Divine beings that are unaware of their own chaotic nature?"

Demeter points to another butterfly and says: "just like the previously mentioned butterfly effect; it is probable that some of the Divine are not aware of the chaos that is within them and that is created through their actions! Therefore we should begin to realise that the Divine that are not totally aware of the consequences of their actions [just like the human race]; could also be unaware of the true reality of their self!"

Lug smiles and says: "the Divine that try to show themselves as perfect and in complete control–through their scriptures–cannot realise their true chaotic design, because the scriptures that have been written are written by the hand of man and that is known to be unreliable and chaotic in tits thought process. Therefore the scriptures that are written can be written by a being that does not realise the true chaotic nature of itself or it's Divine. This becomes problematic, because a being that is not willing to realise; that all that is written is not necessarily correct; will have problems relating to other scriptures or theories that disprove, and/or disagree with what they consider to be their holy word or their holy scripture!"

Gaia smiles and says: "the chaos that is created in scriptures is seen to be an attempt of a Divine being; to create perfection out of imperfection, but this is problematic, because perfection out of imperfection makes evident the chaos that was there in the beginning. Due to this, the religions that create such chaos or have it written in their scriptures, try to blame the origination of the imperfection on an evil being that creates chaos throughout the world, and therefore; chaos is seen as a corruption that is brought upon the human race by demons and/or a devil. This also becomes problematic, because–as we have already explained–chaos comes before order, and if chaos comes before order, the creator must be part chaos and in being part chaos it must have chaotic principles in itself for it to be able to create order."

Sankara smiles and says: "a religion that is not willing to accept that their God does not know all there is to know, cannot accept chaos as part of their God and part of their theology, because chaos shows unpredictability to be present, and if something is unpredictable there cannot be perfect order, because there is no imperfection in something that is perfect and chaos is full of imperfections in its creations!"

Michael smiles and asks: "that would mean that chaos would be the true creator of all, because there is order in a singularity and if chaos is the true beginning of all; would chaos be the true original creator?"

Sankara smiles and replies: "that is what becomes problematic for religions that believe in a singular creator, and that is; that a creator that has arisen from a chaotic form arises from a selection of many unordered circumstances, and as history has proven; these many circumstances create chaos in their attempts to create order and therefore, chaos has many unforeseen circumstances that are unpredictable, and this unpredictability; could not happen if there was perfect order, which makes evident that the idea of perfect order and predictability cannot be present in a creator! Therefore chaos would be the true creator, because for anything to exist there must have been separate and chaotic elements that arose before its orderly state began, and therefore; a singular entity that created the chaos for the beginning of any existence would have the knowledge of the chaotic principles that were needed for order to arise, and in realizing this; it would then realise that for chaos to begin; chaos must already be present within itself!"

Gaia winks at Sankara and then she says: "what we call Mother Nature is the true chaos that begins all creation, and in being so; that true chaos would have many variations, because chaotic creation is dependent on creating what appears to be ordered form from many particles and circumstances; some of which are not yet understood or [probably] have not been discovered."

Morrighan puts her hand on Merlin's shoulder, smiles and then she says: "perhaps everything did start with a single force that became chaotic when it split into an unknown quantity of particles and forces, but in doing so the creation still happened through chaos and the problem of how and where that singular force occurred; still comes into a question that has no answerable probability, for example; we know that something flapping in the air creates a wind current, but without that originator of the air current it would not be there!"

Michael taps Morrighan on the shoulder and then he asks: "does it always take a series of events to create a force?"

Morrighan smiles and replies: "within the natural world it seems to need a series of events to create weather patterns, earthquakes, volcanic eruptions, etc... But the circumstances or events that create a natural force can be reduced to a starting point in some cases, but this in itself becomes problematic, because the creation of a natural event starts with motion, which needs a force for the motion to begin; in other words motion creates motion and what starts that first motion to begin can only be another motion!"

Michael smiles and asks: "can a thought process begin a motion that was not originally there?"

Morrighan smiles and replies: "a thought process or a natural action–like the butterfly that flaps its wings–can create a motion or a force, but the thought process or natural action must come from somewhere and something has put that thought process or motion into action. Therefore the thought process and/or the natural action have been put into motion by something else and that something else must come from somewhere, because a thought process or a natural action is a type of motion in itself."

Michael smiles and asks: "is a thought process a movement or a force in itself; or is it just a thought that has no distinct movement until its thought is transferred into action?"

Merlin smiles and says "just as Morrighan has begun to make evident; thought processes start somewhere and that starting point begins with the motion of the thought processes, for example; the thought of hunger begins with the need or the wanting of food, which is a type of movement within the processes of the body of the individual."

Michael smiles and asks: "is it being suggested; that thought processes flow like water?"

Morrighan smiles and replies: "yes that is being suggested, because the motions of the bodies organs affect the mind, but the physical function of a body does not necessarily effect the thought process, for example; a mind that is concentrating on mathematical problems is looking for an answer that is not related to bodily functions or senses, and therefore; the mind or the thought process does not always relate to functions within the body of the individual, but it does need the brain to be functioning; for the understanding of the problem it wishes to solve!"

Gaia smiles and replies: "all the different parts and particles that make a physical being do not explain what consciousness actually is, but without a functioning body and brain the consciousness—as far as we are aware—has no means by which it can communicate to another physical being; without its physically living matter! Therefore the physical being that incorporates the conscious mind needs to be aware of the presence of other conscious beings in that physical state; for it to be able to communicate with them. But this becomes problematic when the conscious physical being tries to relate to a being that does not have any known physical form, such as; a God or the chaos from which all was created."

Pingala winks at Gaia and then Pingala says: "the consciousness of a God without physical form is hard to imagine, but if we notice the force of the wind in nature we must realise that there are forces that have no apparent physical form. Hence the realization of a conscious force that we cannot see or feel as a solid or fluid form [such as water or another physical being or solid form that is in motion] becomes more plausible."

Demeter smiles and says: "the forces that create a wind can be understood and explained in scientific terms, but a conscious force that creates all things cannot be truly explained or understood—that is if the creative force is actually conscious of its creations—by scientific means at this stage in time, because our understanding is limited by the need of its own evolutionary process, and therefore; the explanation of the emergence of the creative force of consciousness remains a mystery that is unsolved by present scientific and theoretical capabilities!"

Michael smiles and says: "perhaps consciousness is the true chaos and in being so; consciousness would be its own creator through its chaotic thought processes!"

Gaia smiles and says: "chaotic processes need some kind of force for their motion and that force does not need to be conscious of itself, but it is quite feasible that consciousness has always been the process by which chaotic form has been put into some kind of order, because without awareness or consciousness there would be no realization of chaos or anything else. Therefore we should begin to realise that the creation of consciousness; is not within the present capabilities of our understanding, because we are presently limited by the understanding that is available to our present and physical senses. Due to this the consciousness that we understand can only be explained by what has been taught to it in the present physical state, and therefore; the chaotic creation of consciousness cannot be proved or disproved."

Pallas smiles and says: "being unable to prove how the creation of consciousness emerged shows how problematic the world of creation is, because consciousness needs to have developed through some means that is not–as yet–truly understood. Of course this is hugely problematic, because any knowledge that is not presently available to our senses and our thought processes needs investigation, and at this time we do not have the methodology that is needed for such an investigation to begin!"

Sankara smiles and says: "a deep form of meditation would be needed for such an investigation to begin, but this in itself would be problematic, because meditation can lead to hallucination!"

Merlin smiles and replies: "perhaps that hallucination makes evident the creation of consciousness from chaos, because in becoming hallucinated the individual is not in true control of its own consciousness or its thought processes!"

Lug smiles and says: "hallucination is a chaotic creation of the consciousness, which can come through many forms–drugs, starvation, thirst etc… But meditation without any of the previously mentioned forms is the true creator of hallucination through the thought process. Although this may be true, this is problematic, because the creation of a hallucination through the thought forms can be seen as a willed or ordered creation, because if someone is meditating deeply enough they are in control of their meditation and the hallucination that is created whilst in this self induced trance!"

Morrighan winks at Lug and says: "the subconscious dream world is the world that we are not truly in control of, and therefore; the true chaos of the consciousness comes into our realization after we have had an unrelated dream whilst we were asleep.

The worlds that we create in our dream state can relate to things that have already happened, but they can also be of strange and unrelated topics, which can be seen as chaotic in their formation, because whilst we are in a deep sleep we have no control over them."

Pingala smiles and says: "the consciousness of the individual can be just as chaotic in the waking world, because there are many moments when people remember something that is totally unrelated to their present action or discussion, and this suggests that there is much chaos in the thought processes, which in turn could suggest that the creation of a thought form is created by chaos, and if we take this suggestion one step further; we could then assume that chaos and consciousness are one and the same!"

Michael smiles and says: "the Divine must have consciousness to be aware, and with this being so–the Divine and chaos would also be one and the same, or would they?"

Demeter winks at Michael and replies: "that would mean that the Divine and chaos are one and the same, but this becomes problematic, because the human race's consciousness has the same chaotic principles as that of the Divine!"

Pallas smiles and says: "that in itself is problematic, because in true chaotic process it would then be possible that with the Divine and Chaos being one and the same, and the human consciousness and chaos being one an the same; it becomes possible that within the chaotic universe the human race is as much Divine as the Divine, and in that chaos the human race has lost this realization."

Merlin smiles and says: "that is the problem with chaos in religion and that is why religion likes to have its strict rules and order within its scriptures, which need to hold back research and thinking if they are to have their perfection in their creation myths and legends. Therefore some religions must keep science and philosophy in check if they have ideals of perfection that are not able to be modified by present and future thought processes, which mean that the ideas of chaos being the original creator cannot be allowed by such religions."

Gaia winks at Pallas and then Gaia says: "the consciousness of man will need to be kept in check and have some methods disallowed or outlawed by the types of religion that have just been referred to, because the religions that need to set their Divine apart from mankind need to give their Divine qualities that are above the humans abilities, and when chaos becomes the originator of all consciousness it would become impossible for the Divine to have a consciousness and a conscience that is above that of the human being, because if chaos created consciousness and conscience then all consciousness and conscience is part chaos!"

Michael grins and asks: "could there be more than one type or level of conscience and consciousness that is created by chaos?"

Gaia smiles and says: "in the human race there is more than one type of conscience in separate individuals, but they are all conscious on the same level, because if they weren't one would be considered unconscious and therefore consciousness remains the same even if awareness does not!

I make the distinction between awareness and consciousness, because awareness is as dependent on knowledge as it is on consciousness, for example; we could not be aware of the weather outside where we were whilst we were unconscious, but we would also be unaware of the weather in a foreign country in which other woken people were aware of the weather whilst we were awake. Therefore awareness is dependent on knowledge whilst we are conscious!

Conscience on the other hand is totally individualistic which is unlike consciousness, and in being so conscience has many different types and levels."

Morrighan smiles and says: "that is problematic where religion is concerned, because with conscience being individualistic; it is possible that the conscience of a Divine being could be totally different and even below the conscience of the average human being. Therefore the theoretical ideals of a perfect Divine would be unfounded, because if the Divine has a conscience that is below our conscience, that Divine could never live up to our expectations! The inability to live up to these expectations would then lead to the realization that there is a possibility that this Divine being would be considered inferior to the human race!"

Michael smiles and asks: "if the conscience of the Divine was above that of humanity, would humanity be able to understand some of the reasoning behind the judgement of the Divine?"

Sankara smiles and replies: "if there is a conscience or level of consciousness that is greater than that of any of humanity; it would be above any level of understanding, and therefore; there would be some judgements and ideals that would be above our understanding at this present stage in time!"

Morrighan smiles and says: "that begins to make evident why chaos is so realistic within the present system of differentiating religions, and in greater understanding, we begin to realise that the different religions have different types of conscience that is indoctrinated within their beliefs. These beliefs that differ give different levels of understanding and this understanding also effects the conscience of the indidividualistic within these religions, for example; in some religions it would not effect the conscience of a person if they killed someone from another religion in the name of their God, but there are religions that do not believe that killing another is justified unless it is in self defence, which shows that some religions do differ in the ideals that affect their conscience."

Pingala winks at Morrighan and then she replies: "as you have made evident the conscience of an individual is incorporated within its beliefs [or within its lack of belief] that have been taught to it, but this becomes problematic for some religions, because there are many individuals that wish to explore outside the belief structure that they have been taught. Therefore the chaotic lifestyle of the human being becomes evident and this creates another problem for the religions that believe there is some kind of perfect order within the beliefs of their religion, because chaos is evident to those that will not be tied down by a belief structure that believes that it is incorruptible and without mistakes. This unforgiving nature of some of the human race can cause much chaos because in being so deterministic in its nature, it becomes problematic for those that are trying to break free from stubborn and outdated beliefs, and those who are determined to hold on to such outdated beliefs!"

Merlin taps Pingala on the shoulder and then he says: "this deterministic nature of humanity is what causes a lot of the chaos and conflict within the religions and races of mankind, and the main religion to cause controversy is the only religion that tries to find the truth without being indoctrinated by strict codes—and that religion is science.

Scientific exploration has upset many religions in its fact finding processes, but in upsetting many religions science has actually aided some of the religions it has upset."

Gaia smiles and says: "in being deterministic, the human race and its religions become chaotic, because individual determinism will lead to conflict, when the individuals have separate ideals that they are determined to make others become their own. This determinism becomes the cause of chaos and destruction within their species and throughout the natural world!"

Pallas puts her hand on Gaia's shoulder and then Pallas says: "most religions like to believe that they are the only religion that knows what they consider to be the true Divine. But this type of idea becomes problematic, because of the destruction it causes and its inability to realise that other Divine beings are as liable to exist as their own. This again becomes problematic, because when this realization is made evident the separate religions are more likely to go to war with each other, rather than sitting down and discussing the likelihood of both religions having some similarities in their beliefs and agreeing to disagree on certain matters!"

Lug smiles and replies: "that becomes hugely problematic for the religions that are not willing to accept evidence that tells them differently than their holy scriptures, because any evidence that is against some religions scriptures—as we have mentioned before—is seen as an illusion or as works of a devil or demon. Therefore the scientific exploration of chaos would be thought of as works of the devil or even the illusion that is created by misunderstanding, by some religions!"

Demeter winks at Morrighan and then she starts to conclude by saying: "religions always seem to try to find an excuse for the chaotic ideals that we have mentioned, but chaos in itself is probably the most misunderstood and misinterpreted of scientific theories, by the religions, and this would be due to most religions being unable to analyze and alter their own holy teachings, because of their determinism and their apparent–but not really necessary–need for a type of order that is only attainable by their ideas."

Morrighan smiles and concludes by saying: "those ideas have been shown to be false, because all evidence points to many religious beliefs causing chaos through their wars and their so called theories that go against the practical exploration of the natural world, infinity, and the universe; which leads to much destruction within the natural world, and the attempted destruction of exploratory science and philosophy; and where there is destruction there is chaos and therefore, we should now realise that religion is as much a creator of chaos as it is a creator of order. Of course this is not the type of belief and exploration that many religions would allow within their scriptures, because such a belief would mean that any religion that believed that it had a Divine being or beings that knew all there is to know was mistaken, because to know all would mean you must have an infinite knowledge and to have an infinite knowledge would mean that there is an end to infinity. That we know cannot be so because infinity has no ending!"

The firewood is gathered and the players sit in a circle around the newly created fire and the party begins…

9

PREDATORY RELIGIONS

After the food and dance the discussion begin
Gaia smiles and says: "religions that do not allow their scriptures or beliefs to evolve become predatory in their beliefs, because such religions tend to believe that other religions have no place in their world, and this type of attitude makes these religions believe they are superior to other religions."

Lug passes a cup of tea to Gaia and then he says: "predation is a part of most religions, but this predation is more virulent in the One-God religions, because their inability to accept other Gods and Goddesses means that they must destroy the other faiths that have these other Gods and Goddesses, because when they admit to other Gods and Goddesses their One-God becomes one of many and this loses them their superiority!"

Demeter takes a sip of her tea and then she says: "there are many points in the bible that show how vicious their predatory ideals are, for example; in Revelation (16, 1-2) of the New Testament it is said:

And I heard a great voice out of the temple saying to the seven angels: go your ways, and pour out the vials of the wrath of God upon the earth.

And the first went and poured out his vial upon the earth, and there fed a noisome and grievous sore upon the men which had the mark of the beast, and upon them which worshipped his image

This type of ideal is from a predatory belief that thinks that it is going to control all that is, and with such ideals the life of any kind of separate ideal must be destroyed to prove how right they are in their dictatorial belief structure."

Gaia stirs some honey into her tea and then she replies: "the structure that surrounds predatory beliefs comes from acts that are meant to show how powerful their Divine being is, and such structure make people believe that they are invincible, which is problematic for those who do not have this type of controlling principle in mind when they wish to explore the natural world and the universe by scientific means. Therefore the structure of such religions becomes warlike in their dictatorial principles!

War is the main ideal that is part of any religion that believes that it is the only true religion, because it must stamp its beliefs upon other religions and cultures that are not put into bondage by the belief that they are the only truth and that truth is undeniable in its theories!"

Sankara takes a sip of his tea and then he says: "such thought processes are designed to put the individual into a situation that is inescapable, but evolution will always create chaos in such a dogmatic belief structure, because evolution is a system that cannot be held in bondage for ever, because understanding evolves throughout all ages. Hence we must realise that the so called incorruptible and dogmatic belief structures of some religions become undesirable by many other cultures and religions, and therefore; the war process begins and takes upon many forms, for example; the witch trials of past centuries and the terrorist acts of the present century are all part of the predatory religions war machine! This war machine evolves in its devices, but this war machine does not allow its belief structure to evolve, because this war machine has only one purpose and that purpose is to convert or destroy everyone that does not hold its ancient and dogmatic beliefs!"

Pingala winks at Sankara and then she says: "there are many ancient religions with Gods and Goddesses of war, but many of those religions did not have holy wars, because the wars that they had were usually about land, power, and wealth rather than in the name of their Divine, for example; the Romans used to incorporate the Gods and Goddesses of other faiths into their society when they had taken over another race!"

Merlin sips at his tea and then he says: "as we have begun to make evident the predatory religions seem to have–mainly– developed from the emergence of the One-God religions, and I suggest that this predatory ideal has emerged from the corruptible attributes of total power, because when such an ideal of power is put upon a singular person it inevitably corrupts them, just like the many Caesars of the Roman empire!"

Michael smiles and says: "Holy wars and the wars that emerge from a religion are inevitable when conflicting ideals become part of the same culture or are brought into a culture by a neighbouring culture. This neighbouring and cultural warlike manner has been around before the One-God cultures emerged, but the warlike ideals of the One-God cultures have spread, and in spreading; they have made many different cults within their ideals; and when these separate cults have become part of the same culture–of which they separate themselves from–they cause much conflict within their own religion and the chaos of war begins."

Morrighan sips at her tea and then she says: "that shows that the One-God religion is actually evolving into separate cults, and within these cults; separate theologies can emerge from the same scriptures, because there will be some cults that will take and hold onto the original scriptures as the true word and law of the universe, but there will be others that will explore the original scriptures and make new theories out of the old scriptures. This becomes problematic for the beliefs of those that are not willing to evolve and–as we have just made evident–conflicts will occur when differentiating ideals become part of the same culture!"

Merlin smiles and says: "the One-God cultures have fought between themselves for many centuries, but in their origins they were the targets of much larger cultures, and as the One-God cultures managed to expand through the manipulation of other cultures they became more powerful, and the prey evolved into the predator!"

Lug stirs some of Gaia's honey into his tea and then he says: "conflicting ideals within religion–especially the One-God religions–seem to cause many wars [these wars are not only wars in the physical sense they can be wars in the emotional and mental sense as well] amongst many peoples, for example; there is at least one of the Christian cults that goes completely against idolism, which includes the idols that are of their Christ!"

Michael smiles and asks: "would this type of behaviour and ethics also be considered as predatory as the more physical cultures that take up arms and go to war?"

Morrighan smiles and replies: "any religion that tries to control the mind and take over from another culture can be seen as a predatory religion, because it is attempting to destroy other beliefs; to gain ground, and to establish control over a population by fear tactics, and therefore; that type of religion can be seen as predatory, because its aim is for the outright control of the population by the obliteration of other beliefs!"

Gaia smiles and says: that becomes problematic, because there are many scientific theories that emerge that–in a sense– create a new type of religion, and in doing so there are certain aspects of science that religion tries to predate upon, because science will predate upon any religion that is dogmatic in its belief structure! Therefore we must begin to realise that certain aspects of science can turn the predatory religions into the prey! This becomes very disturbing for the predatory religions, and in being so disturbing; the predatory religions try to confine and destroy the scientific understanding that turns them into the prey, which causes predator to turn upon predator."

Lug takes another sip of his tea and then he says: "true science is probably the ultimate predator of religions, because true science and/or philosophy does not care what belief structures it destroys in its search for the understanding of universal truths. This type of action can become intolerable for the religions that are unwilling to evolve, and this intolerance leads to such religions; attempting to hide and destroy the evidence that true science has uncovered in its exploration for universal truths, and the understanding that comes from such truths.

The biggest problem that religion has with true science is that–unlike all the other predatory religions–true science is not afraid of admitting its mistakes and learning from such mistakes."

Sankara finishes his tea and then he says: "predatory religions of a non scientific means are unable to admit to their mistakes, because they believe that their actions are aided by their Divine, and in being so aided they believe that their Divine is the true ruler of all that is, which becomes problematic when these religions–that are so dogmatic in their beliefs–are confronted by truths that are not seen as truths are made evident by other means!"

Pallas takes some biscuits out of her rucksack, passes them round and then she says: "predatory religions depend upon their intolerance for their brainwashing techniques. Such techniques are used for the spread of fear into a population that has other ideals that they cannot comprehend and understand, because their intolerance of other religions makes them believe that they are the only ones that have the truth of creation, and in being so sure of their scriptures; they cannot allow themselves or others; the freedom of the exploratory sciences, because such sciences [and in some cases other religions] will conflict with their beliefs! That becomes undesirable for the dogmatic religions, because the conflict that is caused by some scientific principles is hard to permanently destroy and hide whilst there is free will. Therefore the dogmatic religions that try to hold back scientific exploration and truth tell many lies and untruths to their followers, which in itself becomes problematic, because some lies that are told need further lies to keep the cover up in place, and this type of behaviour is actually against their own beliefs.

Merlin finishes his biscuit and then he replies: "all predatory religions depend on lies to protect their scriptures from other religions, and mainly from the scientific discoveries that are made that conflict with their religious theories and scriptures. This causes many kinds of conflict within their own faiths, and these conflicts can then be used by some religions as acts of evil that are created by their devils and/or demons, which helps to spread fear amongst the general population. But in spreading fear in such a way, the general population will have those amongst them that are not convinced by the tricks of such religions, and this type of person carries on the exploration and the theories of those that conflict with the religions ideals."

Demeter passes a bag of fruit around and then she says: "all conflict starts with opposing ideals, but some conflicts can be avoided if there is compromise, but this becomes impossible for the dogmatic and predatory religions, because those that are predatory and dogmatic have no ideals that would let them sway from their chosen path."

Morrighan takes a pear and then she says: "people are coerced into the ideals of the predatory religions by promises of superiority over other religions, and this superiority becomes predatory in its ideology, because its ideology has no room for other religions in its structure. Therefore we should understand that the One-God religions become the main predator in the religious fields!"

Merlin takes a bite from his pear, finishes it and then he says: "when it is realised that the coercion of such religions causes predation; some of the people that realise this become dissatisfied with the religion that has coerced them into such a belief structure, and these people tend to go against some of the regulations that are put down in such a structure. This can become unfortunate for such people, because the predatory religions try to wipe them out, and in doing so; these predatory religions use many tactics [most of which we have discussed earlier] to dissuade other people from the ideas of those that have strayed from their coercive methods."

Gaia finishes one of her grapes and then she says: "predation within religion relies upon coercion for some of its conversions, but coercion is only possible when the people that are being coerced are willing to become converted into the predatory religion. Therefore we must realise that the ones that cannot be coerced into such religions need to be outcast or destroyed for the predatory religion to reach its goal, for example in Revelation (22, 18-19) in the Bible it is said that:

For I testify unto every man that hears the words of the prophecy of this book; if any man shall add unto these things, God shall add unto him the plagues that are written in this book: and if any man shall take away from the words of the book of this prophecy, God shall take away his part out of the book of life, and out of the holy city, and from the things which are written in this book.

These few words can be used in so many different ways; for the dissolution of scientific discovery and for the destruction of other religions ideals!"

Michael gets an apple out of the bag and then he says: "the aim of such scripts can be used in the way Gaia has described, because science can take many ideas away from the bible and replace them with new ideas and truths, but such scriptures have been used for the idea that this God's word is perfect and final! This becomes problematic for many other cultures that wish to add their knowledge to such a book, because if you are not allowed to change something you are held to a system or belief that could be wrong and in being wrong; it could be creating much more harm than the good it is supposed to produce!"

Pingala finishes a grape and then she says: "that is the problem with predatory religions and that is: the predatory religions do not realise that they are predating and just like any predator; controls are needed for the predators survival, because once the predation of other species has ceased through over predation; the only thing that the predator can turn upon is itself!"

Lug finishes a pear and then he says: "perhaps that is one of the reasons why the One-God faiths have turned upon each other and split into many cults that have different ideals of the same book! History shows this, and that there are many instances where the One-God faiths have come into a war, because one cult cannot agree with the other, and this makes evident the fact that the predator preys upon itself! Therefore we should begin to realise that the predatory nature of the One-God religions could wipe themselves out through their misunderstandings that have been created by their unwillingness to evolve their theories."

Pallas smiles and says: "the predatory religions need to firstly realise that they are predatory and then they need to realise that in being predatory a predator needs prey for its survival. But this is problematic for the predatory religions, because they do not see themselves as a predator, because they believe that they are just in their actions and their actions are in the name of their God, and in being so; they believe that their actions are to destroy what they consider to be evil and against the will of their God, and therefore; they do not realise that they are a predator!"

Michael finishes his apple and then he asks: "if they do not realise they are predators would they be able to realise the consequences of their actions?"

Sankara finishes a piece of his orange and then he says: "if a religion does not realise what it actually is, and if it has such strict codes that it does not allow true philosophy and/or science to evolve its scriptures; it has no means by which it can consider itself as predatory! Therefore we should begin to realise that the predatory religions are just like natural predators, because natural predators predate for their food without thinking of the consequences of their actions, because their actions are needed for their own survival. These types of actions should be understood to be part of a natural cycle, but the predatory religions that are adamant in their ancient scriptural beliefs and understanding are actually creating a means by which they could wipe themselves out, because in being unwilling to evolve they are losing the means by which they can subsist if their prey evolves into a predator that is capable of extinguishing them completely."

Demeter finishes one of her strawberries and says: "science is the latest and most evolutionary of the predatory religions, but science can become just as self destructive as any of the predatory religions, because science is rarely realised as a religion, and therefore; it is seen as a means to an end in many cultures and religious circles. This is hugely problematic, because science is accepted only in parts by most religions, for example; some of medical science and the tools of war are some of the scientific things that religions allow within their order, but the parts of science that show the need for their scriptures to evolve within the latest understanding of the natural world and the universe are shunned, because it shows imperfections within! With this problem another problem arises, and that is the problem that is created when part of a scientific discovery is accepted by a religion; that has no wish to understand the consequences of the usage of such a scientific discovery!"

Pallas smiles and says: "in the natural world the predator, predates for its own survival, but religions predate on one another in such a way that a singular or part of their survival can become a necessary loss for the survival of their cause. Therefore we should realise that the loss of some of their own culture can be considered an acceptable loss for their cause. But this type of loss is not a natural predation, because the people that are lost in wars defending their religion are lost through un-natural means!"

Lug starts to brew some more tea and then he says: "beliefs are constructed around ideals of superiority, for example; in Revelation it refers to the One-God taking over the world and becoming the most superior being of this planet. But this is problematic, because that type of superiority needs mass destruction, and such a destructive ideology shows the dictatorial ideals of a religion that thinks of itself as superior to all other religions and cultures upon the planet, which is un-natural, because no natural predator tries to take over the world in its attempt to survive!"

Michael smiles and asks: "does this mean that the predatory religions are in some ways un-natural?"

Morrighan watches Lug carefully preparing the tea and then she says: "a lot of the predatory religions appear to be un-natural in their approach to the world, but they have grown up within nature without the ability to realise what they are doing is against natural ethics! Therefore it is quite reasonable to think of such practices as un-natural, because when all a religion thinks about is the next coming of its Lord–for the salvation of its people–it does not tend to care about the consequences of its actions upon the natural world, and therefore its beliefs should be realised to be un-natural!"

Gaia smiles and says: "un-natural beliefs do not make the people that believe in such ideals un-natural, but the people that hold on to such beliefs can be thought of as an order that is similar to a plague, because a plague that is spreading does not realise the damage it is causing and eventually the plague will wipe itself out through its own destructive attributes, and through the loss of its prey!"

Morrighan takes a sip of her tea and then she says: "some religions could be seen as such a plague, but plagues seem to have a habit of renewing themselves or evolving into a different form, just like the predatory religions! Therefore we should begin to realise that the religions that are predatory are evolving in their numbers without evolving their beliefs, which can cause many problems! One of these problems is the problem that arises from the lack of understanding of natural processes."

Gaia winks at Sankara as he passes her the pot of tea and then she says: "Mother Nature and the ideals that follow through the understanding of her ecosystems, is probably the greatest predator of all, because every living thing she has created preys on some other living matter or something for its survival, because even the act of taking water for survival purposes is in a sense a predation. But this type of predation is solely for the survival of the living matter, which is unlike the predation of religions, because some religions predate in such a way that their ideals want the extinction of all other religions and belief structures that do not conform to their ideals! Therefore we should begin to realise that such a type of predation is unsustainable where people have the freedom of their own will, and are at the same time; confined to physical needs by the form that Mother Nature has given to them."

Sankara smiles and says: "religions can only predate by the controlling of the individual will that is meant to be free! This is problematic for religions that want to show that their God is the controller of all, because if something controls all it controls the will of the individual and that means the individual does not really have free will!"

Gaia smiles and says: "the human race can never actually have free will whilst it is confined within the physical body, because the physical body has needs for its survival and in having needs for its survival; the will is partly trapped when it is fulfilling the physical body's need for its survival. Therefore we should understand; that the predatory religions are trying to take the natural desires from us; and in doing so they are controlling what the mind wants, for example; predatory religions banish people from certain types of food, and in some cases banish sex before marriage!"

Pingala smiles as the fresh pot of tea is passed to her and then she says: "the controlling of natural desires and needs is a way of controlling the mind of the individual. Those ways of controlling the mind are used in many forms and these forms bring many consequences that are useful to the predatory religions, for instance; the controlling of the sexual desires and the disallowing of contraception is a way of expanding the congregations of a religious order."

Pallas smiles and replies: "a controlled population explosion is a way in which a predatory religion can increase its congregations in a healthy way, but as we have already discussed this can become problematic, because there is a finite amount of space and resources on and within our planet!"

Merlin pours himself some tea and then he says: "to become viable and to be able to expand; a predatory religion must begin by finding an easy explanation for natural events and turn them to its advantage, but this would be difficult to do when the population suddenly realises there are finite resources upon this planet, and therefore the predatory religions need to show that there is some kind of infinite resource that is available to them! This is why the predatory religions try to hold back and destroy some kinds of theories and discoveries, and this type of action has held back mankind for many centuries, and in doing so; mankind has only been able to partly fulfil its true potential–whatever that might be–up to this date."

Demeter smiles and says: "predatory religions that are not willing and able to evolve; have a great need for the holding back of new understanding, because if your beliefs are not able to evolve; any new understanding that compromises them must be hidden, destroyed or in the very least seen as works of a devil or demon!"

Sankara sips at his tea and then he says: "whether or not the human race likes to admit it: the human race is the planets top predator, and therefore the religions that are predatory are part of the nature of the human race. This becomes problematic within religions, because it is their nature to predate upon other religions."

Morrighan pours herself some more tea and then she says: "natural predation is problematic for the religions that are predatory, because in already being the top predator; the human race has a natural need to predate upon that which is not following what it thinks is its need for survival. Therefore the predation of some religions can be thought of as a natural consequence of the nature of the human race! This is a consequence that some religions will never be able to understand, because some predatory religions think of themselves as the only true religion, and in having such a thought process; they are not willing to accept that other religions could be or are as realistic as their own religion, and such religions use many techniques to disguise such a probability!"

Lug smiles and says: "the techniques they use to disguise such a fact are not understood for what they are, because such religions think of themselves as the only true religion, and in thinking so they eliminate the possibility of any other religion having any truth that is not of their understanding! Therefore this process of elimination is not understood as predatory, because once a religion has decided it is the only truth it cannot realise and admit to alternative truths that are against or contradict some of their beliefs!"

Pingala finishes her tea and then she says: "once a religion becomes held in bondage by ancient beliefs; it cannot admit to new ideals without it evolving; and if these ancient beliefs are meant to be undeniable; a type of permanent structured bondage is created; and the only way for such religions to hold on to such a structured bondage; is for them to predate upon other religions or cultures that can undermine their belief structure! Therefore we should begin to realise that such a strict belief structure can only predate upon other belief structures if it is to remain intact!"

Gaia smiles and says: "that is problematic for the many cultures and religion that are willing to evolve, because the structure of evolutionary beliefs need to be predated upon by those that are held in bondage by their beliefs, because if they are not predated upon by those that are held in bondage; those that are held in bondage become the prey of the evolutionary religions and cultures!"

Michael smiles and says: "it is becoming evident that those that are held in bondage by their beliefs are the most predatory of religions, but in being the most predatory of religions they also become the religions that are open to the predatory tactics of those that wish to evolve, because those that wish to evolve will not be easily closed down!"

Morrighan smiles and replies: "predator and prey are needed for the survival of both, but in the natural world prey does not become the predator of its own predator, and if something is over predated in the natural world; the predator starts to starve and balance is restored when the numbers of prey start to increase; through the lack of predators; which is due to the predators starvation through its over predation! But this natural balance is not part of a predatory religions ethics, because a predatory religion is intending to wipe out and make its opposition extinct! Therefore we should realise that the conflicts that arise from beliefs are separate from those that are purely about the survival of a species in the natural world!"

Gaia sips at her tea and then she says: "predatory religions cannot attempt to extinguish humanity, because humanity is what it needs for its own survival, but there are some of the predatory religions that will adopt tactics that are not in the interest of the human race; without the true understanding of their actions. They do this, because their religions have them so bound up and brainwashed by their beliefs that they believe that they do not need to understand the consequences of their actions, for example; in the New Testament of the Bible of the One-God religions it is said that:

And Enoch also, the seventh from Adam, prophesied of these, saying, behold the Lord comes with ten thousands of his saints, to execute judgement upon all, and to convince all that are ungodly among them of all their ungodly deeds, which they have ungodly committed, and of all their hard speeches which ungodly sinners have spoken against him.[52]

For I testify unto every man that hears the words of the prophecy of this book; if any man shall add unto these things, God shall add unto him the plagues that are written in this book: and if any man shall take away from this book of this prophecy, God shall take away his part out of the book of life, and out of the holy city, and from the things that are written in this book.[53]

From this type of scripture the words of this book are locked and are unable to evolve, because if anyone attempts to change the book they are cursed by their God. This is one of the ways in which people can become brainwashed and misled by an ancient religion!"

Pallas smiles, stands up, and says: "once the words of any book are tied and are unable to be altered; the book becomes static and in becoming static it can stagnate, and in stagnating it can become the same as stagnant water–it spreads unwanted pollution and disease! Therefore we should realise that once evolution is lost within a religions text; all that text can do is stagnate, and in this stagnation; it will become as unwanted as the malaria that spreads from the mosquitoes that breed in such conditions–in some countries."

Michael walks up to Pallas and then he says: "that makes evident; that religions that stagnate through the unevolutionary

---

[52] The General Epistle of Jude (1, 14-15)
[53] Revelation (22, 18-19)

ethics of their beliefs can be realised as a destructive force. But in being destructive the stagnant religions can hold up the evolution of other cultures, and in holding up a natural and scientific evolution; they could cause the extinction of mankind or they could affect the natural evolution and cause their own extinction! Although in realizing this we should also realise that the stagnant religions can only remain stagnant within their own belief structure; which is unlikely to brainwash all the minds of humanity, because humanity is constantly evolving!"

Morrighan walks next to Michael and then she says: "the evolution of humanity will always become a problem for the predatory religions that stagnate, because in evolving the scientific evolution within the human race will not allow all of its members to stagnate. Therefore we should realise that the only outcome of permanent stagnation is extinction—even the humble mosquito evolves throughout time!"

Merlin stands up and then he says: "the evolution of the knowledge of the human being is the most destructive and predatory aspect of the human being, because knowledge and the search for the understanding of creation is not bound by ancient beliefs; if it is true in its methods, because true discovery cannot be bound by ancient ethics that were created for an ancient race that did not need such knowledge for the continuation of its existence! Hence we should begin to understand that ancient and stagnant beliefs need to evolve, because if they do not they cannot truly understand the consequences of their actions in a world that has many problems that have been created by such stagnant beliefs!"

Pallas winks at Merlin and then she says: "the problem with stagnant beliefs is that in being unable to evolve and creating situations that they believe their Divine will cure in its next coming, they are avoiding the need for the solution of the problems that they create. That type of avoidance creates many problems as the human race expands, because in some discoveries the expansion of the human race becomes out of control and in becoming out of control; there is much of the important needs of some places and species upon the planet that are not considered and are lost by such foolishness!"

Demeter points to a fox and then she say: "the stagnation of any religion that is not willing to evolve through new discoveries will lose its acceptability, and in losing its acceptability it will be preyed upon by such discoveries! Therefore the religions that were predatory can become the prey through their own stagnation. That is due to the new discovery becoming the new predator, because any new discovery predates upon any old belief that it is attempting to dismiss as ignorant of the true facts!"

Lug smiles and says: "therefore we should realise that any belief; that is held by ancient ideals is going to create much death within its own believers, because they will eventually become undermined by the problems that they have created through their own stagnation. Hence we should begin to realise that the predatory religions need to evolve if they wish to survive and not become stagnated."

Pingala smiles and says: "all predators need the ability to evolve if they are going to survive, because conditions of survival will change, and once these conditions have changed and evolved the predators that survive within the new conditions must also change and evolve to continue their existence! Therefore the predatory beliefs will need to–at some stage– evolve or they will face extinction, because they will not be able to cope with the new conditions! Therefore we should begin to understand that science within religion needs to be examined, and if science shows that there are some serious faults within a religions scriptures; these scriptures should be altered. Most scientists realise that their scripts need to evolve and if in evolution some of their older scripts need altering; they do so, and therefore; the religious scriptures should learn from the scientists and if they did they may not be so dogmatic and foolishly warlike, because it is possible that in evolving the predators could become non predatory religions, just like the giant panda evolved from a carnivorous bear into something that is mainly vegetarian (giant panda's will eat dead animals if the opportunity arises)."

Michael momentarily watches and listens to a blackbird and then he says: "that would be problematic for the religions that are so dogmatic in their beliefs that they cannot alter them, because in being so enslaved; those types of religions are unable to alter and remain part of the same religion. But in realizing that we should also realise that some of the Dogmatic religions have evolved into separate cultures, for example; Christianity has split into many different cultures! Hence we should realise that this predatory culture has split into different predators and when different predators meet, conflict becomes unavoidable!"

Gaia smiles and says: "whereas nature evolves to survive; some religions try to make other religions evolve into them selves through predatory ideals. One thing we must remember is that religions predate mentally and unlike nature they try to turn other non predatory cultures over to themselves, for example; the Christian missionaries that try to convert other cultures are predating upon the mind of that culture and are not trying to destroy their physicality for their food. But in realizing that; we should also realise that the culture whose minds are preyed upon could be thought of as food for the mind. This food for the mind is the way in which religions are taught to people, but the food of true knowledge cannot come from a belief that is not willing to explore outside their belief structure! Therefore this food of the mind or the soul that is taught and used as a weapon by many religions needs to be reassessed; by the cultures that these types of religions are trying to overthrow. But this is problematic when the religions that wish to control the mind of the individual have many that are already under its control, because it is far easier to overwhelm the individual when the mass is against the individual, for example; a single lion could not kill a grown elephant, but there is a pride of 30 or more lions in Africa that are known to hunt elephants. This physical example shows us that physical numbers can overthrow a far stronger physical opponent, and therefore; we should explore the possibility that a greater number of minds would dissuade many separate individuals from their original ideals. But this again can become problematic for religions, because a single mind can become very persuasive and that single mind or will can spread its ideals and become another predatory culture or religion; that could eventually overthrow the first predator."

Morrighan smiles and says: "that is making evident; that the predatory religions that become or are stagnant because of their belief structure; will at some time be replaced or overthrown, because the human mind will evolve and there will always be those that are willing to accept and acknowledge this type of evolution, for example; such scientists as Galileo were held back by religion in the 17th century, but this did not stop people from investigating in this age and in later ages."

Merlin walks alongside Morrighan and then he says: "just like in the natural world, a predator will try to kill or destroy an opposing predator for its survival. Therefore the predators of the mind are trying to make other predators extinct, just as the lion and the hyena are in a constant battle against one another; the stagnant religions are in battle against the evolutionary religions [science and the One-God religions are such opponents], and just like in the natural world [where lions will take prey form hyenas and hyenas will take prey from lions]; they can use one another for some of their own desires! These desires that religions use for their survival are quite often misunderstood concepts that become out of control and go against themselves, due to their misunderstanding of the natural world and the consequences that can arise from such a misunderstanding! This type of misunderstanding cannot be realised by some of the dogmatic and predatory religions, because such religions are unwilling to admit their mistakes, because they believe that their scriptures cannot be mistaken!"

Pallas smiles and says: "in being stagnant in their beliefs these religions have the greatest need of all for predation, because if they do not predate upon others beliefs they will be overcome by their inadequate exploration techniques. Many of these inadequate techniques are the cause of the demonizing of scientific discoveries that they cannot explain by other means, and therefore; we should begin to understand that the demonizing of some finds and discoveries can lead to the coercion of many people's minds!"

Michael points to a pair of buzzards and then he says: "this is making evident; that some of the predatory religions need to attack the mental awareness of the individual for them to remain in power over the mass, and the simplest way to make such an attack successful is to make the individual fearful of the consequences of its actions; by demonizing those actions or discoveries that the predatory religion finds unacceptable."

Sankara smiles and says: "from what has been made evident it becomes obvious that the stagnation of some predatory religions can become self destructive! Therefore it becomes clear that the methods that are used by such predatory religions are those of fear tactics, but the fear element in any religion can only remain whilst people believe in the fear tactic that is devised."

Morrighan smiles and says: "fear can only remain whilst there is reason to fear something, and therefore; the search for truth [by scientific means] must be held in check, and in some cases be destroyed and/or hidden by the stagnant religions, because once the stagnant religions become unstagnated they have evolved and in evolving they will have lost some of their original ideals! Once these stagnated religions have evolved and become unstagnated; they will also lose some of their predatory ways and in losing some of their predatory ways their original ideals will change; and some of those ideals will be dissolved!"

Pallas momentarily watches the buzzards and then she says: "some of the predatory religions will eventually change and accept that their ancient writings are wrong, but there will always be some religions that will not change their ideals, and in being so stubborn they will eventually cause their own and quite possibly some others extinction, for instance; there are may faiths and cultures that were destroyed by the One-God religions, but in being so stubborn in their beliefs the One-God religions tend to turn on themselves!"

Michael smiles and asks: "could the turning in on themselves cause their own extinction?

Gaia smiles and answers: "if any other natural predator turned upon itself for its main prey it would not last long and therefore; the chances of any religion surviving when it splits and wars within itself; becomes improbable!"

Morrighan winks at Michael and then she says: "that is correct, but when predatory religions start to prey upon themselves one of the parties that split could become the top predator within that religion, for example; the Catholic and the Protestant religions are the top predators in Christianity, but they have not wiped each other out and they have caused much destruction to each others people! This destruction has made each religion stronger in its ideals and made them believe they are the ones that are truly right, and increased their predatory fields as the human population has expanded, but this is problematic, because in preying upon each other they are losing ground to other predatory religions, such as; the Muslim faith, and the non predatory religions such as; Buddhism and many of the older Pagan faiths!"

Michael winks back at Morrighan and then he says: "if non predatory religions are increasing over the predatory religions; are they actually becoming a predatory religion without realizing this?"

Morrighan smiles and replies: "the non predatory religions that gain ground on the predatory religion do so because people become dissatisfied with the ethics of the predatory religions. Therefore the dissatisfaction becomes the reason of the peoples change and this cannot be seen as predation, because the religions that such people convert to; do not try to convert them by force and fear tactics!"

Gaia points to some wild strawberries and then she says: "the non predatory religions can appear to become predatory to the predatory religions, because the predatory religions see such religion as predators of the weak, but this idea does not truly make the non predatory religions predators, because the conversion is up to the individual!"

Merlin starts to pick some of the strawberries and then he says: "whether a religion is predatory or not, does not matter to the truly predatory religions, because the truly predatory religions only have one aim; and that is to destroy all other religions that are not of their own kind. This type of destructive attitude does not care what tactics it uses to annihilate and make its opposition extinct! Therefore we should realise that a non predatory religion must be seen as a threat and a predator; if the predatory religion is to exterminate them."

Pallas starts to help Merlin and then she says: "the ideas that surround the predatory religions are for the survival of their faith, but this survival can become problematic when new threats arise; that they had not foreseen! When these new threats arise the predatory religions try to explain the new threats by misusing ancient scriptures. In misusing the ancient scriptures they can see the new threats as an act of their God's displeasure or an act of their devil and/or demons!

Devil and demon are the terms that predatory religions tend to use when they are explaining the rise of what they consider to be an ungodly religion, or culture that is showing some of their ideals to be false, and when they consider a destructive act of Mother Nature [that has affected them] they tend to reason that this type of destruction is due to them displeasing their God."

Pingala smiles and says : "any flood or severe natural disaster can be used as the wrath of any God or Goddess of any religion, because all religions see the Gods as the controllers of the weather and therefore; we should realise that it is not only usable by the predatory religions it is also usable by the non predatory religions. These natural disasters can be used by the non predatory religions for the same ideas of the wrath of a God or Goddess, because if the predatory religion that preys upon the non predatory religion is badly affected it can be seen as the wrath of a non predatory religions God or Goddess!"

Michael picks some strawberries and then he says: "what this would mean is that non predatory religions can use the ideas of a wrathful Divine being; without having to become a predatory religion!"

Lug smiles and says: "because a Divine being has been thought of as enacting some type of wrathful action; to another religion that has been doing wrong to its followers does not mean that the Divine beings religion is predatory. The nature of a religion is not necessarily predatory if its Divine is thought of as capable of a vengeful action, because the religion itself is only considered predatory if it's followers try to exterminate other religions, for example; the Buddhists Lords of Karma seek a type of revenge on those that have defiled their ways, and the followers of Buddhism are not known for predation on other religions. Hence we should realise that the followers of a religion; are the tools of the predatory religions, but they are not used as the tools of a non predatory religion; even if the Divine of a non predatory religion are though of as capable of taking a vengeful action; upon those that have defiled their beliefs and/or their followers! Therefore it becomes evident that; if a

Divine being is capable of revenge upon those that have attempted to destroy those in its religion; it is vengeful in its wrath and in being so it is not predatory; it is defensive!"

Demeter winks at Lug and then she says: "apart from karmic retribution; natural disasters are the things that can be thought of as the Divine retribution of a non predatory religions Divine beings, which is very problematic, because the predatory religions use natural disasters in the same way. Therefore a predatory religion would try to show that a natural disaster was the act of their own Divine for the sins that they or other religions have committed against their own Divine being!"

Sankara grins and says: "predatory religions will always try to use natural disasters as acts of their Divine, because in doing so; they can use such disasters to frighten their own people into the bondage they require, and to frighten those outside their religion into the same bondage as their own people. This type of manipulation is problematic for all other religions without a reasonable scientific and philosophical understanding of the world in which they live, because without the knowledge that has been discovered by the philosophical religions; the religions that do not have such understanding are easier to manipulate!"

Morrighan helps in collecting the strawberries and then she starts to conclude: "from what we have made evident we should realise that all predatory religions need to manipulate anything they can for their cause, but in such manipulations there are non predatory religions that are strong enough to withstand the corruptions of natural events. Those types of non predatory religions are the religions that are able to encompass philosophical and scientific truths. In realizing this we should also realise that the predatory religions tend to be dogmatic and are unable to evolve in their beliefs, which leads to uncomfortable situations; for the cultures and religions that do not hold such beliefs!

The belief structure of predatory and non predatory religions are both constructed by the hand of man, and the predatory religions tend to want their scriptures to be perfect, because they believe that these scriptures were written with the understanding and the aid of their perfect God, but that in itself is problematic, because there are many different ideals that surround perfection."

Pallas smiles and concludes: "predatory religions can only predate whilst their prey accepts their predation, and therefore; the prey must become unwilling to accept the predation and start to predate upon the predator if the prey wishes to survive, and in this wish to survive the prey must, and in many cases already has begun to accept the truth of scientific and philosophical discoveries!"

The players finish their collection and restart the walk.

10

TRUE UNDERSTANDING

The players finish their walk and after entering Morrighan's abode they start to prepare the party that will ensue during this discussion.

Morrighan enters her kitchen and then she says: "during our discussions we have considered many aspects of religion and in considering these aspects it has become evident that some religions do not always want the truth to appear, because the truth can undermine some of their scriptures, for example; a plague of locusts can be used as an act of their God, but if the truth was truly understood they would realise that such a plague is just an act of Mother Nature's chaotic universe! Therefore true understanding can only evolve from unhindered scientific and philosophical processes, because any process of discovery cannot be hampered by beliefs that are ancient and that are unable to evolve through new understanding!"

Pingala walks up to Morrighan and then she says: "any religion that is unable to evolve its understanding will always be hampered by their lack of true knowledge, which is a dangerous position to be in, when a religion is ready to accept technological breakthroughs that are destructive, and in accepting such breakthroughs they are not willing to accept the responsibility or the consequences of their new destructive powers!

Destruction is a part of science that needs full understanding of its consequences if it ever needs to be used, but there are many religions that are not willing to try and understand, because they believe they have Divine inspiration in their actions, and in having such Divine inspiration they believe that what they are doing cannot be wrong."

Lug starts to prepare some food and then he says: "in the eyes of dogmatic religions; scientific discoveries are only useful if they accommodate their beliefs! This is problematic when destructive discoveries are only partly understood by such religions, because in being dogmatic they cannot believe that the consequences of their actions will go against their own kind or their God, which is in their eyes the only thing capable of showing them the absolute truth. When this type of principle is applied to the latest destructive forces that science has made available to them; the consequences of their actions could be catastrophic."

Sankara puts the collected strawberries on the table and then he says: "catastrophic actions are inevitable in any major war of the present age, because scientific technology has increased the destructive powers in such a way that mass destruction is more easily possible. Therefore the major religions of the world need to understand the actions that can cause the extinction of the human race. But this type of understanding is not accommodated by ancient scriptures that were not capable of understanding the power of modern warfare techniques! Such misunderstanding of the present world–by scriptures that are unable to evolve–can and does cause much loss of life and it also creates the destruction of important ecological systems; that we have no true idea of the long term consequences of such actions. Without such understanding the human race could eventually release something that could cause its own extinction or do something that could make the planet uninhabitable for all its present life forms."

Demeter puts the kettle on the stove and then she says: "future consequences are hard to predict, but the scientific communities have realised that the human race is capable of making this planet uninhabitable for many centuries, and if it does so Mother Nature could reinhabit the planet with totally different creatures, for example; the dinosaurs form became extinct and evolved into many species of birdlife without being self destructive!

Even if man does not cause the planet to become uninhabitable, the sun will eventually cause such an action, and therefore; the permanence of the planets life is not as permanent as most religions would like us to believe!

Merlin passes Demeter the milk and then he says: "planets and stars will eventually die, but in dieing the planets and suns can leave a memory behind, for instance; if a star died many millions of years ago the light that shone from it–before its death–could be seen millions of years later. The full understanding of this becomes evident when we realise that light travels at 186,000 miles per second, and our nearest major galaxy [apart from the Milky Way of which we are part of] is Andromeda, which takes 2.2million light years for it to be seen from our planet.[54]"

Morrighan smiles and says: "this makes evident that the only thing that remains permanently in the universe is evolution, because everything evolves even if what has evolved becomes extinct through its evolution, because in becoming extinct the part of space that replaces what is now extinct has in a sense evolved due to the new unoccupied area!"

Michael pours himself some tea and then he says: "when anything evolves it makes its previous form extinct, but the extinction of a solar system seems to have a finality that cannot be recovered!"

Merlin smiles as Michael passes him the pot of tea and then he replies: "the whole universe is full of theoretical problems, and the finite state of the universe is one such problem, because in its creation and its expansion the universe has no known boundaries. Therefore we should explore to our greatest abilities, but in such exploration we should realise that our exploration of such a state of being will never be able to end if the universe is infinite! This infinite being's creation would be an ongoing event if it is constantly expanding, and in being a continuous event it would need limitless and infinite space if it was to continue throughout infinity!"

Pallas smiles and says: "so, the creation continues throughout infinity, but with this being an acceptable theory, the interesting problem of what was before this universe arises and this is hugely problematic, because we all realise that chaos comes before order, but what we do not know is what came before the original chaos. Perhaps what came before the beginning of our universe will always be out of the reach of present understanding!

Pingala smiles as Sankara passes her some biscuits and then she says: "if there were other beings before this universe was created it is possible that those beings would not have realised

---

[54] Bang! The Complete History of the Universe, Brian May, Patrick Moore, Chris Lintott p22 Carlton Books Limited 2006

their own extinction [that is if they ever became extinct], and it is also possible that such beings were and are on a plane of existence that we have not yet reached, and may never be able to reach."

Michael sips at his tea and then he says: "there may be planes of existence that we are not aware of, but if these planes exist it is also possible that those on such planes could not be aware of the life that is on this plane of existence! If that is correct, then the beings on such planes could not have created life on this plane without being aware of it unless what they did was accidental, and if this is also correct it would be highly unlikely that such beings would remain unaware of their creation; unless they became part of it, and in becoming part of it; they lost the memory of what was before the creation of the universe!"

Demeter looks out of the window and sees Gaia gathering some herbs and then Demeter says: "there may be many planes of existence that the human race is unaware of, but in being unaware of them does not mean that the human race will always be unaware of them, because as they evolve they could be able to reach new planes of existence that were unrealised. Hence we should realise that until the human race has evolved into such a state of existence we cannot gain any evidence of such planes of existence, and therefore; the unknown planes of existence cannot be theorized upon, because there is nothing to theorize that is within the abilities of the present understanding!"

Merlin watches Gaia enter the room and then he says: "perhaps in being unaware of what was before the present universe is already locked within the memory of the present universe, because we can only assume that there was no time before the present universe, but if there was a universe that died before the present one began, then there would have been a time before. Perhaps the universe before was some form of pure energy that we cannot understand at this present point in time!"

Gaia starts to prepare the herbs and says: "if there was pure energy before the present universe began, then that pure immortal energy would surely be part of whatever it creates and if part of that creation is living matter; the consciousness of some of that living matter could have the origins; locked within itself if that consciousness is as immortal as some religions believe it to be!"

Pallas smiles and says: "that is possible, but it is not provable and in so being it is not liable to be part of superstitious probability, which is the main basis for the majority of religions and therefore; we must realise that the truths that are supposedly gained through non scientific means will always be questionable! Therefore the questionable superstitions that emerge within religions are always questionable as scientific understanding evolves. This evolution of scientific understanding will evolve alongside the human race's evolution, but this evolution has not proved or disproved the possibilities of the Divine. Henceforth we should not dismiss the probability that the Divine always were and will always be, even if they are in a form that we cannot truly comprehend up to this point in our evolution!"

Sankara starts to help Gaia prepare the herbs and then he says: "as we have already discussed; it is probable that the Divine are chaos and in being chaos in the beginning; anything that is created by the Divine is partly chaotic! Therefore in being chaotic in its creation; the human race will probably always be partly chaotic in its realization of creation, and in its attempts to create what many religions believe to be the one true religion!"

Morrighan smiles and says: "there is a huge problem with chaos and that is; that if reasoning comes from chaotic form [which it must before it has been put into order by reasoning] it is liable to give out just as many untruths as it does truths. But even the amounts of truths are liable to be chaotic and unpredictable, because of unknown circumstances."

Gaia smiles and says: "what creates such chaos within religion is the uncertainty of the future, because past events can be explained by acts of Gods or Demons by many religions, but this is problematic because such explanations do not search for the real truths of past events, and therefore; they can become full of misconceptions and untruths that will affect the future. This will become problematic when religions become created through dogmatic beliefs that are not willing to search for past truths, because if we have no true understanding of the past we can lose some means of predicting some of the future events!"

Lug takes some pans from the cupboard and then he says: "the search for past and future truths are held back, because some religions think that their scriptures cannot be wrong! But this type of thinking is liable to keep and hold contradictions and/or untruths in place and in doing so it can create problems that go against their own faiths, for example; in the book of Exodus; of the One-God religions Bible it is said:

Thou shalt not kill (Exodus 21, 13) and Thou shalt not suffer a witch to live (ibid 23, 18).

Pingala smiles and says: "that type of contradiction is evident in many places within such scriptures, but there are more serious untruths that are present within these and other scriptures that could seriously affect the understanding, for example; in The First Epistle of John (1-5) it is written:

That which was from the beginning, which we have heard, which we have seen with our eyes, which we have looked upon, and our hands have handled of the word of life; (for the life was manifested, and we have seen it, and bear witness, and show unto you that eternal life which was with the Father, and was manifested unto us;) that which we have seen and heard declare we unto you, that ye also may have fellowship with us: and truly our fellowship is with the Father, and with his Son Jesus Christ. And these things write we unto you, thus your joy may be full.

This then is the message which we have heard of him, and declare unto you, that God is light and in him is no darkness at all.

This above script could affect the understanding, because it suggests that everything within our senses was there in the beginning of life, which we know is incorrect, because all things have not lived upon this planet for the same amount of time, and if this is misunderstood the whole of the understanding of the evolutionary process is held back!"

Michael starts to prepare some of the meat and then he asks: "does evolutionary theory hold many untruths?"

Merlin smiles and says: "there are many scientists that disagree with natural evolutionary theories; but once theories are proven wrong within a scientific field; they are admitted to! Hence we should realise that the untruths within any scientific theory can be shown when the truth is discovered, because in its search for truth there are going to be many mistakes and misunderstandings, because true science will admit to the mistakes it has made. These mistakes are usually realised when new techniques and technologies emerge within a scientific field!"

Morrighan winks at Merlin and then she says: "evolutionary theory [like most scientific theories] is liable to start with many untruths, but scientific theories are able to evolve and unlock their own untruths, which is very problematic for many religions, because many religions like to believe they hold a truth that is unquestionable and because it is unquestionable it provides them with a comfortable life in which everything can be explained by the actions of their Divine or their demons, and therefore; they believe that they have no need to search for any truth that is outside their scriptures understanding."

Sankara passes Michael some of the herbs and then he says: "most religions that base their theories around ancient scriptures, and are not willing to let them evolve; are not searching for any truths that are outside their limited understanding! This is problematic, because in being unwilling to seek the truth; they are comfortable within ancient ideals that are not helpful within the modern worlds scientific understanding, for example; there are many of the One-God religions that have used the idea that one should not kill against the ideas of contraception–and even against abortion when the mother to be is in danger of losing her life–when science tells us that we could and probably already are overpopulating the planet."

Gaia smiles and says: "that is probably because scientific understanding is not limited by scriptural ideals; that were produced in an age when mankind was not realised as being able to have the ability to overpopulate the world, because they had no conception of the finite resources that are available on this planet.

The understanding of the finite resources and our ability to be able to overpopulate the planet did not become a realizable and well understood problem until the 20th and 21st centuries!"

Pallas puts some of the vegetables on the stove and then she says: "for many centuries; religion has been the only truth that some people have been able to understand, because religion has been the main power behind the worlds greatest rulers and in being the main power behind such rulers, religion was able to undermine scientific works and in some cases have them banished for many years, decades and centuries! Hence we should realise; that the truths, that some science exposed; became unwanted by rulers that realised that some of the truths could undermine their scriptures, and in doing so; they would show the imperfections within the rulers of the states and of the priests of the religion that ruled the heads of the states."

Lug smiles and says: "the truths that are available to science will always be controversial to those people in religion that do not seek the truth, because such people believe that they know all the truths that are needed, because their God has given them all the truths that they need, and in believing so; they also believe that the word of their God is undeniable and incorruptible! This becomes hugely problematic when science provides evidence of misunderstandings and untruths within such works, because most of these religions believe their God cannot make a mistake, and if parts of the scriptures of such a god are proven incorrect, this God has made a mistake somewhere."

Merlin puts on another pot of water and then he says: "most religions are not concerned with proving their scriptures, because they have no freedom that allows them to search for the truth unless they are of a philosophical nature, which is unlike most of the One-God religions, for example; in Revelation (22, 18-19) it is written:

For I testify unto every man that heareth the words of the prophecy of this book, if any man shall add to these things, God shall add unto him the plagues that are written in this book: and if any man shall take away from the word of the book of this prophecy, God shall take away his part out of the book of life, and out of the holy city, and from things which are written in this book.

When the above script is followed to the extent that most of the One-God religions do: the truth of philosophical or scientific discoveries will not be admitted to if they conflict and/or contradict some of the scriptures within their bible, because they believe that the only truth is written within their ancient scriptures, and if they break such beliefs and add new evidence; they will be cursed by their God!"

Morrighan passes Merlin the tea and then she says: "truth cannot be sought when the people of a religion are held in bondage by a structured system that does not allow true freedom of thought and exploration. The people of that religion are confined and imprisoned by the belief structure that has been put upon them, and such a structure will cause great fear amongst those that are not willing to rebel against those who think they know the greatest truth! Those priests that think they know the greatest truth tend to refer to things that are thought of as miracles and acts of their God that will amaze and manipulate their audience into their way of thinking.

There are many religions that use things they consider as miraculous, as acts of their Divine, but most of the miracles have explanations or are unproven to begin with. Therefore we should understand that miraculous happenings can usually be explained or put down to superstition, for example; the lack of snakes in Ireland can be explained by geological and weather phenomena and not put down to banishment of such creatures by saint Patrick!"

Pingala smile and says: "superstition [as we have already made evident] is what most religions use for the explanation of the unexplained, and others use superstition as a fear tactic to manipulate their followers, and also to manipulate those who do not follow their beliefs, but superstition is also a powerful tool from where many myths and legends can emerge!"

Michael puts the meat in the oven and then he says: "most religions use superstition in such a way, but this is problematic, because superstition is based on events that are unexplainable at the time and some of these events will be explained in later years. When such events have been explained by science and or philosophy; these events can become a reason [for the religions that believe their superstitions are undeniable] for the controlling and the banishment of some scientific discoveries and theories!"

Gaia passes some herbs to Sankara and then she says: "most religions rely on superstition for the creation of their myths and legends, but there are many religions that are willing to accept scientific truths and philosophical discoveries that go against their original beliefs, for example; the early Greek pantheon had Athena as a Goddess of wisdom. Where would this Goddess of wisdom be without new discoveries? She would not be considered as truly wise without being able to evolve within new scientific fields, and because the early Greeks were known for their scientific and philosophical explanations; they would have no place for a Goddess that was held in check by ancient and dogmatic beliefs! Therefore we should realise that there are some religions that are more philosophical than others, but in realizing this we should also realise that the majority–and possibly all–religions are held in bondage by their ideas that surround the death of the physical form, and that the only way to change such ideals is to change religions!"

Demeter starts to prepare the salad and then she says: "what happens after death is only able to be theoretical, but the theoretical ideas that surround an afterlife are wide ranging, because of the uncertainty that is within most human beings. I say within most human beings, because there are those that think they are certain of what will happen to them after their physical death. But those that are certain of what happens after their own death only have the theories and the hallucinatory manifestations that are given to them, and therefore; there is no empirical evidence that is available [at this present stage] to us that can actually prove life after death."

Morrighan smiles and says: "that is problematic in more than that single way, because there is also no empirical evidence to support the theory of physical death being the end of every thing within that life form. With this problem it becomes evident that in this state of understanding we can only theorize on the unknown aspects of what happens after the physical death, but this in itself is problematic, because there are many people that have had strange experiences in-between being medically dead and in being brought back to life!"

Michael smiles and asks "could these experiences be hallucinatory effects of the shock of being brought back to life after death?"

Pallas passes the olive oil to Demeter and then she says: "shock can cause many strange effects, but the experiences of people that occur between death and resurrection are–in many cases–so similar that they are unlikely to be due to the shock of resurrection after death. But in realizing this we should also realise that the many similarities could be due to similar experiences, for example; there are many people that are dying of thirst in a desert that have experienced an illusory or hallucinogenic oasis! Hence it becomes evident that the possibility is there, but this is problematic, because in the after death experience there are some explanations that are so long; that they go against the time frame in which the resurrected person was deceased, for example; a person could give an explanation that lasts over many hours; when they were only dead for a matter of seconds!"

Lug chops some peppers and then he says: "the past death experiences that lose the accountability of time could be due to past memories emerging within the individual but this is also problematic, because some of the happenings can be outside the memory of the people that have such experiences. Although this is possible; it is also possible that the memories of outside experiences could be forgotten memories. This would be very problematic, because forgotten memories could be memories of past lives! Hence the problem of past life experiences starts to emerge and becomes as unexplainable as the momentary death experiences!"

Demeter smiles and says: "there can be many strange and unexplainable events within a person's life and these unexplained events will always be problematic! Therefore we should consider the events that are unexplainable at this present time as just that! Hence the exploration of the unexplained events in their singular form becomes unnecessary at this stage in time, but the exploration of the causes of the unexplained is necessary all through any discussion of a religious theme, because we could find explanations for things that were seen as acts of Gods and demons! Therefore the cause and effect of such matters need to be examined in the greatest possible detail when there is any search for the truth of a matter"

Morrighan starts to cut some cheese and then she says: "we have covered some of the problems of creation in many places in this book, but as yet the problems that surround death have hardly emerged, except in the form of a fear tactic that is used by many religions to control and manipulate their followers and those followers of other religions. Therefore the cause and effect of strange happenings within the death of an individual do need some exploration on a few singular cases; for there to be any kind of explanation; of some of the unexplained events within the death of individuals, but as Demeter pointed out, there is no need for the full event to be explained in fine detail, because it is the cause and the effect that we are after, for example; if a persons experience of death leads them to a beautiful forest, we do not need to know all the separate beautiful things within that forest, because the thought of beauty is enough for us to know, but what caused such an experience and the after effects of that experience are the most important things that we need to know!"

Michael smiles and says: "the after death experiences of many people go against many of the One-God religions beliefs, but even those that do can be manipulated into regions of heaven or hell, and therefore the causes of an after death experience could be dependent on the religious theories of the person that has the experience! This is problematic, because the belief that caused the experience could be then thought of as truthful if the person thinks that they have actually gone to the type of place that they deserve!

The effects of a person's experience of death is not always due to religious experience, but there are those that have turned religious after experiencing death."

Pingala finishes kneading the dough, passes it to Demeter and then she says: "all the experiences of death need resurrection for them to become available to the thought processes of other people, but this in itself is problematic, because if death is not the end result of the humans thought process; it is possible that these experiences could become suggestive, and in becoming suggestive they could affect the evolution of the soul of other individuals!"

Demeter puts some herbs on top of the dough, places it in an oven and then she says: "after death experiences could be similar due to suggestibility, but because they are similar–due to suggestibility–does not mean that they only think along the same ideals, because of manipulation [intended or not]! Therefore the after death experience should be thought of as having many possibilities and these possibilities are linked to the outside influences of the individual."

Merlin smiles and says: "if where you go after death is dependent on actions within this life; the Buddhist and Hindu ideals would explain the many different happenings within the after death experiences, but this is problematic, because such ideals are dependent on a type of resurrection; they either place a person back in the physical world in another situation, or in the spiritual form of which there is no need to return from when the person has reached true enlightenment. This becomes hugely problematic for the people who have after death experiences, because they could not have reached true enlightenment and returned so quickly without the wish to do so! Therefore this type of experience does not show enlightenment or the probable final destination to all religions ideals."

Lug gets some wine glasses, places them on the table and then he says: "in the Buddhist and Hindu religions such experiences would be thought of as part of the illusory world that is created by maya! This illusory world or worlds are created by the physical senses ideals of permanence within the physical world, and therefore; the differences in the after death experiences could be thought of as part of the illusion of permanence in the physical world, because although the body is medically dead in these experiences it is not totally void of life if it comes back to life! In other words the tie between the spiritual self and the physical self is not completely broken and in not being truly broken it is not truly dead, because the spirit returns!"

Sankara puts the wine on the table and then he says: "even if the spirit that has returned to the physical body was still under the control of maya [when the physical body was dead] the spiritual self still went away from the physical world that it knew, and therefore; the spirit travelled away from the physical plane of existence onto another plane of existence! Another plane of existence requires another type of reality that could be as physical as ours, and if it requires such a type of physicality, it would therefore be as open to the illusory world of maya! With this world of maya being present to a spiritual physicality; it is possible that the differences of happenings in the after death experiences, are due to the differences in the way we experience the illusory world of maya in the physical world that we originate from before the after death experience. But this is problematic; because this suggests that there could be an infinite amount of physical worlds or planes of existence that maya could affect the physical being upon. If this is the truth of the matter we must realise that maya in itself is never ending and if it is so: the realization of maya would be to realise that there is no escape from the illusory sensual world of maya!"

Gaia smiles and says: "perhaps the death of an individual is a new beginning that could help the individual realise; there is no escape from the illusion of our senses if we are to remain a sentient being, because our consciousness is dependent on our senses for the realization of itself, for example; we cannot think without language and language must be taught in past tenses, because once a word is spoken or written it becomes a past tense in its construction. Therefore we should begin to realise that illusion must be part of a sentient being, because the entire world that we sense at present is sensed through past events, and therefore; our realization of the present is actually a realization of the past!"

Merlin finishes brewing the pot of tea and then he says: "our realization of past and what we consider as present events is explained through our present physical senses, but the consciousness of an individual cannot be one of them senses if all the physical senses have died, and the consciousness has experienced something else!"

Gaia passes the cups around and then she says: "if the same consciousness comes back to the revived being, and in being away from its physical self has experienced something else; it is possible that the consciousness is not only the free spirit it is a separate sense that can experience the other worlds that are available to it after it is freed from the bondage of the physical body. If this is correct; that consciousness must be able to realise the physical senses in its spiritually free form; if it is able to explain what has happened to it when its physical body has been medically deceased; and it is also possible that in its new state of existence [once its body has died], the consciousness is moving in a different time scale than that of the presently accepted physical state."

Pingala smiles as Merlin pours her the first cup of tea and then she says: "there are many instances where people have been in a coma for a long time and their mental age has not changed, which is unlike their physical age. That would not be the only time difference of when someone has been in a coma for a long time, because when people come out of a coma they tend to have no idea of the passage of the time that they were in such a state. Hence it starts to become evident that the steady state of time is not such a steady state for the consciousness! With the consciousness being able to have different states of time whilst it is connected to the physical body this could suggest that there are different planes of existence that have different time concepts!

Gaia smiles and says: "time only seems to be on a different state whilst in a coma or a dream state! But such a state does not mean that time is not steady, because we are not truly aware of the time that is involved whilst we are in such a state of consciousness. Therefore it does not concur that time is not a steady state, because we lose our awareness of the time that is involved!"

Michael smiles and asks: "would it be possible for time to move at different speeds on different levels of existence; such as that of the Gods?"

Morrighan sips at her tea and then she says: "time would move at the same rate, but in being immortal, the Gods would probably not be as aware of the movement of time, because they would have no particular restraints that time brings upon the mortals, for example; the mortals need things to survive! Therefore the requirements of life that are within a certain time are not required by the Gods for their survival, and in having no such requirements the Gods only awareness of time would be the awareness that is required by their mortal subjects.

Michael pours himself some tea and asks: "if the Gods were here before the creation, would the Gods have had any conception of time before the present universe was created?"

Demeter passes her cup to Michael and then she says: "it depends upon what was before the present universe, because if there was nothing before, there would be no reason to have any measurement of time, but if there was something before that died before this universe came into existence; there would be a need for time to be measured. But this in itself is problematic, because this would suggest that there was a creation before this creation and this is presently beyond our means of understanding!"

Pallas smiles and says: "what is beyond the human's means of understanding does not mean that it will always be so, because it is possible that there is some evidence that has not yet emerged that will at some stage point to a universe; that is presently beyond humanities understanding. Therefore the theoretical ideals that surround creation could be just a beginning of philosophical ideals that could make evident the possibility of other universes that came before, will come after, and are there at present, for example; it is unlikely that we would be able to see anything that is outside our three dimensional perspective, but the thought process can make evident the idea of a fourth dimension that the human race is not able to be aware of at this present state in time! Hence we should begin to realise that the evidence of other universes is only available to the thought process, and this in itself is problematic, because once an idea has emerged, that idea had an origination somewhere, and if that origination is unknown it does not mean that the idea is nonsensical, because any idea has origination and the origination of an idea needs to be found before it is considered nonsense. This again becomes problematic, because the human race does not have the capability of being able to be aware in the fourth dimension or in however many other dimensions [apart from the three that they are aware of] there may be."

Merlin puts a bowl of cherries on the table and then he says: "The understanding of the human race may be confined to the three dimensional awareness it is held within physical bondage, but this does not mean that once the physical bondage has gone, the human race is still confined to the three dimensions! Therefore it is possible that some of the ideas that are outside the human beings awareness come from between past and present physical existences of the self!"

Sankara takes one of the cherries and then he says: "perhaps it is possible that the self could come from many different time spheres in many different dimensions, but it would still be within this universe and around this planet, because as far as I am aware all past life experiences relate to this planet and this universe!"

Michael smiles and asks: "is it possible that the human race could go outside this universe, but not be capable of being aware of such an action whilst it is restrained by its present physical state?"

Morrighan finishes one of the cherries and then she says: "that is highly probable, because whilst the human race is confined by its physical state; it would only have a limited amount of awareness that is available to it, because it would be confined to its own physical abilities whilst it is in such a state of existence. Therefore it is possible that whilst the human being is confined by its own body it is also confined to the amount of knowledge that is storable in such a body, for example; a computer can run out of memory if you try to input too much information into it, but it does not mean that there is not any more information available, and to input the new information some old information has to be wiped out, but that old information was within that system in its origin!"

Michael puts some oranges on the table and then he asks: "does this mean that the human race could have lost the evidence of what was before our universe, because it is so confined?"

Morrighan starts to peel one of the oranges and then she says: "that is possible, but the lost knowledge may not be lost when the human being loses its physical bondage, because in being aware that there are other possibilities makes evident that the origins of these possibilities arose through the evolution of the science of the human race. This evolution becomes hugely problematic for the religions that were and are confined by ancient belief structures; that did not have the awareness of the present day, because these religions–that were in the humans infancy–were only aware of what was evident to them through their senses, and these senses did not have the technological means to discover truths that were outside their abilities. This un-technological background wasn't the only problem for such religions, because another major problem was that they took things on face value, and they did not try to understand what they could explore by using basic scientific and mathematical techniques!"

Lug smiles as Morrighan passes him the freshly peeled orange, and then he says: "the search for truth is not in the interest of any religion that does not have the ability to evolve, because in not having this ability; a religion will not want any truth that is not within and/or contradicts its belief structures, because if their belief structures are meant to be an undeniable truth that has come from their God, they believe that their God cannot be wrong! This type of belief becomes problematic; when other cultures start to evolve and show truths that are not within the guidance of the God; that such non evolutionary religions; believed held undeniable truths within his unalterable scriptures!"

Pingala starts to peel some potatoes and then she says: "many religions believe that the only truth is written in their scriptures, but these scriptures have been rewritten many times, and the original scriptures tend to be from times when the technologies of mankind were not capable of showing them the truths that were beyond their scriptural abilities! Therefore the people of such times used acts of God or demons for the explanation of events that were beyond their scientific understanding. This type of theological reasoning became a standard and in becoming a standard; there became idealised scripts that manipulated people in such a way that scientific exploration had to fight for its works to be published, because the manipulative religions were not looking for any truth that was outside their scriptural teaching!"

Merlin smiles and says: "there are many faults within the teaching of any religion that depends upon fear and manipulation of its followers, and for the conversion of others into its cause, because if you depend on fear to keep the truth away from the followers, truth has a way of finding those that are not happy within the religion they are indoctrinated into! Therefore the hiding of truth by ancient ideals will not always hold those who wish to explore and evolve the scientific capabilities of mankind!"

Morrighan smiles and says: "truth is only available to those that are willing to look beyond ancient ideals, because the truth of a situation or action is only available to the full exploration of that action or situation. Therefore the need to become independent of religious myths within the scientific field becomes absolutely necessary, because the truth needs to be found without the constriction and the bondage of a strict religious belief that will try to stop any scientific theory undermining a religious belief or myth. This undermining of a religious belief is not wanted within religions that are trying to show and convert other people into the truth of their religions ideals, for example; in the Bhagavad-Gita (XVI, 23) of the Hindu religion it is said:

Whoso forsakes the ordinance of scripture, and lives at the whim of his own desires, wins not perfection, [finds] no comfort, [Treads not] the highest way.[55]

Although I use this example from the Hindu religion I must admit that this is no where near the worst religion for undermining scientific and philosophical thought, because this religion is quite open to philosophical and scientific argument, and it does not believe that its Divine are all knowing, because in the Rig Veda (X, cxxix, 7) it is said:

Whence this emanation has arisen, whether God disposed it, or whether he did not,—Only he knows who is its overseer in highest heaven knows. [He only knows] or perhaps he does not know![56]

This type of theology would be hugely problematic, because in relying on scriptures for its truth it admits there are some truths that even their God might not understand! Therefore the later scriptures that show reliance on the scriptures for the reaching of the highest plane of their existence; are not admitting that they are the only truth that is out there, they are just saying that to reach the highest plane of their religions existence; their scriptures must be the norm as in the later verse of the Bhagavad-Gita (XVI, 24):

Therefore let scripture be the norm, determining what is right and wrong. Once thou dost not know what the ordinance scripture bids thee do, then should thou here perform the works [Therein prescribed].[57]"

---

[55] Hindu Scriptures, R. C. Zaehner p394 David Campbell publishers LTD 1992
[56] Ibid p14
[57] Ibid p394

Merlin smiles and says: "the Hindu and Buddhist religions are well known for their philosophical approach to life, but this does not mean that they do not have scriptures that are designed for the enlightenment of their followers by the enslavement of the mind, because if any person lives within any kind of ethical idea, their mind is enslaved by that idea! Therefore the human race should realise that there can be no absolute freedom of the will whilst it is confined by ethical ideals; that are used for the survival of others and its own personal survival! This becomes problematic, because many religions are full of selfish desires that do not wish for such survival techniques when there are those that are not willing to bow down to their ideals, and those that were already partly enslaved by ethics, but not totally enslaved by their scriptures become the main problem for the religions that wish to totally enslave their own followers! When these types of dilemmas meet, the outcome is usually some type of war and in these wars; there is much human sacrifice and lives are needlessly lost and disrupted by those that have selfish desire–and those types of people tend to want to stamp their unethical ideas over the human race! This becomes problematic for those that are in search of the truth, because a true seeker of the truth cannot have his mind totally enslaved by ancient scriptures; that were written in tines of scientific ignorance!"

Gaia finishes chopping the carrots and then she says: "the ignorance of the human races ancestors is quite obvious, but that ignorance has remained, because some religions believe that their scriptures are the truth that is written with the aid of their God. But this type of ideology is known for the untruths that are written within it and these untruths are ignored by some of its followers, because they still believe that these untruths are true. Therefore the human race should realise that those of them that are willing to ignore the untruths within their own works are not seeking the truth, they are looking for ways to dictate and dominate the people of the world! This becomes very uncomfortable for those that are seeking the truth and are being ruled by ignorance, because those that are held enslaved by the ignorance of their scriptures do not believe in the truth of science, and this has been made evident in many of the things that we have discussed on the One-God religions!"

Michael smiles and asks: "are most religions looking to dictate to the individual rather than searching for the truth?"

Sankara sips at his tea and then he says: "all religions want to dominate their follower's belief structure, but there are some religions that are willing to accept the possibility of other religions Gods! Therefore we should realise that the less restrictive religions have more of the free will that people wish for. Although this sounds very compatible with most people, there are always restrictions within any belief structure [just as Morrighan pointed out earlier]. Therefore we must understand that the religions that appear unrestrictive can be as manipulative in their structure as the ones that appear more dictatorial. But in their subtle manipulation [the religions that appear less dictatorial] we must realise that there is actually more freedom of will even if they are manipulative, because in the more subtle manipulations there is more choice in the ways in which you are meant to reach enlightenment, for example; in the Hindu religions Bhagavad-Gita (XVIII, 13-15) the enlightenment can come to fruition by five factors:

In the system of the Samkhyas five factors are laid down, by these all works attain fruition. Learn them form Me.

Material basis, agent, instruments of various kinds, the vast variety of motions, and fate, the fifth and last:

These are the five factors of whatever work a man may undertake, of body, speech or mind, no matter whether right or wrong.[58]

Hence it becomes evident that the more subtle religions are manipulative, but they are not as dictatorial in the way in which their enlightenment is reached!"

Gaia smiles and says: "any religions manipulations are attempts to hide something that is uncomfortable for their beliefs, but some of the more subtle religions are willing to evolve within scientific understanding whilst they hold on to some of their ideals, for example: the caste system of the Hindu religion is held onto whilst the Hindu religion is quite willing to accept new scientific understanding. Hence it becomes evident that old moral codes are the foundation of dogma within many religions, because moral codes are the building blocks of dogma

---

[58] Hindu Scriptures, R. C. Zaehner p400 David Campbell Publishers Ltd 1992

within religions. But this is problematic, because morality issues differ within different religions and when these codes are broken by opposing religions or cultures, conflict will occur. Therefore we should realise that moral issues can hide many truths within many religions, because if a moral code is accepted it becomes an ethic that is hard to break, due to the ideals being thought of as a way to the enlightenment of the individual self or soul!"

Morrighan starts to prepare a fruit salad and then she says: "many truths are overlooked, because of moral issues, but morals can hold on to ideals that are improvable by empirical means, and therefore; metaphysical philosophy becomes the only means by which such beliefs can be approached and disproved if need be! This is hugely problematic, because some philosophers see metaphysics as useless, because there is no empirical evidence that is available to such ideals and if there is no empirical evidence; there can be no provable truth or untruth without such evidence!"

Lug helps Morrighan in her preparation and then he says: "the enlightenment of the soul or the self can only be theorized upon by metaphysics, and therefore; any truth that is beyond the means of empirical evidence must be sought through belief structures that do not confine any sort of reasoning that does not need empirical evidence, for example: murder has obvious consequences and some of these can be assessed using empirical means, but the mental anguish of the family of the murdered individual can never be felt in the same way; by someone who has not experienced such a death in the family–and even if they have there could be other incidents within each family that make their feelings of the murdered individuals totally different. Hence we should begin metaphysical enquiry with an open mind to the individuals or races that the enquiry concerns, because if we do not make such distinctions we will become inadequate in the theoretical means that we need to apply our thought process to!"

Michael smiles and asks: "if there is no empirical evidence, can we truly assess a situation [even murder has the empirical evidence of the dead body and the means by which it died]?"

Demeter chops a pineapple and then she says: "all thought processes require something for them to emerge, but this can be unpredictable and confusing when it is outside the empirical means, because the truth of the spiritual well being can only be assessed by an individuals belief, and this belief can only be fully understood by the individual and those of a similar faith to the individual! Hence it should be realised that metaphysical examination needs to be able to assess the belief structures through a reasoning process that employs some empirical evidence, for example; the previously mentioned murder consequences; is examinable by the actions the victims family take, and their inner feelings that cannot be seen could be assessed by our own feelings of such an event [even if it has not happened to us]. Hence we should begin to realise that an event can be assessed without empirical evidence, because we have imagination and imagination can be truthful or fanciful, and therefore assessment is needed."

Pingala puts the potatoes on the stove and then she says: "whether or not something is truthful within the imagination, it is still not provable if it only has the imagination for evidence. Therefore all the Gods and the beliefs of reincarnation are not provable in a society that depends entirely on empirical evidence. But such a society would have many problems, because the inventions of such a society would have to come from a mind that had theorized upon the invention before it existed. Therefore the realization of the individual that invents must have an imagination to invent something that was not thought of before!"

Pallas smiles and says: "the imagination can be manifested and enhanced in many ways, but the imagination can also be confused by many things and in being so confused; the imagination can see unreal things as real! Therefore the imagination could be seen as the means by which a religion can be indoctrinated into the individual through confusion, for example; the imagination could quite easily put an earthquake down to the act of a vengeful God without the understanding of what created such an event. But even with the realization of what creates such events religions can still use the imagination to show such an event as a cause of the displeasure of their God, and therefore; the accepted empirical evidence of science can still be used as an act of God! This idea of an act of God is used in many explanations that were beyond scientific understanding, but even when science explains the act; the religion that wishes to use it as an act of their God will use the imagination to explain that their God put the pieces in place—that caused such an event—and in effect had the event prophesized!"

Merlin sets the table and then he says: "the truth of metaphysics is hard to distinguish because of the problems of the imagination that we have discussed. But this does not mean that there are no truths to be found by metaphysical reasoning, and this is because metaphysical reasoning is the means by which new understanding begins! Therefore the logic that comes from empirical evidence begins with metaphysics, and that is because until empirical evidence for something is found it remains metaphysical theory. This creates many problems, because the metaphysical theories can only remain metaphysical whilst there is no physical explanation for them!"

Michael smiles and asks: "would that mean that the Gods and the soul can only remain metaphysical theories whilst there is no physical evidence to support their presence?"

Gaia smiles and says: "not necessarily, because physical presence is not always explainable by empirical evidence, for example; the physical presence of a God would not necessarily explain its origins, and therefore; the metaphysical theories about its origins would remain unanswerable by empirical evidence. However, if there was such a physical presence it is not impossible that such a being would be able to tell of its own origination, but until such a presence is available; that is just another metaphysical theory!

The images of Gods present another problem for metaphysical theory, because images of Gods are based on physical beings of either the human or the animal world [in many cases animal and human combined]. The combination of human and animal form for a God is a great feat of the early imagination, but the explanation of how the combination came to be present in the imagination is a question that will probably never be answered!"

Morrighan takes a sip of her tea and then she says: "the search for truth through metaphysical theory will always be problematic, but the truth of a religion is always dependent on the follower's practises; which should always be able to evolve and be open to new theoretical ideas. Unfortunately–as we have pointed out in many places–there are many religions that are not willing to evolve, because they believe that they already understand all truths through their scriptures. This type of thinking creates many problems for theorists, because a religion that believes its scriptures are undeniable has no will to question anything that is outside their scriptural beliefs–why would a religion that thinks it knows the ultimate truth have any need to search for anything else? The answer is: it does not, but this is problematic for such religions, because there are always some people that are stronger willed than others and some of the ones that are stronger willed, will question things that they are uncomfortable with. Problems will arise from such strong willed people, because in being so strong willed their search for the truth [of whatever they are looking into that conflicts with their scripture]; will lead to many conflicts with the hierarchy of a religion that wishes to remain enslaved by its own scriptures!"

Lug passes Gaia some honey and then he says: "as we have made evident; metaphysics searches for theoretical truths; without the confines of religion or empirical evidence. With such an unrestricted search process; the problem of how to assess the evidence occurs, because if there is no empirical evidence to support a truth we enter the realms of transcendental and a priori philosophical reasoning. This is hugely problematic, because both types of reasoning search for truths that are outside the sensual abilities of the human race! Therefore the metaphysical theoretical worlds of a priori and transcendentalism must be realised; as the search for the origination of our thought processes, for example: a good definition of a priori is:

A proposition is knowable a priori if it can be known without experience of the specific course of events in the actual world. It may, however, be allowed that some experience is required to acquire the concepts involved in an a priori proposition. The category of a priori propositions is highly controversial, since it is not clear how pure thought, unaided by experience, can give rise to any knowledge at all, and it has always been a concern of empiricism to deny that it can.[59]

---

[59] Oxford Dictionary of Philosophy, Simon Blackburn p21 Oxford University Press 1996

All through our discussions the empirical proof has been problematic for religions, but the empirical truths still cannot disprove the possibilities of a God or Gods. Therefore the problems that are investigated by *a priori* reasoning should not be discounted if there is no empirical evidence to confirm the truths that such reasoning proposes!"

Pallas smiles and says: "truths and laws should not be completely reliant upon empirical evidence, because empirical evidence is based upon what is known by that evidence at a particular time, and in being so reliant it will conflict with truths that are surmised without any physical evidence at the time of its proposal, and such truths could become evidential when it is too late, for example; a person could summarize that a change in rainfall could cause flooding or drought in an area where it has never been proved to have happened before, which would cause disastrous consequences for those concerned! Although recent science shows what will happen, because it has happened and is happening in many places around the globe, and the true empiricist would not believe it could happen in their area until a climate change started to occur in said area!"

Demeter pours herself some more tea and then she says: "that is problematic, because there would be evidence available that would show an empiricist a possibility, but the possibility would become more problematic for a religion that believes its God knows all there is to know, because if such an event occurred in such a region, without any scriptural prophecy, it would be seen as an act of their Gods displeasure or the act of a devil or demon! Therefore we should begin to realise that most natural events are explainable by empirical evidence, but some religions try to deny the understanding that brings events into an explanation that is satisfactory, and proven to be without the aid of their God or demon kind!"

Michael smiles and says: "all truth requires some kind of knowledge, but how that knowledge is attained can be controversial, because reasoning must start somewhere and that somewhere, that is in the human mind, is not easily understood, because the way in which a person reasons can only be approached theoretically as previously mentioned in the *a priori* reasoning process!"

Sankara puts on the rice and then he says: "truth is unpredictable, because a religious truth can be an untruth in scientific terms. However the scientific untruth that is a religious truth is not made by any logical reasoning, it is made through the misunderstanding of events and the indoctrinated ideals that surround a religion that believes its scriptures are undeniable. Hence it becomes evident that such ideals become a truth that cannot be undermined by any new evidence [even if it is empirical], because the truth that is an untruth is taught in such a way that if that truth is corrupted and denied, the corruption and denial, become a heresy and a work of the devil or a demon! It is becoming evident that this type of demonizing is used as a scapegoat for the untruths that are provable as untruths by empirical means! Once that is realised by the people of such a religion, the people that realise such a truth become outcasts and in becoming outcasts; such people tend to try to find a more suitable religion or they can completely deny the existence of any God!"

Demeter passes Sankara some seasoning and then she says: "a pure empiricist would be an atheist, but many new cults within a religion arise through the dissatisfaction of the ideals within a type of religions theories! Therefore, I suggest that it is more probable that a new cult that believes in the same God is more likely to emerge than atheism from dissatisfaction. Of course this becomes very problematic for dogmatic religions, because as the separate and new ideas evolve within them, there becomes a type of evolution which causes much conflict, because different truths can emerge from the same religious idea; for example; Catholics and Protestants follow the same God, but they have different ideals that surround the path they take in the worship of their God. When those truths become different ideals the true nature of a truth becomes lost, because a truth is a truth and not an untruth!"

Pingala smiles and says: "religious truths are always open to conflicting ideas within a religion, but the untruths that are realised as untruths by some people are always open to being demonized; by the followers that do not believe that their scriptures can be imperfect! Once this has happened the followers of the untruth that still believe it is true have been manipulated without realizing they have been manipulated. This is a type of manipulation that will not be realised by the people that have been so manipulated, because the manipulation entrances them and in becoming entranced they lose the reality that true science and philosophy provide. When the people that are entranced lose the reality that is provided by true science and philosophy; they lose the ability to spot any corruption within their own theories and this can lead to many conflicts!"

Morrighan peels some pineapple and then she says: "most religions are not interested in any truth that conflicts and invalidates their belief structures, because most religions rely on the complete belief of their followers. Therefore we should realise that the people of restrictive religions are held in bondage by their gullibility and their lack of true understanding. This becomes problematic, because there are many things that are open to extinction by the foolishness of people that are not willing to accept the consequences of their actions. Such people do not seem to realise that there is not infinite space upon this planet and even if they do, some of them do not seem to realise the consequences of over breeding [as we have mentioned in many places before]!"

Merlin smiles and says: "most religions [especially the One-God religions] do not see over breeding as a problem, because in their origination they would not realise how successful the human race would become! Therefore the religions of ancient times had no need to think of the problems that would be caused when mankind would start to overrun and overuse the planet and its resources. When this becomes evident to some religions they still do not believe in contraception, because their scriptures tell them that the creation of life is sacred and not to be interfered with. Therefore the act of contraception is seen as a sin, because successful contraception stops the creation of life through sex, for example; in The New Testament it is written *'thou shalt not kill (Romans 13, 9)'* and this can be used against contraception, because contraception can be seen as preventing a life from being born, and in doing so it can be seen as killing that which has not yet been born."

Sankara smiles and says: "if contraception is seen as killing that which has not been born it is avoiding the truth, because in preventing a conception there is nothing to kill, because if a life has not started it cannot be killed! Therefore the act of conception is only a preventative course of action, but this is a problematic theory, because in preventing a life from existence it is losing the possibility of a life and that could be used and manipulated in such a way that it is seen as killing the unconceived! When this type of manipulation is used it can become a means by which sexual controls become a part of religions practises, and the people that are controlled in such a way have no opportunity to seek the truth of the consequences of their actions, which is hugely problematic, because there is a truth in what is said in these controlling factors! Therefore the truth within a controlling ideal does need exploration and evaluation, because all truths are not necessarily beneficial to the human race. Hence the human race should begin to understand that some truths need ethical ideals that are beneficial to the human race, and in being so; the ideals that surround contraception could be shown for what they could really do!"

Michael passes Morrighan some bowls and then he says: "what this makes evident is that some truths can be misused and become destructive to the human race, because the will of a religion can overcome the scientific truths without actually ignoring the truth!"

Morrighan smiles and says: " that type of theoretical practise is used in many ways, but the truth of one individual or one religion is not necessarily the same as another, and this creates many problems, because truthfulness can only become so if it is seen within the individuals religious ethics. This is problematic, because there are many truths that conflict in different religions, and most religions believe that they hold the truth in their scriptures! Therefore all religious truths need examination, and this is, because a truth within a theory is a truth, but that does not mean that the truth is a good and beneficial truth!"

Michael smiles and asks: "is religions truths still a truth if it is found to be incorrect by science and/or other religions?"

Pallas passes Sankara some mint and then she says: "if empirical truth shows a religions truths to be incorrect it would be so, but the religion that has been proved wrong can always use the idea of demons and a devil for the explanation of how that empirical evidence came to be! Therefore a religion that uses such methods can conspire to make their untruth a believable truth to those that are willing to strictly follow their religious practises! This conspiracy would then make a truth out of something that is known to be incorrect, and in doing so it makes an untruth a truth, which would then become a truth in the minds of the people that follow such a manipulative religion. When this type of manipulation is in place an untruth can be made into a truth that is undeniable, because if someone wishes to use empirical evidence that is—by some religions—thought of as a demonic work it would be very difficult to disprove such, because they would need to firstly prove that demons did not do it or that demons do not exist!"

Gaia smiles and says: "that type of reasoning is a part of the magical ideas that have come from many religions and many religions theories, all of which are hard to prove and equally hard to disprove, because there is no empirical evidence for either case! Therefore, I suggest that the religions that are not open to being disproved in their theories will not consider the empirical evidence as a truth whilst they believe that there is some kind of magical creature [such as a devil or demon]; that can be blamed for inconsistencies and untruths within their scriptures!"

Pingala smiles and says: "a truth is only a truth, if it is actually so; but purely theoretical truths are always open to misuse and abuse! Therefore the human race should realise that its religions theories are not necessarily the truths that they appear to be, and this is because when the scriptures were written they were written without the modern technological and scientific capabilities, and in being so unaware they were confined to the situation of their time; which is very problematic, because in being so; their followers became so entranced by what they believed to be so; they carried their beliefs throughout the centuries and some of them still do so! Of course the religions that take such actions, because they believe their ancient beliefs to be the only truth; are denying any counter action against their beliefs whether they are based on empirical evidence or not! Hence the human race should realise that such religions are detrimental to the true needs of humanity, because such religions do not want to or think; that they have to realise the consequences of the actions that their religions beliefs can create!"

Lug puts out the plates and then he says: "what is becoming evident is that some religions were based around untruths that were created by their misunderstandings of the universe and the natural world. These misunderstandings have become areas of conflict within different cultures, and if a religion is going to remain so dogmatic in its beliefs–no matter the consequences of its actions–it needs to be caged before it does irreversible harm to the planetary system!"

Michael smiles and asks: "should such a type of religion be destroyed or caged? I ask this because a religion that is determined to wipe out other religions and other beliefs–before it realises the consequences of its scriptures ideals,–surely has no place in civilized society?"

Lug smiles and says: "you are right in suggesting that such religions have no place in civilized society, but their ancient beliefs still need to be kept for future reference, because the need to remind the human race of how uncivilized they were and presently [in the be beginning of the 21st century] are will always be useful if they are ever going to be truly civilized! Therefore the total destruction of the knowledge of any religion should not be allowed to happen!"

Gaia opens a bottle of wine and then she says: "some of the dogmatic religions depend on misunderstanding and untruths for their beliefs to remain! Therefore such religions have no wish for any evidence that compromises what they see as the truth. This type of behaviour is problematic, because such religions–in thinking that they have no need for any truth outside their scriptures–deny evidence that could prevent much harm coming to their own communities, and the communities of others that they are trying to persuade to follow their beliefs. When this type of denial becomes evident; the religions that use such processes tend to try to convince others; that happenings that affect their community; are because their God is displeased with them. But this will only convince those that are not willing to go and explore the scientific world without the chains of ancient scriptures! Those people that are willing to use science and defy their scriptural ideals–as we have already made evident–are outcast by those of the religions community that are unwilling to evolve and recognize the truth of the scientifically minded communities!"

Merlin smiles and says: "it is becoming evident that the dogmatic practises of some religions are actually dangerous to the evolution of the understanding of the human race. This is because in misunderstanding a situation and/or environment catastrophes can happen. When the catastrophes happen they are lied about when religions use their Gods or demons to cover up the events that were caused by the misunderstanding of the natural world. This type of behaviour can and does cause later catastrophes that could be avoided, but the religions that are so enslaved by their scriptures that they cannot evolve an ancient detrimental practise; are not going to be able to evolve to save themselves and other communities that have been and will be affected by their ancient ideals! Therefore [as Lug mentioned earlier] such religious practices need caging and confining to ancient history!"

Morrighan finishes preparing the fruit salad and then she says: "some religions will never accept scientific evidence that contradicts their scriptures ideals! Therefore the practises of such religions need to be realised for the damage that they could cause within a confined environment, but this is problematic for the religions followers, because they believe that they already know the truth. Therefore the religions that are willing to evolve and realise new truths need to keep such religions away from those; that are willing to see the truth as it evolves within the scientifically aware communities! Of course this is problematic, because the religions that are not willing to accept other possibilities and new truths; tend to defend their practises and cause much conflict within other communities! These other communities that are being thought of as heretical will also start to defend the truths that have evolved through scientific means, and these scientific means will also be seen as works of a devil or even a misunderstanding that is caused by maya! Hence the human race should begin to realise that it is not only the One-God religions that have a means to dismiss scientific understanding."

Sankara smiles and says: "religions have many ways of avoiding scientific truths, but in doing so the empirical evidence should not be allowed to be dismissed by such religions, because it is against their scriptural ideals. In theorizing that way; many of the religions that dismiss the ideas of science because they are against their scriptures would have no need for the conflicts that are caused by their ideals. Although we should realise that this is problematic, because if those types of religions do not dismiss the ideas completely they are going against their religions ideals! Therefore we must realise that the truth of some scriptures can only remain the truth if there is no believable evidence against their scriptures! Hence the human race must understand that a believable truth can only be a believable truth if the people are willing to accept it as a truth! This is hugely problematic, because a truth is a truth whether or not it is believable by its audience. If the audience or the followers are entranced and enslaved by their beliefs, a believable truth that is against their religions scriptures; will remain an untruth for such people, because such people think that they have no need for anything outside their religions scriptural truths!"

Demeter places a bowl of nuts on the table and then she says: "the problem with such people is that they have accepted the enslavement of the mind, by their religions scriptures. This is problematic, because in accepting such enslavement; the people of such a religion lose their free will! Of course the people who have their free will enslaved do not see it as enslavement, because they do not realise that their free will is enslaved in the search for truth! Such a realization would free the mind of such individuals and they could then search for the truth, but they will never do so whilst they are enslaved by the entrancement of their religions preachers and scriptures. Those preachers and scriptures have total control over the followers that are not willing to try to realise any other truth; than that truth they have been taught. The willingness of the individual that is in such enslavement needs to be tightly controlled by the preachers of such religions, because if it is not; the entrancement that is used to control such individuals is broken, and if it is broken a separate cult can arise and take over from the old tradition. When this happens the old religions that are not evolutionary try to destroy the new traditions and use their scriptures against them! Hence we should realise that all the human races religions that are willing to accept truth and evolve are the ones that are the only true religions, because they are the ones that are willing to accept their mistakes and allow their beliefs to evolve!

Michael smiles and asks: "are there actually any religions that will allow their ethics and practises to evolve in such a way?"

Morrighan pulls some freshly baked bread out of the oven and then she says: "any religion that is willing to accept new truth is such a religion, if it is willing to accept new truths that go against its old beliefs which can create problems, for example; there are many schools of philosophy within the Hindu and Buddhist religions, and these schools have many different ideals, but they all come from the original school of thought and they still maintain much of their old principles, be they right or wrong in the minds of others! Hence we should begin to realise that the religions that hold many schools of philosophy can still hold onto a belief; that is incorrect and dangerous to the human race. Although in realizing this, we should also realise that the religions that are willing to evolve are less likely to hold such dangerous principles!"

Michael eats one of the cherries from the fruit bowl and then he says: "if any religion is going to survive it must maintain some of its original beliefs, because if it does not the religion will become extinct. But in realizing this we should also realise that if something evolves and its original form becomes extinct it is not completely extinct, because it is still there although it is in a different form. This different form can become problematic when the dogmatic religions try to stop such evolution occurring within their own ranks, because the only way dogmatic religions survive is through their non acceptance of evolutionary ideas, and the new empirical evidence that science can provide. Such non acceptance is part of many religions belief structure, and such a structure is provided through ancient beliefs that did not have the later scientific reasoning; that evolved within many cultures!"

Pallas smiles and says: "the truth of a dogmatic religion will not be negotiable; because such religions only realise the truth within their scriptures, and in doing so they see anything that contradicts their scriptures as a mistake that is created by another unseen force that is not their God! Therefore we should realise that this type of religion cannot evolve whilst its scriptures are not negotiable and unable to evolve. Hence we should begin to realise that such religions will never realise that there is a need for the truth that is outside their scriptures; until it is too late for them to recover what has been lost!"

Pingala sits at the table as Merlin and Gaia start to serve the food and then Pingala says: "it is becoming evident that a religions truth is a truth unto their religion even if it is not scientifically correct. This becomes problematic, because a truth that is not scientifically correct can become a contentious issue for other religions and cultures! Therefore the religious truths that are in contention with other religions need to be analyzed by a neutral party. But this is problematic, because finding a neutral party will become a contentious issue in itself, because all people have their own beliefs and in having their own beliefs they will strongly defend them unless they are willing to evolve their beliefs. Therefore we should realise that the only truth that can be seen as neutral is that of science, because true science is in search of truth and is not hampered by ancient beliefs in its own research. But this in itself is again problematic, because the dogmatic religions that are liable to be within a scientific person's community will try to dismiss and destroy works that contradict their scriptures! Such actions as those that try to invalidate the truth of science within a community hold up the progress of others within that community, and can keep some of those within that community in the bondage that such religions require. That bondage can be hard to break when the influential people of such a community are held by that bondage, and that same bondage is beneficial to those influential people. Therefore we should realise that the bondage of some of the influential people will not be broken by them whilst they see the immediate benefits of such bondage! Hence we must also realise that the bondage of the people that are being influenced by the influential people becomes harder to break, because the truth is being hidden from none influential people, because it benefits those that are in a position of hierarchy to do so!"

Michael butters some of the freshly baked bread, passes it around and then he says: "whilst a religions hierarchy and people are held in such bondage; the truth of science will always be hidden from them; whilst they are attracted by the religions ideals that make them believe that they have a superior truth to that of other religions or communities. When this superiority is realised as incorrect; the influence of the hierarchy becomes broken. But that is unlikely when the hierarchy holds the majority of the people in the bondage that they have created and become held by!"

Morrighan takes a slice of bread and then she starts to conclude by saying: "from what we have discussed it is evident that some religions are not willing to accept scientific truths when they contradict their scriptures. This is hugely problematic, because some truths can be dismissed and kept from the understanding of their population by influential people and manipulation, e.g. the preachers of religions and those that are willing to support them for some kind of gain over the general population. Hence we should begin to realise that the religions; that use such tactics are actually frightened of losing their hold over a population that is willing to increase its scientific understanding, and dismiss some of the untruths that are within the scriptures. But we must not forget that these untruths were made; in a time when the human race was in its infancy and the truths that appear to such an unscientifically advanced race; will only be made by the means that they have available to them at that moment in time. Therefore we must understand that the means that were available to such a race would affect the writings of their scriptures, and in doing so; the untruths that are within such scriptures become a part of the society in which the religion becomes the answer for many unexplainable happenings!"

Pallas starts to pour the wine and carries on concluding by saying: "some of the past happenings that were unexplainable are part of some religions scriptures and are used for acts of their God. These acts of God were used as a means by which they could control the thoughts and the will of the people, but when science advanced this type of control became less viable. Therefore the dogmatic parts of many religions used a variety of methods to explain the new evidence that was and is being supplied by the real seekers of the truth [true scientists and philosophers]. When this is realised; the human race should begin to realise that many of religions explanation that dismisses scientific evidence are untruths–**or downright lies**–that are designed to keep the people of a certain society in the bondage; that their preachers and hierarchy need to keep control over the population!"

Merlin smiles and concludes by saying: "from what we have discussed it has become evident that untruths within religions are used to control the people of their community, and are also used for the encapsulation of other religions; for the purpose of spreading the message of the warlike religions that wish to control the whole of the human race. These warlike religions only use science to gain greater weaponry superiority over other communities, and they are not interested in the science that shows the untruths within their religions scriptures! Therefore the human race should not become infatuated by ancient scriptures that were made before scientific understanding evolved, and started to show the inadequacies and untruths within their scriptures, because the unscientific scriptures that try to dismiss the truths of science are hampering the human races intellectual evolution. This type of understanding is problematic for the dogmatic religions, because they consider themselves as perfect and in no need of any evolution, and therefore; the human race needs to reassess its religions truths; whether or not they believe that their religions truths show them some kind of perfect understanding of all events within the world!

Truth is only truth if it is actually true, and any manipulation of the truth only creates lies and disharmony within the natural world and the evolution of species which includes the human race!"

The meal is set and the party begins.

11

THE FINAL DEATH OR EVOLUTION! (CONCLUSION)

The meal is finished and the discussion begins…
Gaia takes a sip of her wine and then she says: "We have discussed many ideals within religions, and by now we should have made evident that religions originated through misunderstandings, and these misunderstandings grew and caused much chaos and disharmony within the world that the human beings exist. But in realizing this we must understand that religions; have made many sacrifices of people of their own kind and of other religions kind to make a point of superiority!"

Lug pours himself some wine and then he says: "when such beliefs originated they originated through the need of one religion to prove itself over another religion, and sacrifice, and natural disasters were the ways in which many religions manipulated others into believing that their God was the most powerful of all Gods, and in some cases this most powerful of all Gods was seen as the only true God! Therefore the human race must begin to realise that in the original practises; many religions were manipulating the misunderstanding of the natural world, and they were also using the fear of the unknown within this type of manipulation!"

Pingala smiles as Lug passes her the wine and the she says: "there are many such manipulations within the origination of religion, and one of the major ones for the One-God religions; is that they believe that their God is immortal and all knowing and this is problematic, because this God must have infinite knowledge and infinite knowledge needs infinity for it to be able to exist, and because infinity lasts for ever; infinite knowledge of past and future cannot exist, because if there is no end to future events there can be no end to knowledge! Hence the human race should realise that nothing can know all that will happen within something that never ends!"

Michael smiles and says: "that realization is just as important for the idea of the immortal soul or the self being part of a God, because the immortal soul or the self would be just as infinite as the God, and if the immortal soul or the self comes from such a being it must have been part of the God in the Gods creation, because it would be just as timeless. But this type of philosophy would have been outside the understanding of the creators of the religious scriptures, because in its infancy the human race did not have the scientific capabilities that arose through philosophical practises. Therefore the human race began to see many mysteries as an act of a superior being, and these mysteries became so ingrained within the human practises that they became difficult to break away from; when science showed the truth behind some of the mysteries and the scriptures that used these mysteries as acts of God; were shown to be mistaken!"

Demeter sips at her wine and then she says: "many of those scriptures have been used for the ideas that surround good and evil, but even this has been shown to be problematic, because if a God is perfect and created every thing then the God must be good and evil if both are to exist. Hence the human race should begin to understand that any sole creator must have both within it if both are to exist, and therefore; I suggest that the idea of a world without any evil within it is nonsensical! Although the idea of a creator that has no evil within it is nonsensical the Lords of Karma that punish the ones that break the laws of being seem to be a more ethical type of Gods, because the Lords of Karma seem to have no preference for the type of people they are meant to sentence; and all that defile their laws will undergo the punishment for the acts of misunderstanding or the crimes that they have partaken in; and these punishments apparently lead to what creatures we become when we are reborn after our physical death!"

Sankara smiles and says: "Although the idea of the Lords of Karma seems to be more ethical than a creator that punishes those that do not worship him, neither can be proven to those that have no willingness to explore the beliefs through metaphysical means! Therefore the human race should not dismiss anything that is not bound to empirical evidence, because if the human race relied solely upon empirical evidence; some ideas would not exist at all, for example; how can the idea of infinity remain whilst there can be no way of proving infinity exists, because there can be no empirical evidence of infinity, because it is timeless and without end! This problem of infinity has arose time and again within these discussions, and it is one theoretical problem that would never have arose if the human race relied completely upon empirical evidence, and therefore; the human races metaphysical and empirically related explorations must be as infinite as we think the universe to be! Therefore the emotional state of the human race and of the Gods arose within the next chapter and the theoretical ideas of the Gods being pure emotion, and having a different emotional level than the human race became one of the major topics!"

Morrighan smiles and says: " the emotional states of the human race and the Gods having such a state [even if the Gods emotions are heightened]; led to the possibility that the Gods could actually be ruled by their emotional state rather than the Gods being in total control of their own being. Which is very similar to many of the people–if not all–within the human race, for example; pleasure within a person comes within many forms, just like the pleasures of different Gods and Goddesses within the human races beliefs! Therefore the human race must realise that the Divine they sacrifice their time or energy to; must have similar emotions if it created them and the humans are part of that Divine beings will!"

Lug looks out of the window, smiles and says: "that led onto the realization of the Self; which once the Self is fully realised; the understanding that the only unchangeable reality is that of the Self or the immortal soul emerged. This unchangeable reality must be realised for what it actually is and that is the consciousness of the human being, but not the physical state, because physical states can change as can belief systems, but the consciousness or the Self is changeless and timeless even if its understanding and physical state evolves, the consciousness is still the consciousness–nothing more, nothing less!"

Merlin smiles and says: "it is possible that the human race could evolve and outgrow the Gods, because [as we pointed to in the chapter called The Divine] the Divine seem to be satisfied with what they are [a God of war is satisfied in being such as is a Goddess of wisdom]; which is unlike many of the human race, and therefore; we must realise that the human race wants to continually evolve and become greater than what it is–just like the followers of the One-God religions wish to be greater than what they actually are! Although in realizing this we should also realise that the One-God religions hamper evolution, because they are not willing to evolve their scriptural belief, which is unlike the philosophical view of the Hindu, Buddhist and some other Pagan religions!"

Gaia sips her wine and then she says: "perhaps these Hindu verses in The Hymn of Man; that shows that man is capable of going beyond the realms of the Gods; are verses that show the true potential of mankind is not actually in the hands of the Gods but in the hands of mankind:

1 The man has a thousand heads a thousand eyes, a thousand feet. He pervaded the earth on all sides and extended beyond as far as ten fingers.

2 It is the man who is all this and whatever has been whatever is to be. He is the ruler of immortality, when he grows beyond every thing through food.[60]

This type of scripture could make man appear to be above the Divine when man has realised his true reality, but in realizing his true reality the wisdom of ages would be too much for the human brain to comprehend, and therefore; this complete wisdom could only become available after the death of the physical body."

Michael smiles and says: "the human race could actually be the creators of the Divine and in being such creators they would be Divine in themselves, and such wisdom may actually only be available to those that are enlightened enough after the death of the physical being that holds them in their present bondage!"

Pallas opens the door, smiles and says: "there are many possibilities of how the Divine were created [including self creation], but some religions that believe in the never ending circle of life death and rebirth seem to accept it for what it is, and therefore; they do not see any need to explore that part of creation that cannot be explained by the human being in its present state of evolution. But in realizing this we should realise that such religions do not explore their own evolutionary possibilities at all, and therefore; they do not realise that such an attitude can lead to them being underdeveloped in the philosophical and scientific fields! This type of attitude holds back scientific and philosophical progress, and can be just as

---

[60] The Rig Veda translated by Wendy Doniger O Flaherty p30 Penguin Books 1981

dangerous as the religions that believe that their God will come and put right all that they consider being wrong in this world!"

Lug walks over to Pallas and then he says: "dangerous practises are within all religions, because all the followers of different religions have different ideals of what their God or Gods actually are, and what the Divine are actually capable of, and where these differences occur; different practices occur; and these different practises cause conflicts when two religions disagree. Once these conflicts emerge and one of the religions that caused the conflicts becomes victorious, the victorious religion will try to destroy any understanding that conflicts with the victorious religions ideals!"

Morrighan smiles and says: "these conflicts have led to many problems and one of the main problems within religions is that of the ideals that surround creation. When we explored these ideals the self or the immortal soul could be seen as; the creator of its own universe whilst if is in the physical form, because the soul or the self is held in a type of bondage by its physicality. This physicality creates its own personal reality, and this personal reality was seen as being affected by the beliefs that surround the creation within a persons religious ideals, for example; the Fates, the Lords of Karma or even the One-God was seen as outside agents that could affect the physical beings progress! This progress could only be affected by the actions of the self whilst it is encumbered by the physical form, and whilst it was not enlightened enough to realise the truths that surround the impermanence of the universe that it has created for itself! Therefore the self or the immortal soul should be seen as a creative being that is only contained by its physical constraints. These constraints were seen to be placed upon the self by the controls and the creative ideals that surrounded their particular religions ideals. Hence the ideals that surrounded creation were seen as questionable and in many cases not provable or even scientifically inadequate, and or completely wrong, for example; there are some American Indian myths that saw the creation of the earth coming out of the water and we know this to be scientifically incorrect, but this is problematic, because without the water life upon this planet would not be able to exist. Therefore we must realise that some of the scientific truths that show how incorrect some of the religions are need to be analyzed in the different ways that we have done so!"

Sankara smiles and says: "although many of the more natural religions have been proved to be scientifically inadequate and wrong in their creation theories; their understanding of life being dependent on water for its origins and its existence seem to be greater than those that see a single God as the creator of all, because the One-God religions do not seem to hold the life giving force of water its true respect! Therefore such religions have become more reliant on the pleasing of their God than that of the planetary needs, and in losing such respect and understanding of the planets needs; have undermined many of the natural religions without trying to understand that all physical being upon this planets surface and in its oceans; are dependent upon the waters that support the natural world for their creation and their survival!"

Michael starts to load the rucksacks and then he says: "in the none understanding of the impermanence of living matter; the creation myths that are in the religions that rely solely upon a single deity; are not written with a philosophical or scientific understanding of the natural world, because it has been shown that they believe that their scriptures tell the truth behind the creation and in already thinking that they know the truth—they do not realise; that they need to have any understanding that is not within their scripture. This scriptural dogmatism creates many problems, because in carrying on with unscientific beliefs; many mistakes have and are still being made, and these mistakes have created and are still creating many planetary problems, for instance; the overpopulation of the planet leads to many food and water shortages that are considered catastrophic, but there are many religions that still do not believe in contraception even though science shows what the results of overpopulation are and could become!"

Pingala picks up one of the rucksacks and then she says: "the religions that rely solely upon their scriptures for the truth of creation, and what is being created; have been seen as a major problem for the sciences of many cultures. But the science within the cultures has eventually come to be even if the dominant religion or religions have tried to stop its publication and evolution. Therefore the creation can be seen as an evolutionary process that science can partly explain, but the very beginning of creation is still problematic, and this will not be resolved by these discussions, because science and the beliefs of the many religions have not been shown to be in any position to do so, and whilst some religions try to completely rely on their beliefs; the position of that type of religion will remain the same until its collapse through its lack of understanding! Such a collapse will be inevitable, because the ongoing creation will lead to greater scientific discoveries! Therefore the human race should begin to realise that the religions, that are not willing to be evolutionary and creative; are looking at being nothing more than being a number of pages in the history of the human race. This will happen, because the human race has an ongoing scientific and philosophical process that will uncover, and has uncovered; many truths that show many inadequacies and untruths within many religions beliefs and scriptures. Hence the human race should understand that the religions must evolve and create or they will–as I have already stated–become confined to history and their followers will die out."

Demeter walks up to Pingala and then Demeter says: "many religions are confined to history, and therefore; I suggest that it is possible that in the creative and evolutionary process many more beliefs and religions will be confined in such a way!"

Lug smiles and says: "although religions can be confined to history, the other worlds that have been theorized upon cannot be just put into history books whilst there is a possibility of their existence, because if such worlds really do exist there is a possibility that the spiritual worlds are actually permanent and never ending, because such worlds could rely on a level of existence that is beyond the physicality of the known universe. Therefore it is possible that such worlds are unknown entities until they are reached after the death of the physical being and if this is correct; the death of a physical being could actually be part of an evolutionary creative force–such as the immortal soul or the self–that has no ending, because it is above the physicality that we are aware of whilst in this present state of existence! If this is also correct; the self would be in an ongoing creative process that would have no boundaries–that are set upon it and required whilst it is in the bondage of the physical world–after its physical death. Therefore it is also possible that once the physical being has become enlightened enough to rise to one of the other worlds; all religion changes when they actually reach one of the other worlds and what has gone before may no longer be applicable! But this would only be possible if the self has managed to escape the bondage that was put upon it by their beliefs and superstitions!"

Gaia puts on her rucksack and then she says: "throughout our discussions it has become evident that the creative force of the human race is responsible for all religions and superstitions, because without such an imaginary creative thought process; the human race would never have evolved so many religions and superstitions within its short lifespan upon this planet! But, before we theorized further on the origination of such superstitions and cults we made evident that the thought process is a creative energy that relies on the Fates or past events for the creation to be able to weave the web in which all physical events are created. These past events that are responsible for physical creation and evolution all came from somewhere, but where that origin was or is remained a mystery for those that are willing to evolve their beliefs throughout our discussions, and this is due to the fact that as science evolves it explains how much of creation started, but it still cannot explain why and from where the origination came, for example; what was before the origination of our universe cannot presently be explained by science! Therefore we could surmise that the other world theories of many religions cannot be thoroughly explained, because it is possible that these other worlds that are thought to be on another plane of existence; could have come before the physical universe. Hence we should realise that the only thing that could explain such worlds is not available until after the human being is released from its physical bondage!"

Morrighan smiles and says: "whilst entrapped by the physical realities of the human races being; it has been creative and evolutionary in many of its fields. But many of the religions cults and superstitions have been a force in which the creative and evolutionary powers of the human race have been held at bay throughout their existence! This was and still is problematic in many cultures that were and are upon the planet, because their myths, legends and prophecies were—and in some cases still are—seen as the ultimate and unarguable truth. Therefore such religions have been seen as dogmatic, and in being so; they have also been realised to be hampering the human races progress. These problems led us to discuss the problems that are created by some of the myths and superstitions that believe they hold on to some kind of ultimate truth"

Demeter walks outside and then she says: "within the discussion on the cults and superstitions the demonizing of some of the older religions was seen as a method that could be used for the spread of a religion; that wanted to become dominant and dictatorial to those that were not of its dogmatic belief. One of the methods used was to use some of the Gods of other religions as pictorial or statue like images of the devil and or the demons that are associated with him, for example; the figures such as Pan, Hearne, etc… This type of demonizing was mainly used by the One-God religions, and in being so it helped to coerce the followers of many of the older religions into becoming followers of the One-God faiths. But in being so corruptive of other faiths the One-God religions have become overly destructive without the true realization of the consequences of their actions, and even in the early 21st century (a. c. e) there are still some cults within these dogmatic religions that deny the truth of some of the scientific discoveries. Therefore we should begin to realise that some of the ancient myths that are not able to evolve within such dogmatic religions are not beneficial to the human race, because they were made to coerce and corrupt the followers of other religions through unscientific means. When this is realised the dogmatism of such religions will be broken and such religions could eventually become extinct and left to the pages of history!"

Sankara follows Demeter and then he says: "when we realised that superstitions are founded by the self we made evident that all the writings on the superstitions and scriptures were written by the hand of man; this realization would become problematic for many religions, because of their belief structures that were not based on scientific understanding. This became more obvious throughout the later discussions; when we began to realise that the myths and superstitions of an earlier discussion were made by the human race, and many of these myths and superstitions were made for the coercion of the followers through the demonizing of earlier Gods, and through the misunderstanding of Mother Nature. These types of coercion have become problematic for the human race, because they held on to beliefs that tried to make some scientific theories and other religions; appear untruthful, and in doing so; they made them appear to be works of their devil and demons. Therefore the human race should realise that such religions need to be explored and in some cases need to be left within the pages of history if they are unwilling to evolve their beliefs!"

Pallas smiles and says: "the only way that such beliefs will be left in the pages of history rather than be a totally accepted belief; will be when the self is realised as the creative energy that caused such beliefs to come into existence! But this type of realization needs all the individual selves to realise that their powers of imagination and creation are responsible for their own belief structures; for some of the unfounded ancient beliefs to be left within the pages of history. Unfortunately this is not liable to happen whilst some religions are not willing to evolve their beliefs even though scientific evidence proves some of these beliefs to be wrong! Therefore the human race will carry on defiling the scientific evidence that Mother Nature and the universe provides, and in doing so; they could eventually be forcing their own extinction. Although in saying that it is also possible; that such religions will actually have the intelligence to grow up, evolve and confine some of their beliefs to the pages of history."

Merlin smiles and says: "whilst many religions do not see the self as such a creator it is doubtful that the human race will become able to lose their ideals that surround demons, because [as we have made evident] there are many religious cults within the human race that are not willing to lose their ideals of demons. This is because the religions that use demons as a method of control do not wish to lose such a useful means of domination. Therefore the many religions that use such methods are not liable to evolve whilst they have a major controlling factor that is available to them through their beliefs. Hence the human race must understand that such controlling factors are only kept in place for the dogmatic religions that wish to keep ancient beliefs; without any wish to understand the true consequences of the actions of such beliefs!"

Lug puts on his rucksack, walks out of the door and then he says: "there are many possible consequences to such dogmatism and these consequences can be addressed, but whilst the consequences are held back by religions that are not willing to evolve their belief structures, the human race will only be held to account for its actions by the natural worlds finite resources. But even this realization is problematic for some of the dogmatic religions, because they are unwilling to realise such consequences until it becomes too late! Once this is realised the human race should also begin to realise that any dogmatism within any religion [and the fact that there must be some type of dogmatism within any religion if it is to survive as the religion from whence it came] is there for a purpose, and that purpose is the survival of the religion, for example; the destruction or the defilement of any religions shrines is seen to have dire consequences in most if not all religions, and an example of this was seen in the Greek myth of Medusa; when the beauty of Medusa was turned into something horrific, and her head eventually ended up in the breastplate of the Goddess Athena's armour, because Medusa and another God defiled the Goddess Athena's shrine ! Hence it becomes apparent that any defilement of a Gods or Goddesses sacredness is punishable in a horrific way in the legends of mankind (the One-God religions and the Hindu religions also have been seen to have myths with dire consequences if you go against the wish of their God or Gods)!"

Morrighan smiles and says: "dogmatism has been seen to be within most if not all the religions we have discussed, but all dogmatism needs to be able to evolve and be lost if any religion is to survive, because if any religion remains completely dogmatic in its beliefs it can create much harm to the planet and to the race that it is meant to protect! Therefore the human race needs to realise that many of its myths legends and beliefs need to be confined to history, because if they remain constant the religion will destroy itself through the lack of compliance with other religions belief structures, and instead of evolving it will become completely confined to the pages of history!"

Michael closes the door and then he says: "history is where all of the human races beliefs have emerged from, but this is still problematic, because there still is no answer to the real origination of many beliefs and legends, because the original thought that creates must start from history, and if all starts from history the start of that historical process still has no complete answer."

Gaia walks beside Michael and then she says: "although there is no complete answer there are many myths and legends that would have originated through the acts of Mother Nature, and these acts were seen as either demonic or Godlike actions which could not be explained by the scientific and philosophical reasoning of the times in which they were written! Therefore the human race should realise that the evolution of scientific and philosophical theories should not be dismissed or held back, by the beliefs of cultures that were not as liberal in their ideals as the scientific communities that evolved within them. Although this realization sounds obvious and without problems; there are many ethical issues that create problems; when the realization of the inaccuracies of the myths and legends of many religions become apparent; to the scientific communities within the religions that science proves to be misguided."

Pingala passes a bag of grapes to Michael and then she says: "many of the people within the human race must like to be led by the people that teach them their beliefs, and when these beliefs are questioned and undermined by other races or the scientific communities within their own culture or race; the people who follow loyally do not see that there are other truths that are not within their religion, and try to undermine those that invalidate the truths that the religions loyal followers are either comfortable with or are afraid to go against. Hence the human race should begin to understand that their religious beliefs–that they are comfortable with or afraid to go against–are only able to be so enslaving because they are not willing to philosophically and scientifically question their beliefs in a true and productive manner!"

Michael smiles at Pingala and then he says: "there are many events and animals [of the physical world or the dream world] that have been seen as monstrous creations that were misunderstood and misused by many religions in their own creations, and some of the monstrous ideals could be seen as having a very basic scientific understanding of creation! But some of the myths and legends that we have discussed have been dismissed by other religions and cultures without any philosophical and/or scientific analysis. This has led to the extermination of many cultural beliefs without any applied reasoning. Unfortunately this type of extermination has lost the origins of the creation of many of the myths and legends that could be applied to actual creation myths; and in losing such origins the ideals that surround monsters became confined; to the beliefs of dominant religions and much of the early natural reasoning abilities and possibilities became lost. Therefore the human race became dominated by religions that were selfishly trying to eradicate any reasoning that did not follow their scriptural writings. This early creative domination has been seen to hamper the progress of the human race, and it has also been seen as a destructive force that has had little if any respect for the planetary environments or the scientific practises that prove it to be wrong!"

Demeter takes some of the grapes and then she says: "it became evident that the lack of respect of Mother Nature had many ways in which it could be used, and the main way was for religions to use monsters and demons for their lack of respect for the planets other creatures and the natural systems that Mother Nature creates. Therefore such religions became dogmatic and lost the ability to create any ideals or truths that contradicted their beliefs. In losing the creative aspects within their followers capabilities; these religions have started to lose the respect of other religions and communities that are willing to evolve as science and philosophy evolves! This loss of respect could eventually lead to such religions losing all their followers, and this loss would also be through such religions unrelenting foolishness. This foolishness is due to such religions not being willing to accept that their scriptures were written when mankind was in its infancy, and its scientific and philosophical understanding was severely limited because many fields of science and philosophy were unexplored or in their extreme infancy!"

Morrighan smiles and says: "in mankind's infancy there were many things that were put down to the powers of the One-God or the Gods, and the scriptures that emerged from these are seen to be pretty much incorrect. Such incorrectness within the scriptures has also been realised as a major problem that has hampered the development of the human race, because some of the religions scriptures are thought of as the only true reality; even if they are proven scientifically incorrect. But in hampering the human races development the major religions have lost and are still losing many of their followers to other religions, and the main one of these is the scientific religion that is becoming more predominant in today's communities! When this is realised the religions that try to hold back science should try to incorporate the science that it is trying to invalidate, because if it does not do so it will eventually lead to its own extinction! This is becoming more obvious as mankind develops and evolves through its scientific creations, because within its scientific explorations many of mankind's beliefs have evolved through its creative spirit. This creative evolution may have been hampered by many religions, but it always seems to manage to stay within the mind and the spirit of the human being. If the major religions would realise and incorporate such a creative force they would need to evolve and become less dogmatic if they are to survive the onslaught of the creative will of the human being."

Lug passes Morrighan some of the grapes and then he says: "the creative force of the human race is a part of the spirit or the self that has emerged from the will of the human being, and this will is also responsible for the survival of the dogmatic religions, because without the will to survive; the dogmatic religions and the dogmatic aspects that are within all religions would not be able to survive! With this will to survive many of the dogmatic religions did not wish to evolve, and the creative willpower of such religions became lost and this was because of ancient ideals that were unscientifically founded and written in their scriptures. Some of these scriptures have been seen to be inaccurate and dangerous to the planets environments. This has been realised as a major issue throughout our discussions, because of the harm these dogmatic religions can do to misunderstood environments. This misunderstanding of the environment has led to the destruction and the demonizing of many other cultures and environments."

Gaia smiles and says: "there are many images that have been used–particularly by the One-God faiths–for the demonizing of other religions. This type of demonizing has also been seen to be used for a way of undermining the scientific world's discoveries; that go against some of the unfounded and unscientific scriptural writings that some religions rely upon for their ethical ideals! These ideals have been seen as the cause of much dysfunction within many environments upon this planet, and once this has been realised the religions that cause such problems still use their demons and devils to explain the consequences of their foolish and continuing actions! This foolishness that is the cause of such religions continuing defilement of the planet is partly due to their negligence of the natural world, and their negligence of the creative and destructive powers of the human race!"

Morrighan passes the grapes to Gaia and then Morrighan says: "that type of problem arose through the misunderstanding of Mother Nature, but [although it is] this misunderstanding does not need to be problematic if religion is willing to understand that its scriptures were created in ancient civilizations that were not as scientifically evolved as they became in later centuries, and therefore; the old beliefs need to evolve and their mistakes need to be admitted to. But this will not happen whilst some religions ignore some scientific evidence, and in their ignorance they make some of the scientific evidence seem to be works of the devil and the demons! Therefore the religions that make some scientific evidence seem to be works of the devil and evil should be kept in check and confined to the history books, before they create too much disharmony and destruction through their negligent practises! But as we have made evident this will not happen whilst there are those that are willing to be enslaved by unscientifically founded beliefs; that were written in times of scientific unawareness!"

Gaia smiles and says: "such a lack of knowledge has been realised as being problematic for the human races evolution, because in many places the lack of understanding has been used as a means by which many religions hierarchies have kept control over their followers. This in itself has been seen as a creator of problems, because any religion that uses a lack of knowledge and a misunderstanding of Mother Nature to keep control over its followers; have and are still causing much destruction and harm to the environments in which they live!"

Merlin starts to peel an orange and then he says: "much destruction and many problems have been seen to come from the belief structures that are not willing to evolve; which must be realised as foolishness when science and some other religions actually realise the impermanence of the planet, and the present universe in which the physical being resides. Such foolishness needs to be undermined by those that are willing to evolve, because this foolishness has hampered the human race and will inevitably lead to the whole races destruction; if it is allowed to evolve without true scientific and philosophical understanding. But—as we have pointed out in many places—such understanding has been held back by some religions and those religions have spread and used the destructive powers of new technologies without truly understanding the consequences of their actions. Such ignorance has led to many undesirable consequences, and these consequences have been used for the ideas of a vengeful unsatisfied God; when it is actually the consequences of misunderstanding the chaotic actions and sometimes the predictable actions of Mother Nature!"

Pallas steps over a fallen branch and then she says: "Gods have been used for many explanations of Mother Nature's events, but in using such divine beings for such actions the truth behind Mother Nature's chaotic creations needs to remain hidden, by those that wish to remain in control of the human races scientific progress. This has been realised as being attempted by many religions for their control over their followers, and for the reasoning behind the destruction of other faiths and cultures that remain outside such religions beliefs, and this has been made evident to us by the demonizing and the vengeful Gods tactics that have been used to describe many natural events; that were unexplainable at the times in which they were created. But such creations have fallen to the scientific and philosophical reasoning of many cultures [including some of their own].

Although that is freely evident in many of today's societies (early 21st century a.c.e.); there are still some religions that refuse to fully accept the scientific and philosophical understanding that has emerged throughout the ages. This none acceptance of the evolved understanding has been seen as ways in which the demonic forces; have been used to try to undermine; the evolving evidence of the scientific and the philosophical understanding! Therefore we should realise that such vengeful Gods and demons; are mainly fictitious myths that have been created by those that want to keep the human race in the bondage that was created in the early scriptures. Such a style of bondage should be realised as a danger to the human race, because in being unwilling to evolve it will become extinct–and unlike the dinosaurs that evolved into birds–it will lead to the complete extinction of its species, because in being so trapped it has no means to evolve when this planet becomes inhospitable and eventually dies!"

Pingala looks at the dolphins off the coast and then she says: "it is or has become evident that some religions are heading for extinction, and these religions need to be confined to the history books [as we have mentioned before]. But we must realise that for such religions to be confined to history the human race needs to become released from the bondage that such religions have confined some of them within. Such a release is problematic, because there are many that are unwilling to accept any understanding that undermines some religions ancient scriptures. Although the understanding that undermines some of these scriptures has been made evident; the fanatics of such religions seem unable to accept the truths that are made evident through science, and this is because such religions make many of their followers feel superior, and in feeling superior they believe that their God will take over the world's population. When this feeling of superiority is tantamount to their religions beliefs; the fanatics (and this includes any of the hierarchy of most major religions) have been seen to try to demonize other beliefs (this includes scientific and philosophical discoveries), and destroy them through corrupt practices that have been formed through the misunderstanding of the untruths that are within their scriptures!"

Sankara smiles and says: "therefore the human race should begin to realise that such ideals need to be kept in bondage for them to survive, but in doing so such ideals can only lead to their extinction, because such ideals cannot evolve whilst the species evolves. This evolution can only happen through the true understanding that is available through science and metaphysical philosophy, and this is problematic, because these types of understanding will eventually lead to the destruction of many religions beliefs; which will in turn lead to the extinction of such religions. Such extinction needs to happen, because some of the human race has been held in bondage and had its evolutionary process held back by the misunderstanding, of some ancient races inadequate scientific and philosophical understanding. Although this has been made evident in our discussions; many of the followers of such religions will still try to demonize these thought processes; which will lead to their own extinction; which is inevitable if they are not willing to evolve!"

Demeter walks over to Sankara and then she says: "if any religion is to evolve it must be willing to let go of some of its ancient beliefs, and such a religion would need to have a process; by which enlightenment is not confined and held in bondage by ancient and misguided scriptures. But this has been shown to be problematic, because many religions think that they are superior because of the understanding that is given to them in their ancient scriptures, and in fanatically following these scriptures they are not able to accept any truth that undermines their ideals. This type of fanaticism does not allow them the realities that are given to them that are outside their scriptures, and in being so; their scriptures have been shown to give them the need to dominate other cultures through the untruths that they have blindly followed. The will to dominate through those untruths have and are still leading to many problems within their environment and the environment of others. Therefore we have shown that such religions have been able to dominate through fear and the corruption of other faiths and practices and are still doing so in the early 21st century (a.c.e.). Hence we should begin to realise that such corrupt practices should not be tolerated in a civilized world. But such a realization is problematic; when the world that the human race lives in is not civilized through its own religious creations! This uncivilized creative aspect of the human race has increased as some religions will to dominate has become more potent; with the misuse of technologies that have a highly destructive process!"

Morrighan steps onto the beach and then she says: "such religions have been shown to be detrimental to the human race. But in being shown to be detrimental; such religions will still not be lost to the pages of history whilst the human race is as uncivilized as the followers of such religions allow it to be! This uncivilized structure of many dominant religions will remain part of the human race whilst their followers are dominant within the world's population, and therefore; we have shown that many scientific and ethical values need to be redefined and accepted before the human race makes itself extinct! Even though this understanding has become quite feasible through our discussions; it seems to be more and more likely that the dominant religious hierarchies; will not evolve the beliefs that were written without the understanding of the early 21st centuries (a.c.e.)."

Lug walks beside Morrighan and says: "most religions structures have been shown to accept that there is some kind of afterlife. But this idea is problematic for many religions followers, because in not allowing their beliefs to evolve within some of their religions; the human race has been hampered by structures that have not truly allowed them to evolve. As we are pointing out this could lead to extinction, and these beliefs could be confined to the history books and lose all of their followers. But as Morrighan has pointed to this will not happen whilst the human race remains as uncivilized as it still is. Therefore much exploration is still needed within the realms of spirituality and the afterlife. This type of exploration has proved to be hugely problematic, because as we have shown there are many ideals that surround the afterlife, and these will not be resolved in our discussions, because there are no means by which we can give empirical proof of such a life whilst we are held in bondage by our physical being, and the dogmatism of some false beliefs. Hence some of the human race should begin to realise that some of them are bound and imprisoned by the physical fears that are placed upon them by their religious beliefs! But this is unlikely because most of those that are held in such bondage will remain enslaved by the fear that their religion has placed upon them! Therefore there will be those within the human race that will always remain enslaved by their Gods ideals; whilst they fear the wrath that will befall them if they undermine the scriptures of their Divine."

Morrighan smiles and says: "that fear will remain whilst the dominant religions hierarchies' uncivilized attitude is tolerated by the majority of the human race, but this toleration needs to come to an end if the human race is to truly evolve and realise its evolution before its extinction! This extinction may only be a physical form of extinction and the spirit may survive and be reincarnated into a new being, but if that is the case; the evolution of the race needs to be recorded and when there are those that cannot and will not think beyond the present physical form this is unlikely. Therefore whilst change occurs it should be properly recorded and not demonized as some religions will try to do. Hence the human race should realise that the demonizing of any scientific and philosophical understanding is only used by those; that wish to remain enslaved and compliant to the will of others; that are not able to realise beyond a simplistic belief structure; that was written when some of the human races ancestors were more gullible and more easily led by those that appeared to have the greatest knowledge and power!"

Michael passes a bottle of water to Morrighan and then he says: "as we have seen there are many within the human race that are easily led, and this gullibility is hard to extinguish; when in the making of some religions coercive powers the use of fear is a major factor! Therefore the easily led elements within the human race will remain compliant whilst the fear factor remains within their belief structure. When the fear factor is removed from the belief structure; the easily led will be freed from their religions bondage, but this will not happen whilst their religions hierarchies remain so coercive in their teaching!"

Pallas smiles and says: "many religions have been seen to be coercive and even corrupt in their methods of trying to make other cultures and religions extinct in the process of creating their ideal world. But these types of religions do not want to realise the harm they do whilst they are in the process of denying the human race; the free will and the free thought that much of it desires. The reason that became evident [throughout our discussions] for such an action is that such religions have become enslaved by their beliefs, and in being so enslaved they have lost the awareness that would grant them the knowledge that they are actually a slave, and therefore; they also lost the awareness of the process of extinction within the realms of Mother Nature!"

Gaia passes a pear to Pallas and then Gaia says: "when some of mankind lost the awareness of their enslavement and the respect of Mother Nature; these people seemed to think that they were superior to anything else upon the planet. This type of idealistic superiority has been seen as a destructive force within the world's people, and other species! Therefore; those that are in a religion that is willing to evolve should not let themselves be coerced and conned into a belief structure; that is not willing to evolve, and that will [in its ignorance] cause much destruction! That destruction has been made evident by the past and some of the present actions of such religions, and therefore; the human race should not be fooled by such religions claims, but as we have seen there are many people that like to hold onto beliefs that are not compliant with a truly civilized society. Hence it became obvious that many of the human race blindly follow those that are unsighted by the religious ignorance; that they were taught by those that were as ignorant as they themselves have become! For those that willingly follow such ignorant practices extinction is an inevitable outcome if society ever becomes truly civilized! This would happen, because society would not tolerate any belief structure that thought killing for political or religious desires was acceptable!"

Merlin smiles and says: "as we have seen most of the human race can tolerate much of the grief that their religions have cast upon them. But such a tolerance of hardship that is created by such religions is only tolerated by those; that are enslaved or had their beliefs forced upon them and then enslaved by the enforcers of their religion. Such enforcers have been responsible for the extinction of many cultures and species, and whilst this continues the human race can only be seen as being uncivilized! Once that the human race becomes aware that it is being uncivilized it will begin to realise the foolishness of their actions. But this will not happen whilst the human race believes that the Divine that they think of as the supreme, being, or beings are above themselves. That is why in many places we have pointed to the Self being the creator of the Divine and not the other way round as is usual in most religions, and from this it also becomes plausible that the creators of such Divine are part of the original chaos, because before order is created only chaos can remain. When this is realised the chaotic actions of Mother Nature could suggest that the true Divine is what we refer to as Mother Nature."

Gaia points to the distant natural harbour and then she says: "many of Mother Nature's actions have only been realised as chaotic because of scientific understanding, and this understanding would have become available sooner; if the religions that try to deny some scientific discoveries had not held up their process and in ancient times used such chaos as an act of their Divine [or demons] to keep their followers compliant! Therefore mankind should realise that the ancient beliefs that many of them follow are not as reliable as their religious leaders have led them to believe. But this has been realised to be problematic for many of the dogmatic religions followers, and this is because in being so dogmatic many religions followers have been seen to blindly follow their ancient scriptures! Such scriptures have been seen to be unreliable, because they were written in times of limited understanding! This limited understanding has been realised as a means by which many cultures have been coerced into losing the natural understanding that science and philosophy provides. Therefore any ethics that use such a limited understanding for their laws need to be revised. But as we have shown this is not liable to happen whilst many religions are allowed to keep on coercing and forcing others into beliefs that have been realised to be misinterpretations and untruths! Such misinterpretations and untruths should now be realised as dangerous and leading to the extinction of the human race if they are allowed to go against Mother Nature in the ways that they have been accustomed to.

Therefore the evolution of the human race needs a solid ethical process that is not dependent on ancient and outdated ideals. That type of solid background needs the freedom of science and philosophy to be true and able to follow leads that go against ancient myths. But whilst some religions are able to interfere with the process of discovery; the human race is partly bound by these ancient beliefs!

Sankara smiles and says: "such beliefs have been seen to be orchestrated by the Divine of religion. But as we have made evident this is problematic, because the Divine could actually be the creation of mankind rather than the other way round. Therefore the scientific and philosophical processes need to be held in the same respect as the Divine of any religion, and this is because any religions writing is open to the mistakes and the exaggeration of the human writers, and if the human race is the creator of its own Divine; the Divine would be as open to the mistakes of those that created it! If the Divine was not created by the human race and the Divine did create the human race, the question of whether or not it created the soul within the physical being still remains! Although this problem still remains the possibility of the soul or the self being as divine as the Divine is certain if the soul or the self is immortal."

Pingala passes a peach to Sankara and then she says: "the idea of immortality seems to be the main reason for which many people fear the consequences of the religion that they have been taught, and this is because the fear of the unknown is used by many religions to control their followers, and this fear of the unknown has also been made evident to be the cause of the holding back of science and philosophy by the dogmatic religions. This is because science and philosophy have explored and explained some of the unknown that was put down to acts of Gods and demons! Therefore the human race should realise that many of its scriptures are inaccurate and in being so; the works that show them as inaccurate; should not be demonized by those that are not willing to learn through such mistakes!"

Merlin smiles and says: "most religions have been seen to create chaos through their inabilities to allow their religion to develop and evolve. This chaos has not been realised, because most major religions have evolved through dogmatic beliefs, and whilst they have evolved in numbers their true understanding of the natural world has not evolved. This inability to evolve their beliefs will and has led to extinctions within the cultures of the human race and other species. If this process of extermination is allowed to continue the human race will probably exterminate itself or Mother Nature will have a hand in the process of such extermination! Therefore the human race needs to evolve their ethics before such a process reaches its conclusion! Hence the human race needs to accept; that it came from a chaotic creation and that their Divine are as much a part of chaos as the human race is, and that this chaos is the way of Mother Nature which is the major God whilst the human race is held in the bondage of physical being. If this is not understood and accepted the other Divine of the human race will not be able to stop their extinction, because Mother Nature has the last word in all that happens to the physical being! Therefore the human race should also realise that as its intelligence and understanding evolves the physical body will also evolve and as it evolves the understanding of past ages evolves with it!"

Morrighan walks up to a rock pool and then she says: "the present physical form of the human race is liable to become extinct in the evolutionary process–just as the dinosaurs became extinct and evolved into birds. Hence the human race should realise that its present physical form is liable to become extinct due to the evolutionary process of Mother Nature. In realizing this; the human race should also realise that their intellectual abilities could also evolve far beyond its present understanding– if it is allowed to do so. But this is problematic, because the human race could cause its own extinction before such a process is allowed to evolve! Therefore the human race must allow its religious ideals evolution; if it is to avoid such extinction, and in allowing such a process to evolve the human race must realise that some of its dogmatic beliefs need to be confined–as we have mentioned before–to the history books.

As we have made evident chaos is the creator, and if the Divine come from chaos; the Divine will be part chaos as will all of its creations! Therefore the idea of a chaotic creation emerges and this idea is becoming more relevant as we have shown that the chaotic nature of many religions; has created many problems, and many of these problems have been created by the unwillingness of the intellectual evolution of some major religions. Hence mankind should begin to realise that even the dogmatic religions create chaos in their unwillingness to learn beyond their scriptures! This unwillingness to learn has hampered the intellectual evolution of mankind for many centuries, and the chaos that has been created by such unwillingness has remained unrecognized by the majority of those within the dogmatic religions. Therefore the lack of understanding within such religions grew into a creative chaotic form which they called Divine retribution or the work of demons and devils! Hence many of the human races became enslaved through the fear of the works of devils and/or Divine retribution. But this type of enslavement became problematic, because the human race has many people within it that are willing to enquire beyond their religions teaching. This enquiring mind has started to evolve at a greater pace than many religions; which has caused many problems for the dogmatic scriptures and ideals of many religions. In creating these problems the enquiring mind has caused chaos within the dogmatic religions, because such a mind has undermined their controlling and corrupt structures! Therefore mankind should realise that where there is apparent order chaos can resume if the structure is full of untruths and chaotic in its construction!"

Pallas walks past the rock pool and then she says: "chaos has many causes and consequences and the nature of the human race appears to be as chaotic as the Gods that they worship. Therefore the human race needs to be aware of the chaos that it has and is causing with many of its religions policies. But in becoming so aware the human race needs to realise that the universe that their physical being is part of is a creator of chaos. This creation of chaos within the universe is beyond the control of mankind [whilst it is held in bondage by the physical being], and with this being so; the physical being of mankind needs a certain amount of order [within this chaos] for their survival. Although this may seem quite obvious; many of the religions like to believe that their God can take them away from such chaos, and in their beliefs many religions followers have lost their ability to evolve, and in losing this ability they are threatening their followers and the rest of the human race with a type of extinction that is total (many of the dinosaurs evolved into birds and so their extinction was not total)."

Michael passes Pallas an orange and then he says: "total extinction could be inevitable when the present universe dies. But the death of the universe does not mean that there will not be another one that is created from the chaos that this one was, and therefore; the human race needs to be unconfined in its evolutionary abilities. Hence the human race needs to realise that some of its ancient scriptures are outdated and could lead to the annihilation of the human race, because such scriptures are holding the human race in a type of bondage; that is not beneficial to the being of their race. However apparent this is becoming; there is still many of the followers of the dogmatic religions that do not and will not listen to those that show the inaccuracies and untruths that are written within some of the religions scriptures!"

Gaia smiles and says: "many religions have been realised to be dogmatic in their scriptures, and this dogmatism would not be able to evolve and accept the universal truths that are being uncovered by scientific and philosophical experimentation! Therefore the chaos that is universal will not be accepted by such religions, because in being so dogmatic they have used their devil and demons to undermine the scientific and philosophical truths that have shown some of their scriptures to be incorrect! Hence it has become evident that such religions have and will carry on using such methods even though it causes the extinction of other cultures and species without realizing the chaos that they are creating! Therefore the human race should try to control such religions before they cause the extinction of the physical world that they are part of! But as we have made evident the human race is not likely to control and confine such religions; whilst these religions are allowed to exterminate and cause much misinterpretation of truths through their own misunderstanding, of the universal chaotic and creative process of Mother Nature! As we have shown this type of misunderstanding and purposeful misinterpretation; is used in many aspects of the belief structures of the dogmatic religions, and many fear tactics are created from natural events that are exaggerated and used without any true experimentation! Therefore mankind should begin to realise that dogmatism within a religion is a dangerous tool that is used for the enslavement of the free will, and the exploratory mind of the people that do not wish to be held back by ancient and unscientifically founded beliefs!"

Lug stops to admire the sailing ship that they are approaching and then he says: "religions dogmatism has aroused many suspicions and in turn created the reason for exploring what many religions have tried to hide, and that is the untruths and mistakes that are within their scriptures. Those mistakes cannot be admitted by some religions, because they believe that their God is perfect, and that his scriptures are written with his aid, and that the scriptures are undeniable. Such ideals have been seen to corrupt the true understanding of the scientific and philosophical processes of many cultures. But just like the butterfly that flaps its wings and changes the direction of a future tornado or hurricane; religions interference in the evolutionary process does not stop it happening; it just changes its direction and causation. Therefore the human race should realise that a jealous and destructive God could be the cause of the extinction of the human race, and this would be through the selfish ideals of those that created such a beings religion! This selfishness has been shown to be apparent in many religions, and such selfishness has caused much chaos within the natural world. This creative chaos is not seen for what it is by the religions that believe they have a perfect God. Therefore the human race needs to realise that the follower of a religion that cannot see its own creative chaos needs to be revised if it is to remain. Such a reversionary exercise is not going to happen whilst the dogmatic religions are allowed to maintain their belief structures, and to corrupt others by using such structures to outlaw and undermine scientific and philosophical progress."

Demeter walks up to Morrighan and then Demeter remarks: "the intellectual evolution of the human race has been shown to be held back by ancient misleading, mistaken and chaotic scriptures. Although this is made evident in our previous discussions; there are many followers of many religions; that will still blindly follow their religion into extinction, because they strongly believe that their God will come and save them in some kind of apocalyptic process. Hence it becomes easy for them to undermine and become blinded from scientific truths by saying that such truths are works of the devil and/or demons. In this way such religions have become irresponsible in their actions. This irresponsibility has and is causing much chaos within the world, and the cause of this chaos is unseen by such followers, because they believe that they are creating perfection. Therefore such religions will create their own extinction, because their followers will become less and less satisfied with their lack of intellectual progression, and as this process begins the religion loses its acceptability. When this acceptability is lost its followers become fewer and fewer until the inevitable extinction. This inevitable extinction has happened to many cultures religions, and these religions have usually been taken over by another up and coming religion that has dominating principles. Such domineering religions will inevitably become dominated themselves if they allow themselves to become intellectually inferior through dogmatic beliefs. Hence the reason for their previously mentioned extinction becomes obvious!"

Merlin smiles at Demeter and then he says: "that process of religions extinction has become evident in many of our discussions, and one of the main causes of this is when a religion becomes over confident in its domination of other races. One major principle that seems to have been forgotten by the domineering selfish and dogmatic religions is that power corrupts. Such a principle never seems to become evident to the followers of the One-God religions that believe that their God is the only true God in existence! Therefore these types of religion blindly follow a system that becomes more and more corrupt as it progresses through the destruction of other cultures."

Morrighan smiles and says: "it is without doubt that too much power corrupts, and that such corruption leads to annihilation and attempted extinction if it is thoughtlessly followed. But such attempts of extinction seem to have been unsuccessful, because the free will of the entire human race has been seen to be too strong for the total enslavement of the intellectual evolution of the human race. Although such enslavement has proved unsuccessful; modern science has given the fanatical followers of such religions the ability to cause the extinction of the human race; through the foolish use of weapons that they do not fully understand. Therefore the human race should realise that whilst the self or the immortal soul is the possibility of living for ever; the physical being can be destroyed by foolish actions! Hence mankind needs to reassess some of its ancient ethics and be less selfish when it is trying to express its beliefs. But this is not going to happen until mankind accepts that some of its Gods are over selfish, over domineering and are trying to be the absolute power within the universe; without realizing the cause and effects of their selfish attitudes!"

Sankara passes a pear to Morrighan and then he says: "such ideals will not be broken until the overbearing and domineering religions are realised for what they are! But this type of realization will not become evident to the followers [of such religions] that have been willingly blinded by the untruths that have been taught to them! Therefore the human race needs to realise that whilst there is any kind of free will that is available to all; there will always be those that are willing to be blinded by something that does not leave questions open to them! Hence the realization of the ease by which the dogmatic religions are able to coerce others into a non questionable belief becomes evident whilst free will allows them to do so! This type of coercion is more easily managed by the hierarchies of such religions, because in having an unquestionable belief; the dogmatic religions have no need for scientific progress when their belief tells them all that they believe they need to know. But [as we have made evident in past discussions] such an all knowing belief does not give the truth and in giving believable untruths it becomes chaotic without realizing the chaos it is causing. It also does not realise the chaotic processes of Mother Nature, because it blames unexplainable events on the actions of their displeased God and/or the actions of the devil and demons. Hence mankind should realise that the free will is a problematic area, because as I have just explained if the will is truly free there will always be those who are looking for a simple explanation to their questions, and science and philosophy rarely provides an easy explanation to a universal problem!"

Pingala points to the jumping dolphins and then she says: "as we have discussed; the ethics of the human race; need to be rewritten to accommodate the new understanding that is being constantly upgraded by scientific and philosophical works! When this is understood there may be many beliefs that will become extinct, because; there would be no place in society for a belief structure that hinders the intellectual progress and the evolution of the human race! Although society will lose the need for such negligent belief; the nature of the human race is so self contradictory that the human race is liable to allow such beliefs to remain a part of its society as long as there are those that are willing to follow such beliefs. Therefore it is highly probable that such beliefs will remain somewhere within mankind's cultures. Although these structures may remain they will be manipulated in so many ways they will evolve if they are to remain. Such an evolutionary process will not be understood as evolution by those that follow the ancient belief structures, because they will manipulate their scriptures in such a way that they will believe that they were right in the times that they were written."

Pallas smiles and says: "all throughout our discussions many religions have been shown to be manipulative in their works, and therefore; those types of religion have spread like a murderous disease! I say murderous because many of the manipulative religions try to–purposefully–destroy other cultures and beliefs! Such a type of action should not be allowed in a civilized society. But this is problematic, because the followers of a murderous religion are so entranced by their beliefs that they believe that they are the only society that is truly civilized. Therefore the extermination of races and cultures that do not wish to become enslaved–by such religions–has been shown to be a part of the uncivilized actions of those religions; that believe that the only way to become civilized is to become a part of their uncivilized religion! Hence the human race should realise that the ethics of an uncivilised religion need to evolve if that religion is to become truly civilized. Yet again this is problematic, because if such religions are to evolve some of their beliefs need to be made extinct and confined to the history books!"

Merlin walks up to Morrighan and then he says: "from what we have discussed it is becoming evident that science and philosophy could and is causing the extinction of many ancient beliefs. But some of the beliefs that are due to become extinct; have carried on even though there has been shown to be many falsehoods within their scriptures and beliefs! Therefore the human race needs to revise the ethics and eliminate the stupidity of the cultures and religions that will not allow their beliefs to evolve! The human race needs to do this, because if it does not do so it will lead to much more unnecessary destruction and much more unnecessary annihilation within its own and other species! Hence mankind should understand that all it can accomplish from being dogmatic is its own extermination as a free willed physical being. This extermination may not seem too bad for those that accomplish a spiritual enlightenment, but such enlightenment will never be available to those that are not willing to evolve through a learning process, and no one can truly learn if they are hampered by a dogmatic belief structure that was written in a time of misunderstanding!"

Morrighan steps onto the rocky outcrop and then she says: "it is unnecessary for the human race to carry its dogmatism as the burden that it has been shown to be, but the misunderstandings of ancient times have been blindly followed! When it is realised; how blinded by such misunderstanding the human race is; the dogmatic approach of many religions does not allow new understanding to change their beliefs, and in not doing so; they have been shown as dictatorial and manipulative in their tactics, and many of the natural ethics that we have suggested have been broken! Therefore the demonizing of scientific and philosophical discoveries need to be ignored and realised as a means of corrupting; the means of the evolution; of the intelligence; of the truly civilized people within the human race! Hence mankind needs to admit that some of the scriptures within its holy books are incorrect! Once this is admitted by those uncivilized beings; a truly civilized society may be born! But this will not happen; whilst those that follow the dogmatic religions believe that their God is all knowing! The belief of that all knowing God has one major error and that is its knowledge must be infinite and in being infinite it goes on forever and this is not possible, because if something goes on forever; it has no end, and if the infinite God knows all there is to know; there must be an end to knowledge and that is not possible if infinity goes on forever, because forever can have no end. That is why there can be no all knowing God! Although there can be no all knowing God; this does not mean that the One-God religions God does not exist; it just means they are mistaken in some of their beliefs!"

Gaia steps beside Morrighan and then she says: "mankind makes many mistakes, and if any God actually created mankind; it would be capable of making mistakes or creating chaos. Therefore it is more than likely that all are chaotic within their formation! Such a chaotic formation would then be soul deep and the chaos that is created by the self whilst it is held in bondage in the physical being; will, therefore; always be chaotic in its creations of religion and its understanding of universal truths! Hence the human race should begin to understand that its religious scriptures and ethics are created from chaos, and that intellectual chaos is born through misinterpretation and misunderstanding. Therefore, mankind should realise that all of its religions need to be able to evolve if the human race is going to survive the extermination that it creates for other species! This survival is only possible if universal truths are sought without being hindered and manipulated by the chaotic misunderstandings; that were created in times of racial and religious disharmony!"

Pingala steps into the little boat at the edge of the outcrop and then she says: "that is why the human race needs to let go of the physical and intellectual bonds that are created by some religions, and seek the truth of their actual being! Such a truth cannot be found by looking to a God that is purely dictatorial, because in being so dictatorial that God only has its own interests in mind! Therefore the human race needs to seek understanding that is probably beyond some of their Gods abilities. With this in mind the probability of the self of the human race, being a creator of many of its own Gods becomes highly probable [as we have pointed out in our discussions]! Although this is highly probable [whilst the self is held in bondage by its physical being]; it must be understood that Mother Nature is the true God whilst it is held in this state!"

Michael steps next to Pingala and then he says: "all such truths are presently hidden by chaos, and therefore; mankind will remain captured by the ethics of many of the religions, because most of mankind has a natural fear of what comes after their death! Therefore any simple explanation is feasible to those that are unwilling to explore what is probably beyond the realms of their Gods understanding! Such a realization is problematic for the ones held in bondage by their God, because such a realization would mean that their God is not the overall controller that they assumed it to be. However, when this is realised the scientific and philosophical truths that were already available to them come into being, and many new discoveries are liable to be made when the never ending questions of science and philosophy come into being through old discoveries!"

Demeter steps in front of Michael and then she says: "new ideals evolve from old ideals and such an evolutionary process makes many religions extinct and such extinctions will carry on throughout eternity if the soul or the self is immortal! Therefore the human race should finally realise that the Gods that they worship are not able to hold their soul or the self; in the eternal bondage that they have created for themselves; through their misunderstanding of the creative powers of the chaos that they all originated from whilst they are in the physical form! Hence mankind should begin to understand that their Gods are as much a creation of the self as the physical being is a creation of the Gods and/or Mother Nature, and also the human race should realise that the Gods need to learn from the chaos; that is caused by them and mankind in their search for universal and undeniable truths! Those truths can only be found by evolution and evolution creates new species by making those before them extinct! Therefore extinction of the present nature of the physical beings and the Gods would be inevitable as they make way for the new physical beings and Gods! Such extinction would mean that such beings do not vanish or even cease to be; they just evolve into something new. But it is still possible that the stupidity of some religions could cause the extermination of mankind before it has had chance to evolve, and if the soul or the self is truly immortal; those that created such an extermination; would be liable to be stuck in such a chaotic process for evermore, because if the soul is immortal; it would emerge into new beings and recreate its old desires time and again, and this would be due to the will still being imprisoned by the desire of the old God that wished their enslavement! Therefore mankind needs to be comfortable with the evolutionary process that will make his present physical form and some of his beliefs extinct!"

The rest of the players enter the little boat, and sail it to the ship; before they start a discussion on the nature of reality, but that is for another day.

THE END (for now)

BIBLIOGRAPHY

American Indian Myths and Legends Richard Erdoes & Alfonso Ortiz, Pimlico 1997

Ancient Wisdom, Modern Ethics for a New Millennium Tenzin Gyatso The fourteenth Dalai Lama of Tibet (six times), Little Brown and Company 1999

Bang! The Complete History of the Universe, Brian May, Patrick Moore and Chris Linton, Carlton Books Ltd 2006

Coincidences, Chaos and All That Math Jazz, Edward P Burger and Michael Starbird, Norton Paperback 2006

Encyclopaedia of Science DK 2006

Hindu Scriptures, R. E. Zaehner, David Campbell publishers LTD 1992

Irish Folk and Faery Tales Omnibus Volume 2 Michael Scott, Warner Books 1993

Oxford Dictionary of Philosophy, Simon Blackburn, Oxford University Press 1996

Past Masters Galileo, Stillman Drake, Oxford University Press 1996

The Complete Dictionary of Symbols, In Myth, Art, and Literature, general editor Jack Tresidder, Duncan Baird publishers Ltd 2004

The Holy Qur'An translated by Abdullah Yusuf Ali, Wordsworth Editions LTD 2000

The Lore of the Bard, Arthur Rowan, Llewellyn publications 2003

The Rig Veda Translated by Wendy Doniger O Flaherty, Penguin books 1981

The Tibetan Book of Living and Dying, Sogyal Rinpoche, Rider 2003

The Uddhava Gita Translated by Swami Ambikananda Sarawati, Francis Lincoln Ltd 2000

Shield  Crest

www.ingramcontent.com/pod-product-compliance
Lightning Source LLC
Chambersburg PA
CBHW030129240426
43672CB00005B/81